THE
RULE OF LAW
IN THE
WAKE OF
CLINTON

THE
RULE OF LAW
IN THE
WAKE OF
CLINTON

edited by
Roger Pilon

CATO
INSTITUTE
Washington, D.C.

Library of Congress Cataloging-in-Publication Data

The rule of law in the wake of Clinton / edited by Roger Pilon.
    p. cm.
Includes bibliographical references.
ISBN 1-930865-03-1 (pbk.)
    1. Rule of law—United States. 2. Civil rights—United States. 3. Law
and politics. 4. Clinton, Bill, 1946– I. Pilon, Roger. II. Cato Institute.

KF382.R853 2000
340'.11—dc21   00-063853

Cover design by Elise Rivera.

Printed in the United States of America.

CATO INSTITUTE
1000 Massachusetts Ave., N.W.
Washington, D.C. 20001

Contents

Introduction

Roger Pilon

For millennia, history has taught that civilization and human progress depend on the rule of law. That lesson is evident today in nations around the world in which law barely exists. To the extent that the rule of law is eclipsed by the rule of man, civilization, progress, and real people are the victims. Indeed, America, which arose as a revolt against official disrespect for the law, is a testament to the importance of the rule of law.

Yet even in America, as the reach of government and hence of politics has grown, we have seen increasing indifference to law and legal institutions, coming often from those very institutions, and especially when law stands opposed to political ends. Over the nearly eight years of the Clinton administration, however, the disrespect has grown alarmingly, in many areas, and in ways both obvious and subtle. This volume documents at least some of those abuses.

Based on presentations made at a conference the Cato Institute held on July 12, 2000, the essays that follow draw together, in one place, a host of recent assaults on the rule of law. Taken together, they give us a glimpse of the state of the rule of law in the wake of Clinton. It is not a picture that gives comfort. In area after area, President Clinton and his administration have been indifferent and even hostile to elementary principles central to the rule of law. Their preference, it seems, is for the rule of man, and for the immediate advantage that affords.

When we think of recent assaults on the rule of law, the endless scandals that have surrounded the Clinton administration come immediately to mind, of course, along with the administration's repeated efforts to frustrate investigations of those scandals. But the scandals and the cover-ups are only the tip of the iceberg. In its political agenda, its legal briefs, and its executive actions, this administration has ignored both constitutional limits on government power and constitutional guarantees of individual liberty. In addition, in

1

the name of restraining and even punishing unpopular industries, the administration has variously launched, encouraged, or joined assaults on centuries-old common law principles while abandoning prudence in the application of statutes. And it has politicized the institutions of justice at home while showing studied indifference to limits on its power abroad. Yet in all of that, the guardians one would normally expect to be defending the rule of law have been either ineffective or complicit, raising serious questions about whether respect for the rule of law will long endure.

To develop those conclusions and give evidence supporting them, it is crucial to begin by defining just what we mean by the rule of law, then to explain and justify our allegiance to the idea. With those understandings before us, we can then examine the Clinton record in its many particulars to determine just how far this administration has departed from the rule of law, undermining our first principles as a nation in the process.

Our Heritage—The Rule of Law

In the volume's opening essay, "Civilization, Progress, and the Rule of Law," Lillian BeVier sets the stage for the essays that follow by addressing both the meaning of the rule of law and the rationale for our allegiance to it. From antiquity to the present, she writes, a "government of laws, not of men," has stood for "a legal and political order in which clear, impersonal, universally applicable, general laws constrain the conduct of both individual citizens *and* those who govern them." The rule of law is meant thus to ensure order by securing for all a law that affords "equal impersonal treatment according to known rules and without regard to status, rank, or political persuasion."[1]

But it is not order alone that the rule of law signifies; there is also a substantive element to the idea. For if the rule of law limits government's power in principle, BeVier continues, it does so "to maximize individual liberty." As John Locke wrote, *"the end of the Law is not to abolish or restrain, but to preserve and enlarge Freedom: For ... where there is no Law there is no Freedom."* And, BeVier adds, where there is no freedom, civilization and progress suffer. By contrast, "where freedom sustained by the rule of law persists, human ingenuity thrives and people quite simply live better, richer, longer, healthier lives." The common good that results is thus a function of the freedom of all, not something government aims at. In fact, BeVier concludes with what she calls "the corollary premise of this volume: that what is also dangerous—no, what is likely to be fatal— is to embrace a conception of the common good whose achievement could be won only in disregard of the rule of law." Indeed, one could add that it is precisely that ends-justifies-the-means attitude and approach that one notices repeatedly in the Clinton record, as the essays that follow make clear.

Drawing It All Together—An Outline

With that summation of the meaning and purpose of the rule of law before us, we turn to the application of the principles and to a systematic examination of the state of the rule of law in the wake of Clinton. We do that in two main parts: first, in the area of the Constitution; then, in the area of common law, statute, and legal institutions. As a bridge between those parts, however, we look at what are doubtless the clearest cases of disrespect for the rule of law, those that arose in connection with the scandals and corruption that have so marked the Clinton years. Finally, we look at how and why the institutions one should expect to be defending the rule of law have failed against the Clinton onslaught.

The Constitution is our starting point because our legal order is grounded, after all, in that document. The discussion of the abuse of the Constitution is itself divided into two sections: the first dealing with the assault on limited government, on the fundamental idea that our government is given only limited powers; the second dealing with the assault on individual liberty, on the complementary idea that those powers must be exercised in ways that respect our rights, enumerated and unenumerated alike. And the section treating the assault on limited government is again divided between a discussion of the administration's efforts to expand and defend congressional power and programs, which it would then execute, and a discussion of its efforts to expand and defend its own power, apart from Congress, all in contravention of the rule of law established by the Constitution.

The Assault on Limited Government

My own contribution to this volume begins by outlining America's constitutional framework, focusing especially on the centerpiece of

3

the Constitution, the doctrine of enumerated powers. To better secure liberty, the Founders sought to limit the government they were creating by delegating to it only certain powers, which they enumerated in the document, leaving the rest with the states or the people. A limited government meant a government of limited powers. In 1937, however, following President Franklin Roosevelt's notorious Court-packing threat, the New Deal Court effectively eviscerated the doctrine, enabling Congress thereafter to redistribute and regulate virtually at will. Yet over the past decade, the Rehnquist Court has been reviving the doctrine, albeit only slowly and still at the margins; and even some in Congress have pointed increasingly to constitutional limits on their power. The Clinton administration, however, has fought that effort every step of the way. In Congress it has proposed and promoted one program after another. And in the courts it has fought every move, however modest, to limit the reach of federal power to constitutional bounds. Mr. Clinton has been, I conclude, the consummate government man, constitutional limits on federal power notwithstanding. He has exhibited little but disdain for any such limits, as if the Constitution were an empty vessel to be filled by his plans and programs. That is hardly respect for a rule of law that limits government and maximizes freedom. Indeed, it is the very thing against which BeVier warns—the pursuit of "good" in disregard of law.

But in his own branch too Mr. Clinton has shown little restraint, especially in his efforts to legislate and rule by executive order, oblivious to the need to ground such orders in constitutional or statutory authority. That is the issue Douglas Kmiec examines in his essay, showing that Clinton has no more respect for limits on his own power than he has for limits on Congress's power. Indeed, when Congress repeatedly refused to enact legislation he wanted that would have prohibited employers from hiring permanent striker replacements, Clinton issued an order aimed at blackballing such employers for exercising rights the nation's labor law guarantees them. A federal appeals court made short work of that effort, finding that the president had exceeded constitutional limits on his power. But that has not stopped Clinton from ruling by executive order in many other areas, as Kmiec amply demonstrates. The administration's attitude was put best, perhaps, by Clinton adviser Paul Begala: "Stroke of the pen, law of the land. Kind of cool." At stake here is nothing less than the separation of powers, a principle central to the rule of law. Ignoring that principle, the administration has tried to draw ever more power unto itself—the end of which, of course, is the rule of man.

The Assault on Individual Liberty

We turn next from the powers to the rights side of the constitutional design and to the question of whether the administration, while pursuing its goals, has respected the rights of the people, enumerated and unenumerated alike. Nadine Strossen looks first at that question, focusing on speech and privacy rights. At the outset, however, she takes note of some of the appalling civil rights aspects of the endless War on Drugs, a war Mr. Clinton has pursued assiduously. Although blacks constitute 13 percent of the population, and 13 percent of total drug users (they use prohibited drugs in the same proportion as members of other groups), they constitute 74 percent of imprisoned drug users. That shocking disparity, Strossen shows, has far-reaching implications, including for the right to vote. Since most states disenfranchise convicted felons, in some southern states 30 percent of all black men cannot vote.

But the administration's disregard for rights does not end there. It has worked closely with Congress to reduce access to the courts, for example, leading to outcries from both the Left and the Right. Its respect for privacy—on the Internet, in the Filegate case, with databases—has been all but absent. Its assault on speech led noted First Amendment attorney Floyd Abrams to despair: "Even when the Administration has raised First Amendment concerns, it has done so haltingly and briefly." And in the name of checking terrorism, Strossen concludes, Clinton has promoted such draconian measures as roving wiretaps and deportations based on secret evidence. One could add that in his push for campaign finance "reform," an issue Strossen does not discuss, Clinton has been oblivious to speech rights the Supreme Court has repeatedly had to protect, even as he himself ignored the law we already have on that subject.[2] He apparently believes that in the matter of campaign finance, posture trumps performance.

We look next at Timothy Lynch's analysis of the Clinton record on crime, drugs, and forfeiture, especially as that record implicates such fundamental elements of the rule of law as the Constitution's

Warrant Clause, Jury Trial Clause, Double Jeopardy Clause, and Due Process Clause. The Warrant Clause was written to protect citizens against arbitrary searches "by requiring law enforcement personnel to obtain judicial authorization *before* they demand entrance to a person's home," Lynch writes. Yet that fundamental principle, itself rooted in the separation-of-powers principle, has been repeatedly disparaged or ignored by the Clinton administration. Although Lynch does not discuss the case, the Justice Department's infamous early morning raid on the Miami home of Elian Gonzalez involved an application for a warrant that was little better than fraudulent.[3] But at a more general level, from "national security" searches to public housing searches to drug searches in schools, this administration has all too often been indifferent to the warrant requirement. Moreover, in court it has tried to weaken the right to a jury trial by urging, among other things, that power be shifted from juries to judges. It has sought to further weaken the already limited guarantee against double jeopardy. And it has repeatedly defended the nation's bizarre forfeiture law in court while resisting congressional efforts at reform. When Clinton finally did sign a reform bill in the spring of 2000, it was a significantly weakened version, at the insistence of his Justice Department. If the rule of law is needed anywhere, it is surely in the area of forfeiture law.

Clinton's indifference to our rights is even greater when it comes to property rights and economic liberty, the focus of James Wootton's essay. And there is a perverse consistency about that. For no sooner had the 1937 Court opened the door for the all-but-unlimited federal power President Clinton has promoted than it reduced, a year later, the status of property rights and economic liberty, which otherwise would have blocked that power.[4] Yet here too both Congress and the Rehnquist Court have moved recently to rescue those rights from their current second-class status[5]—and here too the Clinton administration has fought those efforts at every step. Thus, when hearings were held on bills aimed at protecting owners against uncompensated regulatory takings of their property, the administration was on the other side. And in court too Mr. Clinton's Justice Department stood with government, constitutional strictures notwithstanding. Yet where the federal government does have authority to act under a properly interpreted Commerce Clause—to ensure the free flow of interstate commerce against, for example, state tort law that inordinately burdens that flow—the administration was again on the wrong side, Wootton argues. Thus, in both agency actions and litigation, the administration has "sided routinely with the plaintiff's bar to contend that state regulations are not preempted by federal law." Yet in the always uncertain antitrust field, where government should tread lightly, especially in the "new economy," the Clinton Justice Department has been anything but light-footed. Here again the rule of law has succumbed to politics and the rule of man.

Scandal, Corruption, and the Rule of Law

We turn next to what are doubtless the clearest cases of abuse, those in which elementary principles essential to the rule of law were plainly flaunted by the Clinton administration—and for patently political ends. At our conference it fell to Senator Fred Thompson, chairman of the Senate Governmental Affairs Committee, to outline those, which he did in his luncheon address, "Scandal, Corruption, and the Rule of Law." With his experience in 1973 and 1974 as minority counsel to the Senate Watergate Committee, and his more recent experience investigating alleged improper or illegal activities arising out of the 1996 federal campaigns, Thompson is uniquely qualified to address the subject.

He begins by urging that the rule of law is so important a concept that it should not be overused. Thus, for his purposes Thompson reserves the charge of undermining the rule of law "for those whose actions are deliberate, most serious, and go to the heart of, and do harm to, our legal or political institutions or processes." Having thus narrowed his concern, he invokes the Watergate episode, which never gave rise to the feeling "that the system had broken down," he says. With the Clinton administration, however, the list of wrongs is so long that "one is tempted to conclude that there has been virtually a continuous undermining of the rule of law." Those actions raise "serious and troubling concerns," Thompson notes, "especially considering that many of them were carried out by and on behalf of the person with the constitutional responsibility to faithfully execute the law." Nevertheless, Thompson sets them aside to focus on one area of scandal "that allows us to leave ambiguity behind," an area in which "the facts are clear, the duties and obligations of the responsible officials are obvious, and our political and our legal

7

processes were undermined." That area is "the campaign finance scandal emanating from the 1996 presidential election and the way in which it was handled."

Thompson then proceeds to dissect that scandal—from the personal involvement of President Clinton and Vice President Gore, to the "substantial evidence" the FBI found that huge sums of money had been routed to the Democratic National Committee by foreign sources coordinating with the White House, to the recommendations of FBI Director Louis Freeh and others regarding the stark conflict of interest Attorney General Janet Reno faced, to the appalling way she has handled that conflict. "Her arguments are so weak," Thompson notes, "that they are not to be taken seriously." This is not the place to summarize Senator Thompson's account. It should be read in its entirety. Suffice it to say that he concludes that this clear example of the Clinton administration's undermining of the rule of law "is of historic proportions."

Extortion Parading as Law

But there are other clear cases as well, with far-reaching implications, cases in which the Clinton administration has plainly thumbed its nose at fundamental principles central to the rule of law. Waging war on tobacco, guns, and Microsoft, complete with vilification as one of its tactics, the administration is engaged in nothing less than extortion parading as law. In those patently political campaigns, it has abused both common law and statute, undermining centuries-old principles in the process. We move thus from the law of the Constitution to the law that is secured under the Constitution. Yet here too we see the same patterns and the same ends-justify-means rationales.

Robert A. Levy begins this section with a tightly reasoned exposure of the Clinton administration's war on tobacco. For years, plaintiffs lawyers had sued the tobacco industry on behalf of clients claiming to have been harmed by smoking, only to be told by juries that smokers themselves were responsible for their losses. That assumption-of-risk defense and others like it are centuries-old common law principles, aimed at maximizing individual liberty and encouraging individual responsibility. But they also frustrate political agendas of the kind Mr. Clinton had in mind. So he got together with friends in the health community, the state attorneys general offices, and the plaintiffs bar to remove or at least neutralize such impediments. Starting with multiple suits at the state level, often coordinated, the anti-tobacco forces essentially extorted the 1998 quarter-trillion dollar Master Settlement Agreement (MSA) from the big four tobacco companies, effectively cartelizing the industry in the process. Then the federal government jumped in for its share of the plunder, despite Attorney General Reno's having earlier testified that there was no legal ground for federal involvement. Ignoring both common law and statutory limitations, the Justice Department recently filed a 116-count complaint, the plain purpose of which is to extort even more money from the tobacco industry, money that will come ultimately from smokers, of course. Yet while that is going on, Levy notes, the underlying MSA, which amounts to a flagrant violation of federal antitrust law as well as the Constitution's Commerce and Compacts Clauses, remains unchallenged by those sworn to faithfully execute the law. No surprise there, for the billions of dollars the MSA is already generating is now recirculating, through the plaintiffs bar, into the political coffers of Mr. Clinton and his state attorneys general friends. Presumably, the demise of the rule of law is a small price to pay for all of that.

Not every state attorney general went along with the MSA. Our next contributor, Alabama Attorney General Bill Pryor, took a principled position against it—until it was signed and it became clear that further resistance would cost his state a fortune, with no offsetting benefit for resident smokers who ultimately pay the bill. As Pryor and others predicted, however, the novel theories of liability generated for the war on tobacco would not stop there. In fact, they were recast slightly and reused in a war on guns, this time with cities mainly in the lead, but with the Clinton administration again closely behind. At this stage, the gun suits have yet to coerce the gun industry into submission, due in part to judges who have the courage to state plainly what is going on. As one put it, "When conceiving the complaint in this case, the plaintiffs must have envisioned [the tobacco] settlements as the dawning of a new age of litigation during which the gun industry, liquor industry and purveyors of 'junk' food would follow the tobacco industry in reimbursing government expenditures and submitting to judicial regulation."

Here too, as Pryor's essay makes clear, the implications are far reaching. For centuries, we have held individual criminals responsible for their crimes, not those who manufactured whatever implements the criminal may have used. Indeed, it makes no more sense to attribute murder to a gun manufacturer than arson to a match manufacturer. Yet that is the direction in which the anti-gun zealots are headed with their theories of negligent marketing, design defect, and the like. In his analysis of the matter, Pryor contrasts the Madisonian framework with the Clintonian framework, arguing that the latter "erodes both the separation of powers and federalism, undermines the protection of civil rights, denies individual responsibility and, if continued, will lead to a vicious cycle of futile dependence on ever-expanding government power." Those results, of course, are utterly inconsistent with the rule of law.

The vilification tactics the Clinton administration has employed in its tobacco and gun wars have been directed primarily at those industries, although organizations like the National Rifle Association have been constant targets as well. When we turn to the Justice Department's war on Microsoft, however, we find that the vilification has often been personalized, with Microsoft's founder and CEO Bill Gates, until recently the world's richest man, as the main target. That is an unconscionable abuse of government power, yet it is perfectly consistent with the class warfare this administration has so often waged. And it is consistent as well with the fear of private power and the distrust of markets that have animated antitrust doctrine from its inception.

In his brief but trenchant analysis of the administration's war on Microsoft, C. Boyden Gray develops points James Wootton mentioned in his essay while reaching beyond to draw some of the broader implications for administrative law and judicial review more generally. Given the uncertain foundations of antitrust doctrine, when enforcement "migrates beyond the punishment and prevention of collusion to fix prices or divide markets, it constitutes nothing more than economic regulation without a central purpose," Gray writes. And nowhere is that more evident than in the Microsoft suit. Although the administration has tried to sell its case as "a model for regulating the new economy so as to intensify innovation," not only is the new economy not in need of such government help, Gray says, but the central violation the court identified is Microsoft's pattern of "predatory innovation." Yet if the court's remedy were to stand, it would punish innovation, not unleash it. Given the behavior surrounding this suit, it is hard to escape the conclusion that the case "represents nothing more than a successful hijacking

of the government's regulatory power by Microsoft's competitors—
an especially grievous abuse of the rule of law." Indeed, what are we
to say when it emerges, as Gray notes, that Microsoft's competitors,
frustrated that other businesses did not support the department's
action, "hired the same private investigator who had been engaged
by the Clinton White House to denigrate Kenneth Starr?" The Microsoft case is no more about the rule of law than was the raid on the
home of Elian Gonzalez—Janet Reno's protestations to the contrary,
in both cases, notwithstanding.[6] What we have here, plain and simple, is politics parading as law.

Toward the Rule of Man

The politicization of the law goes hand in hand with the politicization of legal institutions, of course, and in this administration no
institution apart from the White House itself has been more politicized than the Department of Justice, the department charged with
seeing that the laws are faithfully executed. Ted Olson, himself a
former assistant attorney general, gives us a glimpse of that with
an essay that simply lists a variety of items, some merely suggestive,
others deeply revealing, about the events that have colored the Justice Department during the long tenure of Janet Reno. The list begins
with the appointment of numerous friends of Bill and Hillary, including the early and prominent appointment of Webster Hubbell, later
convicted and imprisoned for having defrauded his law partners.
It continues with the swift and unprecedented firing of all 93 of the
nation's U.S. attorneys, with 10 days' notice to clear out. It includes
the firing of career employees in the White House Travel Office and
the groundless prosecution of its director; the attorney general's
announcement that she was opening an investigation of Kenneth
Starr, just as he was about to begin the Clinton impeachment trial
in the Senate; her refusal to appoint an independent prosecutor to
investigate alleged 1996 Clinton-Gore fundraising abuses, despite
three separate recommendations from professional prosecutors that
she do so; the department's repeated intrusions into ongoing, politically sensitive investigations; and much, much more. As Olson concludes, "when the Clinton/Reno Justice Department is seriously
investigated, if it ever is, and the full story is told, there is every
indication that we will be stunned—if we are not stunned already—
by what we learn."

The tragedy of that kind of politicization, of course, is not simply that the laws are not enforced, or that the department is demoralized, or that ruthless individuals are able to corrupt and use our legal institutions for their own ends. More important, it is that those actions move us ever closer to the rule of man and to the rank lawlessness that countless generations struggled to overcome with the institution of the rule of law. And nowhere is the potential for that greater than when we move from domestic to foreign affairs, where the stakes are highest, the latitude afforded the president the greatest, the limits on his power the least certain and most dependent on sound judgment and political consultation and cooperation. It is here, in fact, that courts have been most reluctant to intrude, for better or for worse, which means that the risk of succumbing to the rule of man is at its greatest when political restraints are ineffective— or are ignored.

Those are among the issues John Yoo tackles in his thorough and often subtle discussion of the imperial president abroad. The picture he draws does not give comfort. As he writes, "when it comes to using the American military, no president in recent times has had a quicker trigger finger." And it is not in defense of any vital national interests that President Clinton has sent American forces abroad but rather in pursuit of a wide array of other ends—peacekeeping, nation building, and the like. The recent Kosovo operation comes immediately to mind, of course, which Clinton undertook in the face of House opposition and congressional votes that in the aggregate were ambiguous at best. But that is only one of many such operations. What is more, in pursuit of its foreign policy ends the administration has embraced multilateralism with little regard for the implications for American sovereignty. In both war and arms control, "President Clinton has sought to delegate governmental power to international institutions to achieve dubious foreign policy goals," Yoo writes. And with the Chemical Weapons Convention Clinton fought so hard to achieve, "it appears that this administration has the distinction of being the first to transfer public power outside of the American governmental system." In all of this, Yoo concludes, "the administration has played fast and loose with the law to avoid making decisions for which the American people could hold the executive branch accountable." Thus do we move closer to the rule of man, and in this most perilous of areas. If foreign policy is a difficult legal area

12

to begin with, it has been made ever more so by the actions of this administration. When the rule of law is weakened, imperialism invariably follows.

The Guardians of Law Fail

We come then to the question of how and why those institutions one would normally expect to find defending the rule of law have failed. Not only that, they have often been complicit in the administration's assault. Without doubt, this is the most troubling and difficult part of our inquiry, the part that takes us beyond documentation to speculation. Mr. Clinton, seized with power, has behaved like others before him, of course, even if he has indulged excesses from which others have shied. The Founders understood that power tends to corrupt, which is why they limited it constitutionally, leaving most power in private hands where it might be used to check public power. The problems arise when private power fails in that effort, or fails to be exercised toward that end, or, worse still, is used to enhance public power. How and why has that happened? The essays that follow make at least a start in answering those questions.

Daniel Troy looks at the role of the political parties. Our two major parties are always in a certain adversarial relationship, to be sure, each trying to install its own people in positions of power and institute its own policies and programs, often at the expense of the other party. At the same time, the parties share a common interest in the good of the nation—or at least one would hope that they do. Thus, in the Watergate crisis the parties eventually joined ranks for that greater good. In the Clinton impeachment crisis, however, the Democratic Party seemed determined, almost to a man, to give not an inch. Senate Republicans, meanwhile, failed utterly to carry the ball House Republicans handed them, seeming only to wish that the whole matter would simply go away.[7] And when we turn to Clinton's broader assaults on the rule of law—from rule by executive order to unconstitutional legislation to unconstitutional executive appointments and more—Republican forces were often ineffective, nonexistent, or even working hand in hand with Clinton to undermine the rule of law.

Troy lists several reasons that underlay the inability of Democrats to rise above interest, none of which flatters them. Not surprisingly, however, he saves his fire for the Republicans. They failed, he argues, for many reasons, ranging from inexperience at congressional leadership, to Gingrich and the government shutdown, naiveté, fear of risk, poor member and staff work, media hostility, prosperity, and more—including the sheer number of the administration's assaults, the "scandal fatigue." He concludes, however, with a thoughtful note about the basic ideological function of political parties and the inherent danger for democracy when personality replaces principle. It is a lesson we should learn from other nations that have allowed that to happen and have suffered the consequences.

Beyond the realm of politics, however, lie other guardians of the law, or so it once was. Members of the bar and the legal academy, in particular, have always been thought to bear a special responsibility to speak up loudly and clearly when attacks on the rule of law are at hand. That responsibility arises, after all, not simply as a matter of general civic duty but from professional interest and personal understanding beyond that of the layman. During the Clinton years, however, those professionals have been strangely silent, writes Ronald Rotunda, who is a member of the bar and the legal academy and an authority on legal ethics. Worse still, a surprising number have come to the defense of the administration, notwithstanding the plain, overwhelming evidence against it.

Thus, following a *New York Times* story quoting a White House official who called for "coordinated hostilities" as "part of our continuing campaign to destroy Ken Starr," the attorney general said nothing in defense of her appointee, the bar joined in that silence, and many academicians joined in the attack. It fell to a bipartisan group of former attorneys general to come to Starr's defense, which they did in the form of an open letter critical of officials and attorneys appearing "to have the improper purpose of influencing and impeding an ongoing criminal investigation and intimidating possible jurors, witnesses and even investigators." What have we come to when members of the bar and the legal academy condone and even engage in that kind of behavior? Yet the example, as we know, comes from the top. And the corruption it encourages manifests itself in often bizarre ways: in invitations to address ABA conventions, for example, which were extended to President Clinton *after* he was found in contempt of court for lying under oath, to convicted felon and disbarred lawyer Webster Hubbell, and even to Susan McDougal, who could claim only one of Hubbell's labels. Yet when we go beyond the scandals, to more conventional assaults on the rule of law, the response of the bar and the legal academy has been little better, as Rotunda shows. It is a truly disgraceful professional performance. Like so much else that has surrounded this administration, it reeks of politics over principle—as a few who practice that politics are candid enough to admit.

We come finally to the role of the media and the cultural institutions in defending, or failing to defend, the rule of law. David Horowitz minces no words when he speaks of the corruption that has infected our institutions since the cultural revolution of the 1960s. The war on the American legal system is now four decades old, he writes, "and its battles have inflicted incalculable damage on the moral and legal fiber of this nation." Yet for all of that, the media eventually did report all of the sordid details of Clinton's misdeeds, Horowitz believes. "Moreover, 119 newspapers and press institutions, including such sympathetic organs as the *New York Times*, the *Los Angeles Times*, and the *Washington Post*, did call for Clinton's resignation." And even Hollywood produced some implicitly anti-Clinton parables during his reign. The reason Clinton escaped conviction and removal from office, Horowitz continues, brings us back to politics. "Given the failure of the Republicans to convince a decisive majority of the American people that the president's removal was required, the political ramifications of such removal would have been to throw the nation into a constitutional crisis. No believer in the rule of law could wish for such a result."

That is a telling point. Horowitz develops it by noting that after the Lewinsky scandal broke, "Republicans were largely silent for eight months, enabling [Clinton] to define the issues in a manner favorable to his case." He was portrayed "as a victim of government abuse and thus as a defender, ironically, of the rule of law." When Republicans finally did join the fray, they framed the debate in abstract, abstruse legal terms, which the public could not or would not follow, leaving the political arena to the White House and its infamous spin doctors. It should hardly surprise us, therefore, that Clinton won the political battle. Thus, the lesson to be learned is that those who would defend the rule of law cannot focus on law alone to do the job. At the end of the day, law is grounded in a political firmament. If we are to preserve our law, we must attend to that foundation.

And so we close this part where we began, not with law, not even with culture, but with politics, with the idea that law is given life by its operation in the political process. From that, however, it would be a mistake to conclude that culture is little connected with the health of the rule of law. For the political realm that needs our constant attention is intimately connected with the cultural realm—with the principles and the values that define a free society, which must themselves be nourished if the freedom secured by the rule of law is to endure. Thus, the essays that follow should be read not simply as revealing the state of the rule of law in the wake of Clinton but, more important, as revealing what must be done to reinvigorate the climate of ideas and the cultural values that are essential to preserving the rule of law and the freedom it secures.

Notes

1. In this introduction I omit citations for passages, points, and quotations drawn from the essays that follow.

2. Senator Fred Thompson outlines some of those campaign finance abuses in Chapter 7 of this volume.

3. See, for example, Matthew M. Hoffman, "When They Came For Elian: INS Was Armed With a Shaky Warrant," *Legal Times*, May 8, 2000, p. 68.

4. The Court diminished property rights and economic liberty most systematically in *United States v. Carolene Products Co.*, 303 U.S. 144 (1938). See Roger Pilon, "On the Foundations of Economic Liberty," *Cato Policy Report*, vol. 11, no. 4, July/August 1989, pp. 6–11.

5. See, for example, *Dolan v. City of Tigard*, 512 U.S. 374 (1994).

6. The United States Court of Appeals for the Eleventh Circuit made short work of the Justice Department's rule-of-law claims in *Gonzalez v. Reno*, 212 F.3d 1338 (2000). See Roger Pilon, "Hiding Behind the Rule of Law," Letters, *Wall Street Journal*, April 17, 2000, p. A35, and Roger Pilon, "A Much Too Deferential Court," Letters, *Wall Street Journal*, June 9, 2000, p. A19.

7. For a devastating critique of the behavior of Senate Republicans after the House managers brought them the impeachment matter, see David Shippers, *Sell-Out: The Inside Story of President Clinton's Impeachment* (Washington, DC: Regnery Publishing, Inc., 2000).

PART I

OUR HERITAGE

1. Civilization, Progress, and the Rule of Law

Lillian R. BeVier

Throughout history, adherence to the rule of law has sustained civilization and nourished progress. The essays that follow discuss a wide array of recent inroads on the rule of law. To set the stage for them, I offer a template that defines the attributes of the principle and justifies our allegiance to it. I begin by making explicit the implicit bedrock premise of this volume, which is that human freedom and the material prosperity that it enables owe their very existence to the rule of law.

In articulating the particulars of the rule-of-law ideal, my first task is to fix precisely upon what rule-of-law advocates have in mind when they sing the praises of a "government of laws, not of men." In a recent law review article, my colleague, John Jeffries, conveyed with a unique combination of clarity, precision, and economy of phrase what the rule of law is all about. I pause here to note that in selecting Professor Jeffries' summary, I have (for the time being at least) left some fine prose on the cutting room floor, prose from the pens of thinkers as profound and eloquent—and as far removed in time from one another—as Aristotle, Cicero, John Locke, John Marshall, John Adams, and the redoubtable Friedrich Hayek. I chose Professor Jeffries' text not merely because it is apt but also because it is timely, since it sprang from his effort to work through a contemporary legal problem by applying to it the perennial wisdom inherent in rule-of-law principles. As he writes,

> The rule of law signifies the constraint of arbitrariness in the exercise of government power. . . . It means that the agencies of official coercion should, to the extent feasible, be guided by rules—that is, by openly acknowledged, relatively stable, and generally applicable statements [of proscribed conduct]. The evils to be retarded are caprice and whim, the misuse

of government power for private ends, and the unacknowl-
edged reliance on illegitimate criteria of selection. The goals
to be advanced are regularity and even-handedness in the
administration of justice and accountability in the use of
government power. In short, the "rule of law" designates
the cluster of values associated with conformity to law by
government.[1]

Thus, a "government of laws, not of men," refers to a legal and
political order in which clear, impersonal, universally applicable,
general laws constrain the conduct of both individual citizens *and*
those who govern them; in which no act is punished except pursuant
to a pre-existing rule; and in which a stable, relatively permanent
organic law, such as a written constitution, constrains and separates
the institutions that exercise its everyday law-making, law-execut-
ing, and law-applying powers. In other words, a government of
laws and not of men is a government that is limited in principle; it
is not a government that may act as it pleases and simply deem its
actions law: "all [the] actions of such a state would be legal but [that
government] would certainly not be under the rule of law."[2] By
limiting *in principle* the legitimate authority of those who wield the
power of the state, the rule of law secures to all citizens the promise
that law itself will exhibit qualities of regularity, certainty, transpar-
ency, predictability, evenhandedness, and equal impersonal treatment according to known general rules and without regard to status,
rank, or political persuasion.

What is the rationale for embracing such an ideal? What ultimate
end do we seek? Hayek described it well. We seek "that condition
of men in which coercion of some by others is reduced as much as
possible in society"[3]—in other words, we seek to maximize individual liberty consistent with the recognition of reciprocal rights in all.
Anyone who deems personal freedom to be a good in itself, and
who simultaneously recognizes that the task of government is to
secure freedom, must inevitably ask how to constrain government
power. As it turns out, the best answer is to hold fast to the rule of
law. "Freedom of men under government is to have a standing rule
to live by," wrote Locke. And he elaborated,

> The end of the Law is not to abolish or restrain, but *to preserve
> and enlarge Freedom*: For in all the states of created beings
> capable of Laws, *where there is no Law, there is no Freedom.*

> For *Liberty* is to be free from restraint and violence from others which cannot be, where there is no Law: But Freedom is not, as we are told, *a Liberty for every Man to do what he lists:* (For who could be free, when every other Man's Humour might domineer over him?) But a *Liberty* to dispose, and order, as he lists, his Person, Actions, Possessions, and his whole Property, within the Allowance of those Laws under which he is; and therein not to be the subject of the arbitrary Will of another, but freely follow his own.[4]

This volume describes real events. Many of the authors will invite us, at least implicitly, to pass judgment on those events, and on the conduct of the public officials who engaged in them, on the precise ground that the officials' behavior departed from rule-of-law norms. In evaluating matters for ourselves, I think it important that if we condemn those departures we do so not merely because they vary from a theoretically ideal standard of conduct but, more significant, because they sap the very foundation of liberty—an effect that is impossible to justify. History teaches that we have less to fear even from the rough seas of anarchy than from the chains of tyranny. From ancient times to 17th century England to 18th century America to 20th century battles against fascist and communist totalitarian dictatorships, the struggles against rulers who claimed unchecked power over their citizens' lives—men who refused to be bound by the laws they imposed on others—has continued. Those struggles must continue, for they are the price of freedom.

Government officials who possess unlimited power exhibit an inexorable propensity to exert their authority arbitrarily, unpredictably, and for their own personal enrichment. Sometimes they go so far as to loot their country's treasury. Sometimes, as in the 20th century, they stoop so low as to order the murder of millions of their own citizens.[5] Our present concerns do not feed upon the butchery of unchecked state power that the last century witnessed, of course. It is enough today that we contemplate only the first phrase of Lord Acton's observation: *all* "power tends to corrupt."[6] For by this iron law of human nature does the state inexorably expand, straining to increase its control over the people and resources subject to its rule and to inflate the personal and political power of those who rule.

This volume represents an exercise neither in political histrionics nor in partisanship; rather, it is a set of lessons impelled by the necessity for vigilance. Many of the authors raise specific instances from the recent past of actions by those entrusted with power who have demonstrably ignored—even flaunted—the rule of law. Freedom is unlikely to survive complacency in the face of such conduct, for power, abused and unchecked, expands relentlessly.

The rule of law that anchors our discussion today has its critics—principally, "legal realists" and persons on the political Left.[7] The critics decry the rule of law's rigidity and inflexibility; they strain in principle against the limits that principled rules impose, preferring instead the luxury of being free to negotiate an endless series of ends-justify-means compromises. They celebrate the virtues of official discretion and insist that all law is so irreducibly indeterminate that to strive for regularity or certainty of application is to pursue a will-o'-the-wisp. They insist that there is an inevitable tension between adherence to the rule of law and the full realization of democratic values, because the rule of law dictates that today's majorities be bound by limitations imposed by a written constitution whose meaning does not change with every shift of the political wind. Indeed, the critics seem to think it inevitable, and apparently consider it desirable, that our Supreme Court be "a court of politicians enforcing a policy, not a court of judges administering the law"—which is how the legal historian F. W. Maitland described the infamous Star Chamber.[8]

The rule of law's critics contrast the advantages of the ideal of flexible beneficent government with the disadvantages of the supposedly rigid rule of law. Yet to consider life as it is actually lived by citizens in regimes in which the rule of law has been abandoned is simultaneously to render its supposed disadvantages insignificant while bringing its quite stunning advantages into view. With conspicuous understatement, David Hume commented on England's evolution from a government of will to a government of law: "though some inconveniences arise from the maxim of adhering strictly to the law, yet the advantages overbalance them."[9] In fact, it is the answer to the "compared-to-what" question that reveals just how advantageous the rule of law is, how fundamental it has been—and continues to be—to the progress of civilization and the preservation of freedom.

The rule of law is thus instrumental; without it, freedom cannot survive. But what of freedom? Is freedom a matter of natural right, as Locke and Jefferson believed? Or does freedom too need to be defended on instrumental grounds? Those who work in the natural-law tradition claim to discern in individual liberty immutable aspects of any good legal order. The natural-law claim is that freedom provides the essential foundation of a good legal order quite without regard to its social consequences—and perhaps it does. But it is noteworthy that when natural-law theorists turn their attention to devising the rules that would actually comprise a good legal order, they end up prescribing rules that guarantee individual autonomy, protect private property, and enforce freedom of contract—rules that in themselves constitute the indispensable ingredients for an ever-expanding social pie.[10] The undeniable truth turns out to be that although such a regime might not be *dictated* by a utilitarian calculus, it can be persuasively *defended* on such terms.

Thus, from a purely practical, consequentialist perspective, preserving individual liberty and personal freedom—the ends to which securing the rule of law is but a means—are worthy goals because where freedom sustained by the rule of law persists, human ingenuity thrives and people quite simply live better, richer, longer, healthier lives. Reflect for just a moment on the vast creative power that the engine of human freedom unleashes. Give credit to the beneficent synergies that can be exploited only by voluntary cooperation. One must conclude that individual freedom "is best understood . . . as the embodiment of principles that, when consistently applied, will work to the advantage of all (or almost all) members of society simultaneously."[11]

But be clear: those who embrace freedom neither endorse human selfishness nor glorify greed. Rather they seek the common good and a better life for all. Those who embrace freedom do not, however, conceive of the common good "as an attribute of some premier disembodied entity that rightly tramples all individual or private interests"; rather they think of it as "the summation of [all] those individuals subject to state power." And on this second account, a prescription for achieving the common good must be justified "solely by how [it] advances the individual welfare of each and every citizen, be he friend or foe, popular or despised. So understood, their happiness, their pains, their successes, and their emotions matter; what is irrelevant, and dangerous, is some distant conception of the public good that is not anchored to the utility of any human being . . . that disregards the separateness of persons,"[12] and that fails to guarantee their individual freedom. To which I would add the corollary premise of this volume: that what is also dangerous—no, what is likely to be fatal—is to embrace a conception of the common good whose achievement could be won only in disregard of the rule of law.

Notes

1. John Calvin Jeffries Jr., "Legality, Vagueness and the Construction of Penal Statutes," *Virginia Law Review* 71 (1985): 189, 212–13.

2. Friedrich A. Hayek, *The Constitution of Liberty* (Chicago: University of Chicago Press, 1960), p. 205.

3. Ibid, p. 1.

4. John Locke, "Second Treatise of Government," in *Two Treatises of Government*, ed. Peter Laslett (New York: Mentor Books, 1965), para. 57.

5. See generally Stephan Courtois, et al. *The Black Book of Communism* (Cambridge, Mass.: Harvard University Press, 1999).

6. Letter to Bishop Mandell Creighton, April 3, 1887, in Louise Creighton, *Life and Letters of Mandell Creighton*, vol. 1, ch. 13 (1904). (Quoted in *The Oxford Dictionary of Quotations*, 4th ed.[Oxford: 1992], p. 1).

7. See Ian Shapiro, Introduction, in *Nomos XXXVI: The Rule of Law* (New York: NYU Press, 1994), p. 1.

8. F. W. Maitland, *The Constitutional History of England* (Cambridge: Cambridge University Press, 1909), p. 263.

9. David Hume, *The History of England* (New York: Harper & Bros., 1855), 5: 171.

10. See generally, for example, Randy E. Barnett, *The Structure of Liberty: Justice and the Rule of Law* (New York: Oxford University Press, 1998).

11. Richard A. Epstein, *Principles of a Free Society: Reconciling Individual Liberty with the Common Good* (New York: Perseus Books, 1998), p. 2.

12. Ibid, p. 4.

PART II

THE ABUSE OF THE CONSTITUTION

2. Ignoring Constitutional Limits

Roger Pilon

With Lillian BeVier's review of the meaning and point of the rule of law now before us, we can begin to examine the state of the rule of law in the wake of Clinton. We do that in several parts. In this chapter, we look at President Clinton's record regarding that most basic of issues, limited government. My thesis, in essence, is quite simple: For nearly eight years, in both its actions and its proposals, the Clinton administration has utterly ignored constitutional limits on the power and purposes of the federal government. Those limits, fundamental to the rule of law, are there to guard against both overweening government and the rule of man. Yet Mr. Clinton has repeatedly acted as if the Constitution were an empty vessel to be filled by his policies and programs. In a word, he has been indifferent, even hostile, to the idea of limited government.

For present purposes, it matters little that Clinton's disregard for constitutional limits has differed only in degree from the disregard shown by most of his predecessors for nearly 70 years. Nor does it matter that his programs and proposals have enjoyed a measure of popular support. For neither politics nor popular opinion has any direct bearing on the contention of this chapter. The point, rather, is one of law. Fortunately, the Supreme Court has begun recently to rediscover that point, if only at the margins. And even some in Congress have begun again to speak of constitutional limits on their power. It may be some time before constitutionally limited government is restored, of course, if ever it is. That should not stop us, however, from examining how far this administration has strayed from that ideal—and the law—to say nothing of how far it has undermined respect for the ideal itself.

Authority Flows from the Constitution

We begin this chapter with an outline of the Constitution, and a brief discussion of fundamental constitutional principles, because our legal order rests, after all, on that document. Once the Constitution was ratified, it drew both state and common law under its umbrella. It is the supreme law of the land. That means that whatever authority any official may claim must be derived from or permitted under the Constitution. Indeed, one of the most important reasons for having a written constitution is to enable an examination of such claims to determine if they are or are not justified. When government officials act without authority, their actions are illegal. Thus, they undermine the rule of law.

There are essentially two ways an official can act without authority. First, he can exercise some power or pursue some end that is not authorized or otherwise permitted. Second, he can exercise some power or pursue some end that may be authorized but do so in a way that is not authorized or permitted. The second sort of wrong—pertaining to means, and largely concerning violations of rights—will be treated in chapters four, five, and six, in which the assault on liberty is the main concern. Here and in the next chapter we focus on authority in the most immediate sense—on the question of whether an official has authority in the first place to exercise a power or pursue a given end. Our concern is thus with limited government, government limited to certain ends or functions. We focus on a single, simple question: Quite apart from any violation of rights, where in the Constitution does Mr. Clinton find authority for what he is doing or what he is proposing to do?

Chapter three looks at Clinton's efforts, independent of Congress, to expand *executive* power beyond the limits set by the Constitution or by statute. In the present chapter we look at Clinton's efforts to expand *congressional* power beyond constitutional limits, creating programs he would then implement and oversee. Thus, the executive branch can expand its power without the aid of Congress—by simply ignoring constitutional or statutory limits on its own power. But the president can expand his power also by going to Congress—by proposing, promoting, and signing legislation that ignores constitutional limits on Congress's power, legislation the executive branch then implements, thus expanding its own power in the process. In that case, both Congress and the executive branch exceed constitutional limits on their power. This chapter treats this second kind of case—the efforts of the Clinton administration to expand its own power by expanding the programs of the federal government beyond constitutional limits.

To show just how that has happened, it will be necessary first to outline the basic theory of the Constitution—especially the doctrine of enumerated powers—thereby showing how the Founders intended to limit government through the rule of law the Constitution establishes. I will then show how the Supreme Court is at last rediscovering those "first principles," if only in a limited way, and how even some in Congress are doing so as well. With that framework in place—that foundation for analyzing whether the administration's programs and proposals have exceeded constitutional bounds—I will then simply look at a small sample of the endless array of programs Mr. Clinton has proposed since he took office, drawing those from his Castro-length State of the Union Addresses. As we will see, the power to enact and execute most of those programs is nowhere to be found in the Constitution.

But in addition to proposing, promoting, and signing legislation that exceeds Congress's authority, Mr. Clinton has also repeatedly defended such legislation with his legal arguments in the courts. Thus, we will look also at a sample of those arguments. We will see that Mr. Clinton's understanding of the Constitution is far removed from the Founders' understanding—and even, increasingly, from the Supreme Court's. In sum, although Clinton may have once said that the era of big government is over, his political agenda and his legal arguments give a lie to any such assertion. Both in Congress and in the courts, he has shown an utter disregard for the limits the Constitution sets on federal power, an utter indifference to the rule of law imposed by our founding document.

Before proceeding, let me note again that Clinton's posture—his general approach to government—is not all that different from that of most of his predecessors since the New Deal, except in degree. But I would argue that a frank assessment of the record reveals that the difference in degree amounts almost to a difference in kind. Put it this way: Most prior administrations at least talked about constitutional limits on government and sometimes acted pursuant to such limits. The Clinton administration, by contrast, seems to recognize no such limits. To listen to its rhetoric and witness the sheer volume and scope of its proposals, one imagines there to be no problem too trivial or too personal for government attention—in fact, for federal attention. Of Mr. Clinton it can truly be said that he is "a government man." Because ours is a government constitutionally limited to certain enumerated ends, Clinton's posture

29

amounts to a rank disregard for the rule of law. It is that posture, that attitude toward constitutional limits, that needs to be highlighted in any discussion of respect for the rule of law.

A Government of Limited Powers

Let us begin, then, with a brief overview of the constitutional context—and the place, in particular, of the rule of law in that context. The rule of law stands opposed to the rule of man, of course, as captured most poignantly, perhaps, by Louis XIV of the ancien régime: "*L'état, c'est moi.*" For centuries, especially in the West, men fought to overthrow the rule of man and replace it with the rule of law, driven by the basic question of political philosophy: By what right does one man have power over another? Thus, the rule of law is not simply about order or regularity; the idea has a normative side, too. It is about justice as well as order, about substance as well as procedure. In a word, it is about legitimacy. And nowhere is that fuller understanding of the rule of law better captured than in our own founding documents.

Individual Liberty, Limited Government

In answering that basic question about political legitimacy, it is crucial to appreciate that the Founders did not say simply that government's just powers are derived from the consent of the governed. If that were all they had said, we would be living not under the rule of man but under the rule of men, not under the will of a king but under the will of some dominant group, whether a majority or not. Perhaps rule by men is better than rule by man, but it is still a far cry from justice—as the Founders understood when they warned against majoritarian tyranny.[1]

No, the Founders did not give us a mere democracy. Wisely, they gave us a constitutional republic, grounded in a written document that authorizes, institutes, and empowers government, then limits that power far beyond the limits afforded by mere popular will. That is clear from a plain reading of the Constitution. But it is made even clearer when the document is read in the light cast upon it by the Declaration of Independence, which sets forth the philosophy of government the Founders brought with them when they met in Philadelphia in 1776. In that document one finds the idea that government derives its just powers from the consent of the governed only at the end of the argument, only after the moral order has first been established, from which that conclusion follows.

It is crucial to understand, therefore, that the Founders saw legitimacy as flowing not simply from will or consent but from reason, and they saw reason as the foundation of morality. In fact, they were quite clear about that from the start. Thus, they began the Declaration by expressing the need they felt, based on "a decent Respect to the Opinions of Mankind," to give a reasoned justification for the separation they were declaring. And they grounded that justification not in any morality but in the morality of natural rights. Thus, they started with certain "self-evident" truths, truths of reason: In essence, we are all morally equal, as defined by our rights to life, liberty, and the pursuit of happiness. That means that no one has rights superior to those of anyone else. And it means that each of us has a right to pursue happiness, by his own lights, provided only that he respect the equal rights of others to do the same. There, in a nutshell, is the moral foundation of the nation. That it happens also to be the foundation of the classic common law is no accident, for the Founders understood the common law to be the very essence of the rule of law. Grounded in two basic rights—property, broadly understood as "lives, liberties, and estates," as John Locke put it;[2] and contract, which describes the way people come together legitimately—the common law was long thought to be grounded in "right reason."[3] Its principles define moral relationships among individuals and, by implication, between individuals and any government they may create.

Only after they had set forth the prior moral order did the Founders turn to government. And here again they were quite clear: The purpose of government, they wrote, is to secure our rights. They did not write that government is created to provide us with all manner of goods and services—by implication, that is our personal or private business, not the government's. Rather, they wrote, "That to secure these Rights, Governments are instituted among Men." They were then in a position to add that the powers government might need toward that end, to be just, must be derived from the consent of the governed, a conclusion that follows necessarily from our right to be free. Government is thus twice limited: By its end, to secure our rights; and by its means, which require our consent if they are to be legitimate.

The vision that emerges from the Declaration of Independence, then, is one of individual liberty. People are born free, with a right to plan and live their lives free from the interference of others, including the government. Government is instituted for the limited purpose of securing that right. Thus, the Founders envisioned a world of free people and institutions—a vast sea of private activity— with a small government of limited powers, dedicated to securing that freedom.[4]

The Doctrine of Enumerated Powers

Clearly, that vision is a far cry from what we have today. Yet it is the vision that inspired the Founders as they gathered again in Philadelphia, 11 years later, to draft a new Constitution. And here again, we see it right from the start, in the Preamble of the Constitution: "We the People," for the purposes listed, "do ordain and establish this Constitution." The people come first, logically and temporally, the government comes second. Government is established by the people; they give it whatever powers it has. That fundamental point is made in the very first sentence of Article I: "All legislative Powers *herein granted* shall be vested in a Congress." By implication, not all powers were "herein granted," as the rest of the document, especially Article I, section 8, makes clear. And the point is recapitulated, as if for emphasis, in the final documentary statement of the founding period, the Tenth Amendment: "The powers not delegated to the United States by the Constitution, nor prohibited by it to the States, are reserved to the States respectively, or to the people."

Thus the central, the core principle of the document: The Constitution establishes a government of delegated, enumerated, and hence limited powers. The Bill of Rights, added two years after the government established by the Constitution was up and running, has rightly been called an afterthought. For the doctrine of enumerated powers, not the Bill of Rights, was meant to be our principal defense against overweening government.[5] The best way to restrain power, the Founders believed, was to give it sparingly in the first place. Thus, they left most power with the states or, still more, with the people. James Madison, the principal author of the Constitution, put it simply when he wrote in *Federalist No. 45* that the powers of the federal government were to be "few and defined." That is a government of limited powers.[6]

The Court Rediscovers Limited Government, Clinton Resists

It will doubtless be objected that those quaint principles are all well and good, but much has happened over the past 200 and more years. Much indeed has happened. It is all the more remarkable, therefore, that when we come to the present—to 1995, in particular— we discover that those principles have been rediscovered by no less than the Supreme Court of the United States. And even some in Congress have spoken lately about constitutional limits on congressional power.

The Court's rediscovery occurred most strikingly in *United States v. Lopez*,[7] which posed the question: Does the power of Congress to regulate commerce among the states, which was given primarily to ensure that states would not interfere with interstate commerce, entail a power to enact the Gun-Free School Zones Act of 1990,[8] which prohibits gun possession near schools? For the first time since 1937, when the New Deal Court essentially eviscerated the doctrine of enumerated powers, the Court held that Congress had exceeded its power under the Commerce Clause. In other words, the people, either in the beginning or since, have never given the federal government the power to regulate guns around schools. However worthy that end might be, Congress is without power to achieve it. The states might have such a power—and in this instance all states do— but that is a matter of state, not federal, law.

In his opinion for the Court, Chief Justice William Rehnquist began with a ringing statement: "We start with first principles. The Constitution establishes a government of enumerated powers."[9] For a government long unused to such candor, that came as something of a shock. Yet in so speaking, Rehnquist brought us only part of the way back to first principles. It was a major step, to be sure, and more recent opinions have shown that the Court was serious.[10] But Rehnquist's statement leaves us with an essentially positivist reading of the Constitution. For by failing to say that the powers enumerated in the Constitution are first delegated by the people, the statement fails to articulate the basis of those powers, suggesting that the founding generation could have enumerated any powers in the document—making it, in effect, a product merely of their will. That was not the Founders' view. The whole point of delegation—as distinct from enumeration—was to ground the document in the *natural* law. For one can delegate only those powers one *has*, by

33

nature, to delegate. That is the *natural* limit on the scope of government power, which enumeration alone does not provide. Thus, Rehnquist failed to connect the positive law of enumeration with the natural law of delegation, as captured in the very first sentence of the Constitution, after the Preamble, and in the very last documentary sentence of the founding period, the Tenth Amendment.

Notwithstanding that critical omission, however, the Court is clearly moving in the right direction. But where has the Clinton administration been in all of this? Far from having urged the Court to take the next step and ground the Constitution once again in its natural law roots, the administration was on the other side in the *Lopez* case. In fact, in his opening statement in oral argument in the case, Solicitor General Drew Days, speaking for the administration, admonished the lower court for having taken "the extraordinary step of invalidating an act of Congress as being beyond its power under the Commerce Clause."[11] Indeed, he went so far as to speak of Congress's "plenary powers under the Constitution."[12] When Justice Sandra Day O'Connor interrupted with a concern "that the original understandings and structural theories that underlay the Federal system have been so eroded that that whole system is in danger,"[13] Days minimized the concern, then suggested that Congress could regulate all violent crime under the commerce power[14]—despite the Court's having said repeatedly over the years that there is no general federal police power.[15] The assumptions that the Court, and he, were proceeding from, he continued, were "that Congress was given the power under the Constitution to legislate directly upon private individuals, and that there are no built-in limitations on the Constitution."[16] When Justice Anthony Kennedy later objected that the view Days offered left decisions about the extent of Congress's power in the hands of Congress, the solicitor general responded—with nearly 60 years of case law to support him: "It's not an argument that I concocted, Justice Kennedy. It's one that I think flows from this Court's decisions."[17]

The Crux of the Problem

We come, then, to the crux of the modern problem. Days was right. The post–New Deal Court has pretty much, as Justice Kennedy put it, "left decisions about the extent of Congress's power in the hands of Congress." Judicial deference to the political branches—

especially on so fundamental an issue as the scope of federal power, fraught as it is with the perils of self-interest—is inconsistent, of course, with judicial responsibility, to say nothing of judicial independence, the separation of powers, and the rule of law established by the Constitution. But there it is, a modern reality. Deference was the product of President Franklin Roosevelt's notorious 1937 Court-packing scheme.[18] Following that threat, an intimidated Court effectively rewrote the Constitution, without benefit of amendment. The Court's main target, not surprisingly, was the centerpiece of the Constitution, the doctrine of enumerated powers. In a pair of cases,[19] the Court effectively eviscerated the doctrine, freeing Congress to redistribute and regulate virtually at will. Because the story is familiar to students of the Constitution, I will simply highlight it here, the better to show how Clinton's conduct is inconsistent with the Constitution we lived under for most of our history.

Two clauses of the Constitution are at issue, both found in Article I, section 8, of the document, the General Welfare Clause and the Commerce Clause. Unfortunately, neither was carefully drafted, which means that interpretation must be guided by constitutional theory and structure and by writings revealing the original understanding of the clauses, especially as those writings go to the essential theory and structure of the document.

Taking the General Welfare Clause first, Alexander Hamilton was of the view that Congress had an *independent* power to spend for the general welfare.[20] Madison, Jefferson, and most others, however, raised a telling objection to that view, namely, that if that were the proper reading, there would have been no point in enumerating Congress's powers—as a limit on Congress—because Congress could do virtually anything it wanted under the General Welfare Clause by saying simply that it was spending for the general welfare. As South Carolina's William Drayton put it on the floor of the House in 1828, "if Congress can determine what constitutes the general welfare and can appropriate money for its advancement, where is the limitation to carrying into execution whatever can be effected by money?"[21] Hamilton's reading, in short, undermines the very point of enumeration, which both the Constitution itself and the writings that surround it make clear was to be the principal restraint on federal power. The better reading, which prevailed, for the most part, for most of our history, was that Congress could spend only for *enumerated* ends and that that spending was further limited by having to serve the general welfare, not just the welfare of particular parties or sections. Thus, the clause was a further *restraint* on power, not a source of power.[22]

In 1936, however, the Court came down for the first time on Hamilton's side, but only in *dicta*—and in a case in which the statute at issue was found to be unconstitutional.[23] A year later, however, following Roosevelt's Court-packing threat, the Court elevated its previous *dicta* to a holding.[24] Congress did have an independent power to spend for the general welfare, the Court said. It added, however, that that spending must be limited to serving the general welfare—but that the Court would not itself police that limit. Rather, "the discretion belongs to Congress,"[25] the very Congress that was spending with ever-greater particularity. Not even Hamilton had called for that.[26] Needless to say, with the Court now out of the way, deferring to Congress, that trend has continued. Neither enumeration nor the word "general" restrains Congress's spending today.

The Commerce Clause suffered a similar fate. Here, however, the Founders were in general agreement about its meaning and purpose. Written as states were erecting protectionist barriers to interstate commerce, the clause was meant to enable Congress to override such barriers. Indeed, one of the main reasons for drafting a new Constitution at all was to give the national Congress the power to ensure free trade. Congress was given power to regulate—or "make regular"—commerce among the states. The clause was meant to enable Congress to ensure the free flow of goods and services among the states, to ensure a national market. In fact, that is exactly how the clause was read and applied in the Court's first great Commerce Clause case.[27]

In 1937, however, the Court effectively eliminated that functional reading of the clause, holding that Congress could regulate anything that "affects" interstate commerce.[28] Since there is nothing that does not affect interstate commerce at some level, that amounted to giving Congress a power to regulate anything and everything, for any purpose whatever. Not surprisingly, Congress has been not at all reluctant to exercise that power. It has used the Commerce Clause to regulate everything under the sun—including, for example, the possession of guns near schools.

Through its novel readings of those two clauses, then, the New Deal Court effectively eviscerated the doctrine of enumerated powers, the Founders' principal measure for restraining federal power. Indeed, the Court took clauses that were meant to be shields against power and turned them into swords of power. The result is the modern welfare state, with essentially unlimited redistributive and regulatory power.

The incongruity between the welfare state and the state envisioned by the Founders, as authorized by the Constitution, is so clear that even the Court today can no longer avoid noticing it. But members of Congress have also been heard lately to complain that Congress acts often as if there were no constitutional limits at all on its power. Thus, in 1995 over 100 members of the House formed a constitutional caucus, the purpose of which was nothing less than to work toward restoring constitutional government.[29] And in academia too, constitutional scholars today are willing to step forward to say things like, "the post–New Deal administrative state is unconstitutional, and its validation by the legal system amounts to nothing less than a bloodless constitutional revolution."[30]

Yet even during the New Deal itself the constitutional question did not go unnoticed—even among those who promoted the New Deal revolution. Thus, in 1935 President Roosevelt wrote to the chairman of the House Ways and Means Committee, "I hope your committee will not permit doubts as to constitutionality, however reasonable, to block the suggested legislation."[31] And some 30 years after the event, Rexford G. Tugwell, one of the principal architects of the New Deal, could be found writing, "To the extent that these [New Deal policies] developed, they were tortured interpretations of a document [i.e., the Constitution] intended to prevent them."[32] That is a fairly clear admission that the New Deal was skating not simply on thin but on no constitutional ice at all. At the least, statements like those stand in stark contrast with presidential statements like that of President Grover Cleveland, who in 1887, 100 years after the Constitution was written, vetoed a bill for the relief of Texas farmers suffering from a drought by saying, "I can find no warrant for such an appropriation in the Constitution."[33]

The Court and the Climate of Ideas

Here we are today, then, increasingly able to say, as a matter of simple candor, that we need to address the constitutional illegitimacy that surrounds us. The Constitution authorizes a limited government, with powers that are "few and defined." Yet the federal government today is anything but limited, its powers anything but few and defined. The Court is at last addressing the problem, but it is able to do so, it seems, only in the clearest and easiest cases, the cases in which federal power is not only lacking but redundant because state power is already sufficient for the matter at hand. Thus, even in its most recent cases, which have secured the *Lopez* decision, the Court is still working at the margins of the New Deal revolution.

There are several reasons why the Court, by itself, is probably unable yet to move more sweepingly toward restoring constitutional government, but they all concern the climate of ideas in the nation. The Court, with neither purse nor sword, has been called our "least dangerous branch."[34] As such, its authority rests in significant part on the credibility of its arguments. But credibility is a complex matter. To be sure, a growing number of people, including members of the Court itself, are now saying that the Court's enumerated powers jurisprudence of the past 60 years is less than credible.[35] And those who cling to that errant jurisprudence—the dissenters in *Lopez*, for example, who recognize the doctrine of enumerated powers but are unable to think of a thing Congress cannot regulate—are increasingly less than credible.[36] But it takes time for the shifts at play today to fully unfold. And we are not there yet, not at a point at which one can say confidently that the arguments of the Court's majority have carried the day—far from it.

None of that is to say, of course, that this is all a matter of politics: indeed, the natural law view, at bottom, is *not* about politics but about reason. But neither is it to say that politics plays *no* role in changing the climate of ideas—and in bringing people back to reason as the foundation of law, in particular, and away from politics as the foundation. In fact, it is because politics is so important for changing the climate of ideas—and for making that climate more conducive to law grounded in reason—that those who are concerned to see the shift through to the end need to attend to the political climate in which the law rests.

The Administration and the Climate of Ideas

We return, then, to that climate. Clearly, although the Court and some in Congress and academia are at last pointing to our constitutional dilemma, the man who has spoken from the nation's bully pulpit for nearly eight years now is very much on the other side, not only oblivious to the dilemma but hostile to any suggestion that there is one. With extraordinary power to set the political tone of the nation, Mr. Clinton has shown himself to be unconcerned about our fundamental constitutional problem—in fact, determined, by implication, only to exacerbate it. Indeed, whether it concerns taxing, spending, or regulating, his very raison d'être appears to be to promise more and more from government and make more and more people dependent on government, not to restore government to its constitutional bounds, thus freeing people to plan and live their own lives.

In the Political Realm

Look at Clinton's State of the Union Addresses, not to mention the universal health care plan that he and his wife so assiduously promoted, which would have socialized one-seventh of the American economy if it had been enacted. When you go down the list of the hundreds of policies and programs Mr. Clinton has proposed or helped bring into being over the years—from Americorps, to 100,000 new teachers, to family leave, to protection for tobacco farmers, to a patients' bill of rights, to a Lands Legacy Initiative, to juvenile boot camps, to a flextime proposal, to extended hospital stays for mastectomy patients, to a program to help schools make repairs, and on and on and on—you soon realize that there is indeed no problem too personal or trivial for his, and the federal government's, attention. "Got a problem? We've got a program" could truly serve as the slogan of this administration.

Take any one of those programs—federal funds for more teachers, for example—and ask where the authority for the expenditure or the regulation is found in the Constitution. From beginning to end, the document never mentions the word "education." The people, in 1787 or since, have never given the federal government any power over the subject—despite a concern for education that surely predates the Constitution. Thus, no such power is enumerated in the document. Plainly, the administration will point to the General Welfare Clause. But as noted above, until 1937, few thought that that clause afforded Congress a power to spend for "the general welfare" apart from Congress's enumerated powers or ends. That idea was a product of the politics of the New Deal, not the law of the Constitution.

Or take a patients' bill of rights, for which authority is found, the administration no doubt believes, in both the General Welfare Clause and the Commerce Clause. Again, one imagines that the founding generation was no less concerned about health care than is the present generation, but that concern did not find its way into the Constitution. The general welfare arguments just noted apply with equal force here, of course. As for the Commerce Clause, recall that it was meant to enable Congress to ensure that commerce would be free from impediments, especially those coming from the states. No one is suggesting that the states are interfering with the health care or health insurance markets—if states are, Congress has the power to override such impediments. No, the schemes at issue are aimed not at state interference with the market but at redistribution through regulation. They are aimed not at freeing markets but, just the opposite, at burdening markets with all manner of regulatory restrictions—to serve the administration's conception of "social justice," if not its political ambitions.

That is not the kind of "justice" the Constitution was written to establish. In fact, it is no justice at all, but the very opposite, as the simplest of examples will show. Since government's legitimate powers come from the people, we have to ask, in any given case, whether people have a particular power in the first place to give to government to exercise on their behalf. The power here at issue, the redistributive power, is a power to take from some for the benefit of others. But if A has no rightful power to take from B for the benefit of C, then he has no such power to give to government to exercise on his behalf. Nor does it add anything if A and C combine toward that end—if they "vote" to take from B—for that amounts simply to the tyranny of the majority against the minority. Those elementary principles have long been understood. Indeed, the Founders understood them, which is why they constituted our government as they did.[37] Yet there is the Clinton administration promoting one redistributive scheme after another, over and over again, none of which is authorized by the Constitution.

In the Judicial Realm

But when we leave the political arena and return to the courts, we still find Mr. Clinton fighting the Court—and the Constitution—at every step, thus promoting a climate of ideas there too that undermines constitutionally limited government. One of the most recent examples can be found in the government's brief in *United States v. Morrison*,[38] a case the Court handed down on May 15, 2000, finding that Congress once again had exceeded its authority when it passed the Violence Against Women Act.[39] At its core, the case was about little but the doctrine of enumerated powers. It raised a simple question: Did Congress have power under the Commerce Clause or under section 5 of the Fourteenth Amendment to grant victims of gender-motivated violence a federal right of action against their assailants? (Here again, that right has long been recognized under state common law and statute.)

Despite the simplicity of the question, and the all but exclusive focus of the case on the doctrine of enumerated powers, the administration's brief—except in a single footnote, not really on point—never even mentions "enumerated powers."[40] Instead of addressing that fundamental doctrine head-on, and the constitutional framework it implies, the brief reads almost like a policy statement, with page after page devoted to showing that violence against women affects commerce (as if violence against men, which is greater, did not). The brief argues, in essence, that Congress has virtually plenary power to regulate things that affect commerce; gender-motivated violence affects commerce; therefore, Congress has the power to regulate it. Never mind that at some level, as noted above, everything affects commerce—the point the Court had raised five years earlier in *Lopez*. The clear implication—that Congress has the power to regulate anything and everything—is simply dismissed in the administration's brief, as if constitutional limits on Congress did not exist.

But it is no different when we turn to the Fourteenth Amendment rationale for the act, for the administration's brief dismisses the law on this point too—here, the plain language of the amendment. Section 1 of the Fourteenth Amendment prohibits *states*, not private citizens, from violating the rights of citizens. Yet the Violence Against Women Act gives victims of gender-motivated violence federal remedies against *private* parties, not against states. Thus, Congress has no authority under the Fourteenth Amendment to enact such a statute. Yet there was Mr. Clinton's Justice Department, defending the act all the same.

And it continues. A week after *Morrison* came down, the Court decided yet another case involving the Commerce Clause, *Jones v.*

United States.[41] There the question was whether a federal arson statute limited in its application to buildings "used in interstate or foreign commerce or in any activity affecting interstate or foreign commerce" could be used to prosecute a person who burned a residence that happened to have a mortgage and insurance from out-of-state companies and received gas from another state. Those were the links to interstate commerce that gave the government authority under the statute, the administration argued. Set aside the question of whether Congress can use the Commerce Clause to make *any* arson a federal crime and consider simply the lengths the administration was willing to go in *this* case to stretch the reach of the statute— and of the Commerce Clause as well. Again the Court made short work of the administration's argument. In fact, at oral argument the Court even made light of it. When pressed to name something, just one thing, that Congress could not regulate or make a federal crime, Deputy Solicitor General Michael Dreeben, like his *Lopez* predecessor, Drew Days, could think of nothing, until Chief Justice Rehnquist chimed in, "How about an example like a gun-free school district?"[42]

The Rule of Law: Freedom—or Empowerment?

One could go on, of course, but by now the picture should be clear. At the same time, we need also to be clear, once again, about the complicity of others: Mr. Clinton has not been alone in his efforts to expand government by ignoring the limits imposed by the Constitution. Congress has played its part too, after all. And previous administrations also have been less than solicitous about constitutional limits on federal power. Indeed, Kenneth Starr, when he was solicitor general for President George Bush, defended Congress in *United States v. New York*,[43] the 1992 case that was the first of the series of recent cases in which the Rehnquist Court has at last begun to revive the doctrine of enumerated powers.

Still, the sheer scope of the Clinton administration's ambition sets this president apart from most of his predecessors. Perhaps Solicitor General Days captured that best in his oral argument in *Lopez* when he said that "the commerce power is one of the heads of authority under the Constitution that transformed our country from an agrarian society to one that was a powerful commercial enterprise."[44] Even if that was a rhetorical slip, made in the heat of oral argument, it was a breathtaking slip. Doubtless there are those who believe that it was the federal government, acting under the Commerce Clause, that brought about our transformation from an agrarian to a commercial society. Certainly there are people in Mr. Clinton's administration who act as if they believe that it was government, not the private sector, that so transformed the nation. For them, the rule of law is little but a rule of empowerment, a warrant "to do great things" through government. Their disrespect is not simply for the Constitution but for the very idea of limited government. Their vision could not be further from that of the Founders, who saw the rule of law, rightly, as a limit on government. It confined government to its proper sphere, leaving individuals free to pursue happiness, by their own lights, by their own powers, free even from the "beneficent" interference of government. If we want the freedom and prosperity that the rule of law ensures, it is that vision that must be restored.

Notes

1. For a more complete discussion of the relationship between democracy and legitimacy, see Roger Pilon, "On the First Principles of Constitutionalism: Liberty, Then Democracy," *American University Journal of International Law and Policy* 8, nos. 2 and 3 (Winter–Spring 1992–93): 531–49; and Roger Pilon, "Individual Rights, Democracy, and Constitutional Order: On the Foundations of Legitimacy," *Cato Journal* 11, no. 3 (Winter 1992): 373–90.

2. John Locke, "Second Treatise of Government," in *Two Treatises of Government*, ed. Peter Laslett (New York: Mentor, 1965), para. 123.

3. "The notion that the common law embodied right reason furnished from the fourteenth century its chief claim to be regarded as higher law." Edward S. Corwin, *The "Higher Law" Background of American Constitutional Law* (Ithaca, N.Y.: Cornell University Press, 1955), p. 26.

4. I have discussed the theory of the Declaration of Independence more fully in Roger Pilon, *The Purpose and Limits of Government*, Cato's Letters no. 13 (Washington: Cato Institute, 1999).

5. Thus, Alexander Hamilton, arguing against the addition of a bill of rights: "Why declare that things shall not be done which there is no power to do? Why, for instance, should it be said that the liberty of the press shall not be restrained, when no power is given by which restrictions may be imposed?" *Federalist No. 84*, ed. Clinton Rossiter (New York: Mentor, 1961), pp. 513–14. And James Wilson, to the same effect: ". . . everything which is not given is reserved." James Wilson, Address to a meeting of the citizens of Philadelphia (1787), in Bernard Schwartz, *The Bill of Rights: A Documentary History*, vol. 1 (New York: Chelsea House, 1971), p. 529.

6. For a more complete discussion of the foregoing issues, see Roger Pilon, "Freedom, Responsibility, and the Constitution: On Recovering Our Founding Principles," *Notre Dame Law Review* 68, no. 3 (1993): 507–47; and Roger Pilon, "On the Folly and Illegitimacy of Industrial Policy," *Stanford Law & Policy Review* 5, no. 1 (Fall 1993): 103–18.

7. 514 U.S. 549 (1995).

8. 18 U.S.C. § 922(q)(1)(A) (1988 ed., Supp. V).

9. 514 U.S. 549, 552 (1995).

10. See, for example, *United States v. Morrison*, 120 S.Ct. 1740 (2000), and *Jones v. United States*, 120 S.Ct. 1904 (2000). Both cases will be discussed briefly below.

11. Drew S. Days and John R. Carter, Oral argument before the Supreme Court, *United States v. Lopez*, U.S. Supreme Court Official Transcript no. 93-1260, November 8, 1994, p. 3.

12. Ibid., p. 4.

13. Ibid.

14. Ibid., p. 10.

15. Thus, as far back as *Cohens v. Virginia*, 6 Wheat. 264 (1821), Chief Justice John Marshall said that it was "clear that congress cannot punish felonies generally." Ibid. at 428.

16. Days and Carter, p. 10.

17. Ibid., p. 19.

18. See Alfred H. Kelly et al., *The American Constitution: Its Origins and Development*, 6th ed. (New York: Norton, 1983), pp. 487–500; and Merlo J. Pusey, *The Supreme Court Crisis* (New York: Macmillian, 1937).

19. *Helvering v. Davis*, 301 U.S. 619 (1937); and *NLRB v. Jones & Laughlin Steel Corp.*, 301 U.S. 1 (1937).

20. See Arthur Harrison Cole, ed., *Industrial and Commercial Correspondence of Alexander Hamilton* (New York: A. M. Kelly, 1968), p. 247.

21. *Congressional Debates*, 1828, vol. 4, pp. 1632–34. Drayton continued, "How few objects are there which money cannot accomplish! . . . Can it be conceived that the great and wise men who devised our Constitution . . . should have failed so egregiously . . . as to grant a power which rendered restriction upon power practically unavailing?"

Madison made a similar point on several occasions. See, for example, James Madison, "Report on Resolutions," in *The Writings of James Madison*, ed. Gaillard Hunt (New York: Putnam Sons, 1900), vol. 6, p. 357:

> Money cannot be applied to the *general welfare*, otherwise than by an application of it to some *particular* measure conducive to the general welfare. Whenever, therefore, money has been raised by the general authority, and is to be applied to a particular measure, a question arises whether the particular measure be within the enumerated authorities vested in Congress. If it be, the money requisite for it may be applied to it; if it be not, no such application can be made. [Emphasis in the original.]

And Jefferson also addressed the issue. See, for example, Thomas Jefferson, "Letter from Thomas Jefferson to Albert Gallatin (June 16, 1817)," in *Writings of Thomas Jefferson*, ed. Paul Leicester Ford (1899), vol. 10, p. 91:

> . . . our tenet ever was, and, indeed, it is almost the only landmark which now divides the federalists from the republicans, that Congress had not unlimited powers to provide for the general welfare, but were restrained to those specifically enumerated; and that, as it was never meant they should raise money for purposes which the enumeration did not place under their action; consequently, that the specification of powers is a limitation of the purpose for which they may raise money.

22. See generally Charles Warren, *Congress as Santa Clause: Or National Donations and the General Welfare Clause of the Constitution* (1932; reprint, New York: Arno Press, 1978).

23. *United States v. Butler*, 262 U.S. 1, 65–66 (1936).

24. *Helvering v. Davis*, 301 U.S. 619 (1937).

25. Ibid. at 640.

26. For Hamilton's thoughts on the role of the judiciary, see *The Federalist Nos. 78–83*.

27. *Gibbons v. Ogden*, 22 U.S. 1 (1824). Justice William Johnson wrote in his concurrence, "If there was any one object riding over every other in the adoption of the constitution, it was to keep the commercial intercourse among the States free from all invidious and partial restraints." Ibid. at 231. See Richard A. Epstein, "The Proper Scope of the Commerce Power," *Virginia Law Review* 73 (1987): 1387–1455; and Cato Institute, Amicus curiae brief, *Jones v. United States*, 120 S.Ct. 1904 (2000), ⟨http://www.cato.org/pubs/legalbriefs/jvsusa.pdf⟩.

28. 301 U.S. 1 (1937).

29. That was the "firebrand" 104th Congress, of course. The freshman Republicans who so animated that Congress seem since then to have been tamed, for the most part. Nevertheless, many still do speak up for the Constitution. Thus, when Congress repassed a slightly revised Gun-Free School Zones Act, after the *Lopez* Court found the first version unconstitutional, Sen. Fred Thompson rose on the floor of the Senate to condemn the "attempt at the Federal level to federalize another State and local matter," citing *Lopez* as his authority. See Fred Thompson, Statement on Gun-Free School Zones Act, U.S. Senate, 104th Cong., 2d sess., September 12, 1996.

30. Gary Lawson, "The Rise and Rise of the Administrative State," *Harvard Law Review* 107 (1994): 1231. See also Epstein, "The Proper Scope," p. 1388, n. 27: "I think that the expansive construction of the [commerce] clause accepted by the New Deal Supreme Court is wrong, and clearly so."

31. Franklin D. Roosevelt, Letter to Rep. Samuel B. Hill (July 6, 1935), in *The Public Papers and Addresses of Franklin D. Roosevelt*, ed. Samuel I. Rosenman, vol. 4 (New York: Random House, 1938), pp. 91–92.

32. Rexford G. Tugwell, "A Center Report: Rewriting the Constitution," *Center Magazine*, March 1968, p. 20.

33. *Congressional Record*, 49th Cong., 1887, vol. 18, pt. 2:1875.

34. Alexander M. Bickel, *The Least Dangerous Branch: The Supreme Court at the Bar of Politics* (Indianapolis: Bobbs-Merrill, 1962).

35. Thus, Justice Clarence Thomas wrote in his concurrence in *Lopez*, "I write separately to observe that our case law has drifted far from the original understanding of the Commerce Clause." 514 U.S. 549, 584 (1995).

36. "When asked at oral argument if there were *any* limits to the Commerce Clause, the Government was at a loss for words." Ibid. at 600. See also Lawrence Tribe, *American Constitutional Law* (New York: Foundation Press, 2000), p. 816: "The Court's application of its substantial effect and aggregation principles in the period between 1937 and 1995, combined with its deference to congressional findings, placed it in the increasingly untenable position of claiming the power to strike down invocations of the Commerce Clause, while at the same time applying a set of doctrines that made it virtually impossible actually to exercise this power."

37. Thus, Justice Oliver Wendell Holmes was simply wrong when he implied in his dissent in the famous *Lochner* case that our Constitution did not "embody a particular economic theory, whether of paternalism and the organic relation of the

citizen to the state or of laissez faire." *Lochner v. New York*, 198 U.S. 45, 75 (1905). The Constitution explicitly recognizes the rights of property and contract, the foundations of laissez-faire capitalism. See Roger Pilon, "On the Foundations of Economic Liberty," *Cato Policy Report*, vol. 11, no. 4, July–August 1989, pp. 6–11.

38. 120 S.Ct. 1740 (2000).

39. 42 U.S.C. § 13981 (1994).

40. Department of Justice, Brief for the United States, *United States v. Morrison*, 120 S.Ct. 1740 (2000).

41. 120 S.Ct. 1904 (2000).

42. Quoted in Donald M. Falk and Michael R. Dreeben, Oral argument before the Supreme Court, *Jones v. United States*, U.S. Supreme Court Official Transcript no. 99-5739, March 21, 2000, p. 28.

43. 505 U.S. 144 (1992).

44. Days and Carter, p. 20.

3. Expanding Executive Power
Douglas W. Kmiec

I am a defender of executive power. No one who has headed the Office of Legal Counsel, designed to preserve the office and authority of the presidency, could be otherwise. But defending the constitutional parameters of presidential power is fundamentally different from defending assertions of power inclined toward excess or abuse.

Having been impeached by the House of Representatives and found in contempt by a federal judge for misleading a federal court in a civil rights suit brought against him, President Clinton has had some difficulty with the requirements of the rule of law. Whether or not one thinks the personal behavior of the president is a fit subject for judicial and congressional scrutiny, one cannot help but be concerned about the extent to which this president, in carrying out his governmental functions, has directed the executive beyond the boundaries of lawful authority. This chapter focuses on the use of executive orders and other presidential directives, but the excesses outlined here take on greater magnitude when coupled with the president's willingness to engage his nation in undeclared wars, circumvent the advise-and-consent functions of the Senate, or employ the White House as a fund-raising prize.

Executive Power Is Duty, Not Grant

It is significant that presidential power in the Constitution is cast mostly in the language of duty: to "take Care that the Laws be faithfully executed."[1] As one presidential scholar has written, "[t]he duty to execute the laws 'faithfully' means that American presidents may not—whether by revocation, suspension, dispensation, inaction or otherwise—refuse to honor and enforce statutes that were enacted with their consent or over their veto. Many scholars have agreed that the Take Care Clause was meant to deny the president a suspending or dispensing power [like that exercised, before American independence, by the Stuart Kings]."[2]

Executive orders are not mentioned in the Constitution, yet they have a long history dating back to President Washington's proclamation of neutrality.[3] As a practical matter, they are a necessary aspect of governance. To be accorded the respect of law, however, they must be anchored in the Constitution or in a statute. The duty of the president is to faithfully execute, not invent, the law. Yes, the extent of executive power can be debated,[4] and yes, some political scientists complacently claim that all modern presidents have pressed or exceeded the boundaries of Article II authority.[5] Yet, those sworn to "taking care" of the execution of the law must be held to a high standard. This is not a partisan issue, but a legal and constitutional one. As the head of Lyndon Johnson's Office of Legal Counsel once observed, "[t]he authority of the President to 'make law' by executive order does not exist in mid-air. It must find its taproot in Article II of the Constitution or in statutes enacted by the Congress."[6]

President Clinton's Troubling Executive Order Bravado

In the issuance of executive orders, conformance to the rule of law has not always been President Clinton's uppermost aspiration. As widely reported, and upon highly sensitive issues, Mr. Clinton employed this administrative device not to implement the will of the people but to circumvent it. Employing what one seasoned observer termed a "blitz of executive orders,"[7] the president signaled that his strategy was to make progress on his ideological agenda "with or without congressional help"[8]—that is, regardless of the will of the people's representatives. As of June 2000, President Clinton had issued some 324 executive orders.[9] Although that number is comparable to those of Presidents Johnson, Nixon, and Reagan, and far smaller than, say, FDR's (3,522),[10] who virtually governed by executive order during the war years, it is obviously not only the frequency of use but the legitimacy of presidential orders that matters. Here, Mr. Clinton falls well short of the ideal. His advisers have been brazenly boastful of the usurpation of authority, conceiving even the most extravagant legal position as clever policy achievement.[11] Revealing is the remark of one-time Clinton adviser Paul Begala, cavalierly dismissing challenges to Mr. Clinton's executive order practice: "Stroke of the pen, law of the land. Kind of cool."[12]

48

The Lack of Specific Authority and Judicial Review

One indicator of abuse is the extent to which President Clinton employed executive orders without *any* citation of specific authority—beyond, of course, the general assertion of power vested in the president. A recent count done by some of my law students reveals that nearly one-third of Mr. Clinton's executive orders rely on no statutory reference whatsoever. Even if some of these orders are amendments of earlier ones, the number is startling. Unspecific claims of executive authority were condemned almost a half-century ago by the Supreme Court, making it plain that presidential action, even in time of military emergency, is not immune from judicial review. In *Youngstown Sheet & Tube Co. v. Sawyer*,[13] President Truman had seized the nation's steel mills by executive order to maintain supplies for the military engagement in Korea in the face of an impending labor shutdown. Leaning heavily on the contextual justification, Truman had merely recited as authority the Constitution's general conferral of executive power. The Court was unimpressed, invalidating the seizure order as an unconstitutional exercise of lawmaking authority reserved to Congress.

Justice Jackson's concurring opinion in *Youngstown* has thereafter provided a template for measuring the adequacy of presidential assertions of power. Jackson reasoned that a president has maximum authority when he acts pursuant to express or implied authority from Congress; he possesses ambivalent or equivocal ("zone of twilight") authority when Congress has neither granted nor denied the president the authority to act; he enjoys the least latitude (principally that inherent in the office itself) when he acts contrary to the express or implied will of Congress.

It is sometimes mistakenly thought that presidential action in excess of statutory (as opposed to constitutional) authority is not subject to judicial review. This misconception is most often traced to *Dalton v. Specter*.[14] Writing for the Court in *Dalton*, Chief Justice Rehnquist drew the obvious distinction between *Youngstown*, where the president explicitly renounced statutory reliance, and *Dalton*, where the president, in making certain military base-closing decisions, claimed to be operating pursuant to congressional enactment. The Chief Justice wrote that executive action in excess of statutory authority is not *ipso facto* unconstitutional—a quite misleading statement if taken out of context. The statement is true only if the president has constitutionally explicit authority independent of Congress or if a statute confers unfettered discretion upon the president—which, as it happened, was the case in *Dalton*. Where the president lacks such independent constitutional authority or statutory discretion, executive branch action or regulation premised on presidential direction is judicially reviewable.

Specific Examples—The Repeal of Labor Law

An important recent survey[15] from the Cato Institute highlighted how Mr. Clinton's executive order practice has exceeded the bounds of constitutional, statutory, or discretionary authority with enough frequency to merit the concern of anyone who understands how liberty is preserved through the separation of powers. My own research confirms the Cato study. But perhaps such confirmation is not needed insofar as Mr. Clinton is the only peacetime president to have had an order voided in federal court.[16]

In that case, Mr. Clinton used Executive Order 12954 to subvert both established labor law[17] and a Supreme Court decision[18] securing the right of employers to continue business in the midst of labor disputes by hiring permanent replacements. The Clinton order would have blackballed businesses for exercising this lawful right. The order stated bluntly that "[i]t is the policy of the executive branch in procuring goods and services that . . . contracting agencies shall not contract with employers that permanently replace lawfully striking employees."[19] Remarkable in its affront to the democratic process, the order ignored the fact that in the previous four years "Congress had considered and rejected legislation that would have amended the NLRA (National Labor Relations Act) to prohibit employers from hiring permanent striker replacements."[20] Given this context, the Court of Appeals for the District of Columbia Circuit found the order to be preempted by the NLRA. Even one of the most temperate and respected members of the Senate, the now-retired Nancy Kassebaum, reflected that Mr. Clinton's executive order was "by its very nature a troubling effort by the executive branch to, by executive fiat, change what has been the law of the land, and a major part of labor law, for some 60 years."[21]

The president's disregard for the constitutional limits on his power permeated his brash and legally dubious effort to defend EO 12954. Mr. Clinton first sought to deny the court's jurisdiction by arguing that because presidential decisions are not formally reviewable under the Administrative Procedure Act (APA),[22] no APA challenge could be made to executive regulations implementing his order. Although the appellate court found it unnecessary to resolve this wholly "unsupported interpretation" of the APA, it did state that merely because "the [Labor] Secretary's regulations are based on the President's Executive Order hardly seems to insulate them from judicial review under the APA, even if the validity of the Order [was] thereby drawn into question."[23] As the court further noted in considering whether there was a non-APA (that is, a nonstatutory) basis for challenging the president's action, "[e]ven if the Secretary [was] acting at the behest of the President, this 'does not leave the courts without power to review the legality [of the action], for courts have power to compel subordinate executive officials to disobey illegal Presidential commands.'"[24] The appellate court thus made short work of the president's assertion of sovereign immunity. When the president directed the secretary to go beyond the limitations of the NLRA, the president and the secretary were no longer acting for the United States, but for themselves. As the court concluded, the president advanced "a breathtakingly broad claim of non-reviewability of presidential actions"[25] that could not be "seriously press[ed]."

Turning to the merits of this issue, did the president have *any* statutory basis for rewriting labor law? The short answer: no. Indeed, the president could not even muster a substantively related source of authority. Instead, he turned to a wholly unrelated procurement statute.[26] Although the Procurement Act is a broad grant of discretion to "provide for the Government an economical and efficient system for . . . procurement and supply . . . ,"[27] it is not an authorization to regulate the nonprocurement practices, including especially the labor practices, of anyone who just happens to supply goods and services to the government. Yes, prior lower court decisions upheld presidential sanctions for noncompliance with wage and price standards under this statute;[28] but procurement and prices are at least factually related. The Procurement Act is not "a blank check for the President to fill in at his will."[29] Whatever the appropriate limits of the Procurement Act, it could not be disingenuously applied to supersede labor law protections secured by a more specific statute.[30]

An "Acting" Defense of the Unauthorized

Before leaving this example, it is worth noting that much of the president's "breathtakingly broad" defense of Executive Order

12954 was articulated by a likable and highly regarded lawyer, but nevertheless one of the Clinton administration's numerous "acting" officials serving without nomination and confirmation as prescribed by the Constitution.[31] The constitutional disregard and danger of being governed by "acting" officials unaccountable to the people through the confirmation process is beyond the scope of this chapter. However, it has been well documented that Mr. Clinton has not taken the advice-and-consent function of the Senate seriously.[32] Such disregard is especially acute when it extends to the office of solicitor general, the highest ranking legal advocate charged with fashioning the litigation strategy for the United States.

Without belaboring this example, the speciousness of Mr. Clinton's legal reasoning is evidenced by mere recitation. First, it was opined that there was no difference, under the Procurement Act, between an order denying agencies the authority to acquire unreliable machines and an order barring agencies from dealing with private contractors with "unreliable" labor policies. Continuing to turn the gears of legal fantasy, the Clinton legal opinion then asserted the unbelievable: namely, that "we do not understand the action of Congress [refusing to authorize the President's direction] to bear on the President's authority to issue Executive Order 12954 [effectively doing that which the Congress denied him]." To assume the president has authority after contemporary and repeated congressional refusal is, of course, nothing short of a Forrest Gumpian denial of political reality.

But Mr. Clinton's legal mischief proceeds from the unbelievable to the unthinkable by turning the question inside out. It was suddenly not up to the president to locate proper lawful authority, it was up to Congress to explain why he needed it. Indeed, a congressional refusal to give the president what he wanted was even characterized by Clinton legal thinking as unconstitutional. According to the Justice Department apologetics written to rationalize the president's action,[33] "[t]o contend that Congress's inaction on legislation to prohibit all employers from hiring replacement workers deprived the president of authority he had possessed is to contend for the validity of the legislative veto."[34] The memo thus begs the very question at issue—whether the president has authority. The Clinton legal brain trust's assertion that there is "no indication in the legislative history that those opposing the proposed amendments to the NLRA (sought by the President) even considered the specialized context of government procurement"[35] is thus akin to expressing feigned surprise that no one references a local zoning ordinance to interpret an international treaty.

Environmental Adventures—Congress's Need for an Overarching Response

On another high-profile topic, environmental protection, numerous Clinton initiatives are based on executive orders or proclamations having a questionable legal foundation. For example, the *New York Times* recently reported how Mr. Clinton has been deploying sweeping interpretations of the Antiquities Act of 1906 to designate millions of acres of public land as "monuments," with little or no consultation with state and local officials and little consideration of the profound effects such designation has on local economies and grazing rights.[36] Ten governors are urging the president to follow the law and not circumvent the statutorily contemplated review and consultation process.[37]

The president's monument and other environmental designations have been formally challenged. For example, Executive Order 13061 established the American Heritage Rivers Initiative (AHRI),[38] a program designed ostensibly to preserve the natural resources of selected major rivers but, in its vagueness, inviting the transference of local land use decisionmaking to the federal government. Members of Congress sought to terminate the initiative via legislation and lawsuit. H.R. 1842, for example, assessed the executive order as a violation of the separation of powers insofar as it bypasses Congress in the creation of a new government agency (or the reorganization of existing ones) and improperly redirects federal monies. The legislation was reported favorably to the House by the Committee on Resources,[39] but, given other legislative priorities, ended there. The litigation ended, as many congressional lawsuits do, at the standing stage. Without a showing that executive action inflicts personal injury or denies a specific congressional function, such as the nullification of a legislative vote for a specific statutory proposal, judicial redress is frequently denied individual members of Congress.[40] A unitary executive capable of acting "with dispatch" is salutary when within his proper constitutional sphere, but is seldom countermanded easily or readily by a larger, more deliberate, bicameral body.

If Congress has any chance of correcting excessive presidential exercise, it will need to act as an institution and prophylactically, addressing more than a single occurrence. H.R. 2655,[41] presently pending in the House, is such a measure. If enacted, it would rescind the open-ended nature of various presidential emergency powers and require presidential orders to provide "a statement of the specific statutory or constitutional provision which in fact grants the President the authority claimed for such action."[42] Perhaps the most significant aspect of this legislative proposal is its confinement of the effect of presidential orders to the executive branch alone, unless the order is buttressed by particular congressional enactment. The legislation also contains specific grants of standing, some of which may prove constitutionally problematic if they exceed the Court's present conception of legislative standing. With less difficulty, H.R. 2655 acknowledges the standing of aggrieved private parties as well as state and local officials whose authority may be improperly curtailed by executive decree.

Sacrificing State and Local Government—"Suspensions" of Federalism

That state and local authority has been sacrificed by Mr. Clinton is illustrated no better than by his rescission of Reagan-era executive orders that clearly demarcated the respective powers of the federal and state governments and invited consultation between the two sovereigns.[43] As one recent law review assessment observed, President Reagan's "earlier executive orders reflect[ed] sincere regard for state sovereignty and distrust of agency discretion with respect to federalism. [Mr. Clinton's] EO 13083,[44] in contrast, disfavored state policymaking competence and preferred federal agency intervention."[45] Specifically, the Reagan orders, most notably Executive Order 12612, enunciated federalism principles that created a presumption in favor of state authority and instituted important preemption rules that denied regulatory preemption absent firm evidence of Congress's intent to preempt, while forbidding agencies from seeking such preemptive authority contrary to the principles stated. Both provisions, together with a requirement that agencies undertake federalism impact assessments when proposing new regulation, were omitted from the Clinton order, which "permitted federal agency regulation under almost any imaginable scenario" and arguably even bound states to unratified international agreements.[46] As the Cato Report noted, Mr. Clinton faced an "outcry" over his calculated snub of constitutional federalism and he suspended the order.[47] Indeed, "Clinton suspended it . . . on the very day the House voted, 417 to 2, to withhold funds for its implementation."[48]

Mr. Clinton has since issued a new federalism executive order, No. 13132, which is perceived as returning to a more orthodox conception of the constitutional structure.[49] It is patterned largely on President Reagan's earlier direction. Still, Mr. Clinton's disregard of federalism predated his controversial federalism order, and it continues, after his *mea culpa*, in less direct but still costly and profoundly troubling ways. Take, for example, President Clinton's EO 12898 addressing "environmental racism,"[50] a theory holding that a disproportionate number of environmental burdens are intentionally placed in poor and often minority neighborhoods. The research surrounding this subject is highly controverted,[51] which itself makes it unfit for top-down presidential direction. It is far from clear, for example, whether intentional racial discrimination or the availability of suitable sites, transportation corridors, and other geological conditions is what results in these environmental consequences.[52] Those casting a skeptical eye upon the label "environmental racism" doubt that addressing environmental problems under an emotionally charged civil rights rubric actually helps eradicate either environmental degradation or subtle racism.

One does not have to take sides on whether environmental racism is real or counterfeit to recognize that the Clinton administration, without the support of Congress, again employed an executive order to stretch and arguably disregard the accepted meaning of enacted law. When Executive Order 12898 declared it part of the mission of each federal agency to achieve environmental justice, Mr. Clinton cleverly hid the legal coercion implicit in this rhetoric by a separately circulated memorandum to department heads. As Phillip J. Cooper testified in the House, "[the executive order] did not make mention of Title VI of the Civil Rights [Act], nor did it refer to state or local permitting processes. However, on the same day, the administration released 'Memorandum for the Heads of All Departments and Agencies' "[53] that purported to create a wholly new civil rights action under Section 602 of Title VI for state and local permitting decisions.

Title VI provides that "[n]o person in the United States shall, on the ground of race, color, or national origin, be excluded from participation in, be denied the benefits of, or be subjected to discrimination under any program or activity receiving Federal financial assistance."[54] Before the Clinton executive order, numerous cases had established that, absent a showing of intent or valid regulations that allow the inference of intent from a sufficient showing of discriminatory impact, state and local siting decisions cannot be challenged under Title VI.[55] Nevertheless, in February 1998, under the auspices of President Clinton's executive order, the Environmental Protection Agency (EPA) departed from settled legal doctrine by issuing its so-called "interim guidance."[56] The "guidance" purported to create the very cause of action under Title VI that the cases found not to exist and probably cannot exist under the statute or the Constitution's equal protection doctrine.[57] Nevertheless, in disregard of statute, constitutional jurisprudence, and federalism, the Clinton EPA put the burden of disproving a negative (the absence of environmental racism) on state and local governments.

Mr. Clinton's "hidden" memorandum, it turns out, was an attempt to codify a now-vacated Third Circuit decision favored by Clinton policymakers. *Chester Residents Concerned for Quality Living v. Seif*[58] purported to find the right of action President Clinton and his advisers pretended to be the law. But again, Title VI does not expressly authorize such a right of action, and neither courts nor commentators believe it can be implied.[59] No persuasive legal theory was forthcoming from the president for such an implication.

The interim guidance of the Clinton EPA caused yet another firestorm of controversy. Mayors and governors concerned with the overall economic well-being of urban areas urged its revocation.[60] Congress prohibited the EPA from spending any funds to carry out its initiative, and the EPA took its "interim" guidance back to the drawing board.[61]

Again, the point of raising this additional example of President Clinton's disregard of federalism is not to debate the merits of one environmental position over another, but rather to illustrate the difficulty of an executive order lacking a sufficient statutory or constitutional foundation. The substantive infirmities of Mr. Clinton's

directive were compounded by presidential and agency noncompliance with APA requirements designed to promote accountable governmental decisionmaking. "Administrative law has evolved over
a long period precisely to provide processes that are open, orderly,
and participative with respect to rulemaking and that seek to ensure
fundamental fairness in adjudications."[62] In the Clinton administration, however, "the nature of executive orders and the processes by
which they are issued run in a very different direction. They are
usually not open, provide little or no procedural regularity, and
have limited participation. Indeed, they invite political appeals to
do off the record and behind closed doors that which would be on the
record and public in an agency proceeding."[63] As one commentator
reflected upon the "injustice" of Mr. Clinton's "environmental justice" order,

> Nobody was expecting it. Using cloak and dagger tactics . . .
> the [Clinton] Environmental Protection Agency lashed out in
> a historically unprecedented manner. State and local agencies
> were stunned at the new responsibilities thrust upon them
> by the EPA. Industrial leaders . . . fear[ed] . . . lost profits
> and future litigation. . . .[64]

For the Clinton administration, "re-inventing government" seems
to mean unilaterally imposed policies, not those democratically
determined or showing respect for the sovereign units of the
United States.[65]

Disregarding Established Civil Rights Categories

President Clinton's willingness to expand the terms of enacted
law for political ends is illustrated also by his executive orders
adding sexual orientation (EO 13087)[66] and status as a parent (EO
13152)[67] to the list of characteristics prohibited for consideration by
federal civilian employers. Again, the merits of these additions are
not in issue. Conservative and liberal alike have supported (and
opposed) each.[68] What is in issue is whether an executive order
changing present legal standards, or adding to them, is warranted
without congressional approval.

There is presently an ongoing and closely divided legislative
debate over whether "sexual orientation" should be added as a
protected category under the nation's civil rights laws.[69] This debate
concerns the obligation of private employers. Congress has said

nothing explicitly about this topic regarding the federal civilian workplace or public sector.

As former U.S. Office of Personnel Management Director Donald Devine points out, the Clinton order on sexual orientation does not have the "slightest basis in the law" and does not even contain a definition of "sexual orientation."[70] When Richard Nixon directed "equal employment opportunity" in the federal workforce in 1969,[71] the use of race and related protected categories was already part of enacted civil rights law. By contrast, however Congress may decide in the future (and after full democratic debate) to dispose of the issue of private or public employment practice and sexual orientation, the legislative process is today quite incomplete. Presidents are not empowered by the Constitution to add provisions to existing law at will, especially when it is understood by all that the pending legislative proposals are far more nuanced—directed at a different segment of the workforce or proposing to add sexual orientation as a protected category while prohibiting preferential treatment and the related governmental collection of statistics.

As a parent, and at the level of general theory, I welcome President Clinton's policy adding status as a parent as a protected category within the federal workforce, and if the president of the United States were chief legislator, rather than chief executive, I would have no constitutional qualms. In truth, however, Mr. Clinton cites no legal authority for his sensitivity to my parental needs (or those of others) and his action is not supported by enacted law or precedent. Again, the president's action precedes the deliberation of Congress, which has related legislation under consideration.[72] Parents are not presently a protected class under Title VII of the 1964 Civil Rights Act, even as parents do receive indirect protection when gender distinctions affecting parenting are drawn by covered employers.[73] Mr. Clinton may or may not be right that sexual orientation and status as a parent should be as categorically irrelevant to the assignment of work duties as race, sex, and religion, but respect for the rule of law should deny the gratuitous addition of these classifications until Congress has spoken.

Clinton Declares War

Others in this volume discuss Mr. Clinton's foreign policy, so little time will be devoted to that subject here. It is not surprising to find that President Clinton's willingness to act without lawful authority in the domestic field carries over to that quarter. Of course, no order in U.S. history is more infamous than Franklin Roosevelt's EO 9066, coercing more than 112,000 U.S. citizens and residents of Japanese ancestry into relocation camps during World War II. Yet, President Clinton's waging of an undeclared war in Kosovo is cut from the same cloth and fits modern sensibility more easily only because— thankfully—American military casualties were few and the locus of the battle remote. As recently disclosed, however, the president was just hours away from directing a constitutionally unauthorized ground invasion of the former Yugoslavia, involving some 175,000 military personnel, despite international leaders' predictions that such an invasion would result in "waves of blood."[74]

President Clinton's disdain for congressional authorization of the use of force did not begin with Kosovo. At a 1995 news conference, while preparing to use military force to invade Haiti and remove its military regime, Mr. Clinton denied any need for congressional support: "I have not agreed that I was constitutionally mandated to get it," he asserted.[75] This disregard for the law of the Constitution laid the tenuous foundation for Mr. Clinton's later foreign adventures involving the use of force in Bosnia, Afghanistan, Sudan, Iraq, and, most notably, Kosovo. In each instance, the Clinton administration "has yet to receive ex ante congressional authorization for any of these military activities."[76]

In late March 1999, President Clinton, relying solely on the authority derived from his role as commander in chief, directed American forces to take part in NATO bombings to force Serbia's withdrawal from Kosovo. Congress did not ignore this decision; instead, it refused to authorize the NATO-led action. The House of Representatives, "virtually forced" to vote on whether to remove U.S. armed forces by House Republicans' invocation of the War Powers Resolution, rejected resolutions "both to disown and support the NATO bombing."[77] Although some defenders of the administration point to the Senate resolution in support of the bombing[78] and the House's subsequent refusal to defund our participation in the action, it is undisputed that the constitutionally mandated declaration never came. In a military campaign that greatly miscalculated the enemy's resolve, inflicted substantial civilian casualties, dislocated thousands, fractured international relations with neutral nations, and expended billions of dollars of American weaponry, Mr. Clinton's knowing refusal to engage Congress and seek the necessary mandate before waging war was constitutionally evasive and deeply troubling. This is not to say that other presidents have fully complied with the constitutional requirements for pursuing warfare; they clearly have not.[79] However, two things are true. First, Mr. Clinton's noncompliance is premised on a more dangerous rationalization than that employed by earlier presidents. The Persian Gulf, Vietnam, Korea, and several hundred other far more limited military actions have been premised on the implicit authority of the executive to protect American citizens or property abroad, as a matter of defense. President Clinton's undeclared warfare was unabashedly massive in nature, and his tendered line of distinction was between an offensive war conducted only with low-risk air strike or "smart-bomb" technology and an offensive ground invasion. Second, unlike the United States, other NATO member nations had no trouble following their internal laws: Italy's involvement in the bombings was predicated on parliamentary approval, for example, and the German Supreme Court ordered that the Bundestag be recalled in order to consider the deployment of German forces to Kosovo.[80]

Conclusion

The separation and enumeration of powers is intended "to minimize the risk of arbitrary government."[81] The practices of the Clinton presidency outlined here, expanding executive power beyond its constitutional limits, greatly magnified that risk. As Madison warned, the "accumulation of all powers, legislative, executive, and judiciary, in the same hands, . . . whether hereditary, self-appointed, or elective, may justly be pronounced the very definition of tyranny."[82] Madison believed that the interior structure of government needed to be fashioned to check the accumulation of power. "The great security against a gradual concentration of the several powers in the same department consists in giving to those who administer each department the necessary constitutional means and personal motives to resist the encroachments of the others."[83] For the most part, this wonderful system has worked as planned, but we must be concerned over the length, breadth, and subtlety of the attack it sustained during the Clinton administration. Yes, ambition can be made to check ambition, but those seeking to defend the Constitution against a president lacking prudence, temperance, and respect for law, can in the short term be painted as obstructionist or worse. Moreover, scarce resources can be used in support of the constitutional structure only so often, and with respect to the most egregious abuses, or the checking mechanism becomes worn like a machine repaired once too often.[84] When constitutionally dubious executive orders are issued recurrently over a myriad of subjects, and implemented by officers without proper appointment, it is questionable whether the constituent parts of government can contain each individual part to its proper sphere. We may aspire to a rule of law, but that aspiration ultimately depends on the responsibility and fidelity of good men and women.

We have been warned about what lies ahead. Mr. Clinton's domestic policy adviser vows openly that President Clinton "will be signing executive orders right up until the morning of January 20, 2001."[85] It appears that much of that effort will be crassly political, aimed at "aid[ing] Vice President Al Gore's presidential bid."[86] That would be true to form. When President Clinton confronted a Congress unwilling to do his bidding—and shortly thereafter issued an executive order against the will of the people's representatives—Vice President Gore brashly told the administration's political and financial backers: "[m]ake no mistake: this is just a temporary setback. We're going to find a way to solve this problem."[87] An illegal executive order was the path Clinton and Gore found.

Americans admire problem solving—but not, one hopes, at the expense of the Constitution. If we are to preserve our liberties against an overweening executive, the American people must insist that future presidents be more respectful of constitutional limits than William Clinton has been during his tenure.

Notes

1. The president "shall take Care that the Laws be faithfully executed. . . ." U.S. Constitution, Article II, § 3. Of course, lawmaking is not vested in the president. Rather, "[a]ll legislative Powers herein granted shall be vested in a Congress of the United States . . ." U.S. Constitution, Article I, § 1.

2. Christopher N. May, *Presidential Defiance of "Unconstitutional Laws"* (Westport, Conn.: Greenwood Press, 1998), p. 16.

3. See generally Harold C. Relyea, *Presidential Directives: Background and Overview*, [98–611 GOV] Congressional Research Service (CRS) (an annual report providing a historical overview of presidential directives used by 20th-century presidents, including executive orders and proclamations), July 16, 1998.

4. See generally Robert F. Durant, *The Administrative Presidency: Retrospect and Prospect*, Presidency Research Group of the American Political Science Association, Washington, D.C., Fall 1998, p. 1, arguing that "the administrative presidency is neither as politically potent a force in the American political system as its proponents suggest or its critics fear, nor as Lilliputian in potency under all conditions as its detractors allege."

5. Joel D. Aberbach, "A Reinvented Government, or the Same Old Government?" in Colin Campbell and Bert A. Rockman, ed. *The Clinton Legacy*, pp. 118, 129, 2000, (citing Louis Fisher of the Congressional Research Service). Dr. Fisher, a superb scholar, opines that "Clinton is doing what a lot of presidents do in a second term when the legislature doesn't look too inviting." Ibid. The point can be argued, but as a careful student of the Constitution, Dr. Fisher would likely readily admit that the legitimacy of a practice cannot be determined simply by a variant of the child's refrain "everybody does it."

6. Frank M. Wozencraft, "OLC: The Unfamiliar Acronym," *American Bar Association Journal* 57 (1971): 33, 35. See also Dean Alfange Jr., "The Supreme Court and the Separation of Powers: A Welcome Return to Normalcy?," *George Washington Law Review* 58 (1990): 668, 703–4 ("In issuing regulations and indeed in all his official acts, the President needs congressional [or constitutional] authorization. He cannot exceed any limits that Congress has laid down.")

7. Elizabeth Shogren, "Clinton to Bypass Congress in Blitz of Executive Orders," *Los Angeles Times*, July 4, 1998, p. A1.

8. Ibid.

9. Some reports put the number at 450. Marc Lacey, "Blocked by Congress, Clinton Wields a Pen," *New York Times*, July 5, 2000, p. A11. Mr. Lacey derives his number from the Office of Management and Budget, but it seems to include various forms of presidential directives beyond executive orders, such as presidential memoranda, proclamations, and the like. Calculated in this fashion, Lacey argues that the number "far exceeds the executive actions taken by former Presidents George Bush and Ronald Reagan." See ibid.

10. John Contrubis, *Executive Orders and Proclamations*, [95–772 A] Congressional Research Service, March 9, 1999, p. 25, table 1.

11. Aberbach, in *The Clinton Legacy*, p. 128 (citing Rahm I. Emmanuel, a senior Clinton adviser).

12. Frank J. Murray, "Clinton's Executive Orders Are Packing a Punch," *Washington Times*, August 23, 1999, p. A1 (quoting Mr. Begala).

13. 343 U.S. 579 (1952).

14. 512 U.S. 1247 (1994). The *Dalton* Court made reference to the Court's decision in *Franklin v. Massachusetts*, 505 U.S. 788 (1992), involving a suit against the president, the Secretary of Commerce, and various other officials challenging the census-based apportionment of House seats. The *Franklin* Court held that the president was not an "agency" within the meaning of the Administrative Procedure Act, and thus was not subject to review under the act's terms. Nevertheless, referencing *Youngstown*, the *Franklin* Court further held that presidential actions may, of course, be reviewed for constitutionality.

15. See William J. Olson and Alan Woll, *Executive Orders and National Emergencies: How Presidents Have Come to "Run the Country" by Usurping Legislative Power*, Cato Policy Analysis No. 358, October 28, 1999 [hereinafter Cato Report].

16. *U.S. Chamber of Commerce v. Reich*, 74 F.3d 1322 (D.C. Cir. 1996), holding that Clinton's executive order barring the federal government from contracting with employers who hire permanent replacements during lawful strikes was preempted by the National Labor Relations Act, which guarantees management that right.

17. It has long been the NLRB position that "an employer who has neither caused nor prolonged a strike through unfair labor practices, can take full advantage of economic forces working for his victory in a labor dispute. The Act clearly does not forbid him, in the absence of such unfair labor practices, to replace the striking employees with new employees. . . . [T]he strikers are not 'guaranteed' reinstatement by the Act. . . . Admittedly an employer is fully within his rights under the statute in refusing to reinstate striking employees when he has legally filled their positions." See Brief for NLRB, *NLRB v. Mackay Radio & Tel. Co.*, 304 U.S. 333 (1938), quoted in Samuel Estreicher, "Collective Bargaining or 'Collective Begging?': Reflections on Antistrikebreaker Legislation," *Michigan Law Review* 93 (1994): 577, 584.

18. *NLRB v. Mackay Radio & Tel. Co.*, 304 U.S. 333 (1938), holding that an employer may lawfully hire permanent replacements for striking employees and legally deny the striking employees' request for immediate reinstatement if they were permanently replaced before the end of the strike.

19. Executive Order No. 12954, *Federal Register* 60 (March 8, 1995): 13,023.

20. Cato Report, p. 4. See also Ronald Turner, "Banning the Permanent Replacement of Strikers by Executive Order: The Conflict Between Executive Order 12954 and the NLRA," *Journal of Law & Politics* 12 (1995): 1, 10. ("When no legislation was forthcoming, President Clinton issued Executive Order 12954 and, by stroke of the executive pen, changed well-established law without congressional action and without adjudicative or policy rulings by the NLRB.")

21. *Congressional Record* 141: S3831–3, S3836 (1995).

22. See supra note 14 discussing *Franklin v. Massachusetts*, 505 U.S. 788 (1992).

23. *U.S. Chamber of Commerce v. Reich*, 74 F.3d 1327.

24. Ibid., 1328, citing *Soucie v. David*, 448 F.2d 1067, 1072 n.12 (D.C. Cir. 1971).

25. *U.S. Chamber of Commerce v. Reich*, 74 F.3d 1329.

26. 40 U.S.C. § 471 et seq. (1986), formally called the Federal Property and Administrative Services Act of 1949.

27. Ibid. Section 486(a) further gives the president authority to prescribe policies for procurement "as he shall deem necessary to effectuate the provisions" of the Procurement Act. See 40 U.S.C. § 486(a). As interpreted by President Clinton, this provided him with discretionary authority to devise policies about virtually any subject that might be loosely tied to the goods and services supplied to the government (at least those valued in excess of $100,000), or anybody working for others making or supplying those goods and services.

28. See, for example, *AFL–CIO v. Kahn*, 618 F.2d 784 (D.C. Cir. 1979) (en banc).

29. Ibid., 793.

30. See generally Gordon M. Clay, Comment, "Executive (Ab)use of the Procurement Power: *Chamber of Commerce v. Reich*," *Georgetown Law Journal* 84 (1996): 2573.

31. Walter Dellinger first served in the Clinton White House Counsel's office and then as head of the Justice Department's Office of Legal Counsel (where he was confirmed) before serving an extended period of years as "acting solicitor general" (a post for which he was not confirmed).

32. In this regard, the president's actions have been in disregard of the 1868 Vacancies Act, as amended, 5 U.S.C. sections 3345–3349d (1998), which generally limits to 120 days the time an official in an executive branch post subject to Senate confirmation may fill that position in an "acting" capacity—that is, without Senate approval. See generally, Daniel E. Troy, "At the Highest Levels; Lip Service; President Clinton swore an oath to preserve, protect, and defend the Constitution. He didn't mean it." *National Review*, vol. 50, no. 14 (August 3, 1998). President Clinton routinely refused to bring his nominees before the Senate. Mr. Troy noted, on the basis of a *National Journal* count, that the Clinton administration has had at least one temporary officer in every department who served more than 120 days before the president submitted the nominee's name to the Senate. Of the 64 acting officials tallied up by the Congressional Research Service in late February 1998, 43 had served beyond the 120-day limit. Particularly troubling was President Clinton's appointment of Bill Lann Lee as "acting" assistant attorney general in charge of the Justice Department's Civil Rights Division in the face of the Senate Judiciary Committee's blocking of his nomination. The Clinton administration argues that highly general statutory authority supports its acting appointments; namely, 28 U.S.C. section 509, which vests the Department of Justice functions in the attorney general and allows her to delegate those functions to others "from time to time." This line of argument has much in common with Mr. Clinton's questionable defense of his reformation of labor law contrary to the will of Congress.

33. Justice Department Memorandum on Executive Order 12954, reprinted in *Daily Labor Report* no. 48 (Bureau of National Affairs, 1995), p. D-28 (March 13, 1995) [hereinafter Memorandum]. This memorandum was prepared by the Office of Legal Counsel (OLC), which is the same office that has traditionally reviewed executive orders for "form and legality." This is an office expected to deliver objective and cautious legal advice, even when it means disappointing the policy preferences of presidents. See Douglas W. Kmiec, *The Attorney General's Lawyer*, 89–92 (1992), explaining in detail the workings of OLC, and specifically, how the office cautioned President Reagan against issuing a particular draft of an executive order limiting access to sexually explicit (but nonobscene) materials on military bases because of the constitutional questions surrounding the wording of the proposed order and then-existing Supreme Court precedent. Insofar as President Reagan was morally inclined toward a responsible limitation of denigrating pornographic material and was being pressured by influential members of Congress to issue such an order, and given the closeness of the constitutional questions presented, Reagan's fidelity to the rule of law in not issuing the order stands in stark relief to the "breathtakingly broad" claims of the Clinton administration.

34. Memorandum, p. D-28.

35. Ibid.

36. Lacey, "Blocked by Congress," p. A11.

37. Ibid.

38. Executive Order No. 13061, *Federal Register* 62 (1997): 48445.

39. See H.R. Rep. No. 105–781, 1998, 1–3.

40. See *Chenoweth v. Clinton*, 997 F. Supp. 36 (D.C. Cir. 1998) relying on the discussion of congressional standing in *Raines v. Byrd*, 117 S. Ct. 2312 (1997).

41. *Separation of Powers Restoration Act*, 106th Cong. H.R. 2655 (1999).

42. Ibid. § 4(a).

43. See, for example, Executive Order No. 12612, 3 C.F.R. 252 (1988), entitled "Federalism."

44. Executive Order No. 13083, 3 C.F.R. 146 (1999).

45. Brian E. Bailey, Note, "Federalism: An Antidote to Congress's Separation of Powers Anxiety and Executive Order 13083," *Indiana Law Journal* 73 (2000): 333, 334.

46. Ibid, 340.

47. See Executive Order No. 13095, 3 C.F.R. 202 (1999).

48. Cato Report, p. 7.

49. Executive Order No. 13132, *Federal Register* 64 (1999): 43,255.

50. Executive Order No. 12898, 3 C.F.R. 859 (1995).

51. Indeed, the label can be wholly counterproductive, hurting the minority communities it is presumably intended to assist. According to Stephen Huebner,

> The reason is that such a standard is not suited to address the underlying economic source of the problem. Recent evidence indicates that minority and poor populations tend to locate near industrial facilities after the facilities are sited, possibly due to lower property values. If this economic phenomenon is responsible for perceived environmental injustice, then this "injustice" will likely continue, in spite of siting prohibitions. Furthermore, a disparate impact standard would be detrimental to minority and low-income communities because it would deny them the right to host beneficial economic activity, which in many cases they welcome.

Stephen Huebner, "Are Storm Clouds Brewing on the Environmental Justice Horizon?" Center for the Study of American Business, Policy Study Number 145 (April 1998), available on line at: ⟨http://csab.wustl.edu/research/66.asp⟩.

52. As one author notes, proving racial intent has been "an insurmountable obstacle for the environmental justice movement." See Willie G. Hernandez, Note, "Environmental Justice: Looking Beyond Executive Order No. 12,898," *UCLA Journal of Environmental Law & Policy* 14 (1995/96): 181, 186 n.24, 208.

53. *Executive Orders Separation of Powers, 1999: Hearings on H.R. 2655 before the Subcommittee on Commercial and Administrative Law of the House of Representatives Committee on the Judiciary,* 106th Congress (1999). Statement of Phillip J. Cooper, Professor of Liberal Arts, University of Vermont, referencing the President's Memorandum on Environmental Justice, *Weekly Compilation of Presidential Documents* 30 (February 11, 1994) [hereinafter Cooper testimony]: 279, 280.

54. 42 U.S.C. § 2000(d) (1994).

55. See, for example, *Bean v. Southwestern Waste Management Corp.,* 482 F. Supp. 673 (S.D. Tex. 1979), holding that a waste facility within 1,700 feet of an African–American high school could not be enjoined because plaintiffs failed to show that the siting decision was motivated by discriminatory intent. See also *East Bob Twiggs Neighborhood Association v. Macon-Bibb County Planning and Zoning Commission,* 706 F. Supp. 880 (M.D. Ga. 1989).

56. The interim and revised guidance is available at the EPA's Web site. See Environmental Protection Agency, Office of Civil Rights, *Interim Guidance for Investigating Title VI Administrative Complaints Challenging Permits* (last modified June 12, 2000) ⟨http://www.epa.gov/ocrpage1/reviguide2.htm⟩.

57. Section 602 of Title VI (42 U.S.C. § 2000d-1) directs and authorizes federal agencies to effectuate the provisions of section 601, and this is contended to authorize federal agencies to promulgate regulations prohibiting actions which have a "disparate impact" on minorities. The EPA has had a disparate impact rule in place at least since 1984, *Federal Register* 49 (January 12, 1984): 1656 [no federally funded agency may use "criteria or methods of administering its program which have the effect of subjecting individuals to discrimination because of their race, color, national origin, or sex"], but as discussed in the text, before the Clinton administration, it was never claimed to create a private cause of action for permitting decisions.

58. 132 F.3d 925 (3d Cir. 1997), *vacated as moot* 524 U.S. 974 (1998).

59. See, for example, *New York City Environmental Justice Alliance v. Giuliani*, 50 F. Supp. 2d 250, 253–54 (S.D. N.Y. 1999), in which the court writes,

> In *Cannon v. University of Chicago*, 441 U.S. 677, 694–97, 99 S. Ct. 1946, 60 L.Ed.2d 560 (1979), the Supreme Court stated that a private right of action exists when bringing suit directly under Title VI, but said nothing about actions brought under agency regulations promulgated pursuant to Title VI. *Chester Residents Concerned for Quality Living v. Seif*, 132 F.3d 925, 937 (3d Cir. 1997), did hold that a private right of action is available under EPA regulations, but was vacated by the Supreme Court and remanded to the Third Circuit with instructions to dismiss. See *Seif v. Chester Residents Concerned for Quality Living*, 524 U.S. 974, 119 S. Ct. 22, 141 L.Ed.2d 783 (1998). Finally, although *Chester Residents* states that five justices . . . implicitly recognized a private right of action under regulations promulgated under Section 602, this court finds that the *Chester Residents* court's reading of [the cases] (see *Chester Residents*, 132 F.3d p. 930) is insupportable, and the court declines to accept that interpretation.

"Insupportable interpretation" apparently did not impede the Clinton administration. See also Gregory L. Maxim, Comment, "The EPA's Title VI Bout—Remedying One Injustice with Another," *McGeorge Law Review* 30 (1999): 1091.

60. See Ora Fred Harris Jr., "Environmental Justice: The Path to a Remedy that Hits the Mark," *University of Arkansas at Little Rock Law Review* 21 (1999): 797, 803.

61. See Thomas A. Lambert, "Revised Guidance for Implementing Title VI: Environmental Justice on Faulty Legal Footing," a July 2000 report of the Center for the Study of American Business. The report is available on line at ⟨http://csab.wustl.edu⟩. Mr. Lambert argues that the interim and revised guidance are both unlawful, questioning whether there is any actual holding finding Title VI violated under a disparate impact theory. It is not necessary to resolve that issue, however, to challenge the covert manner in which the Clinton administration not only assumed such theory to be valid, but also imposed and enlarged it with a would-be private right of action not authorized in federal law. The revised guidance does appear to have deleted reference to the supposed private right of action, again demonstrating that the Clinton administration can be made to follow the law if caught red-handed.

62. Cooper testimony, p. 9. The Administrative Procedure Act requires that certain procedures be followed when an agency implements a rule. These procedures include, among others, notice of the proposed rulemaking, a public comment period, and *Federal Register* publication of the rule. These procedures are in place so that parties

affected by an agency's decision are given an opportunity to influence that decision-making at a point when alternative views may still be considered. See Maxim, Comment, 1103 (citing *NLRB v. Wyman-Gordon Co.*, 394 U.S. 759, 764 [1969] and *United States Steel Corp. v. EPA*, 595 F.2d 207 [5th Cir. 1979]). Section 551(4) of the APA defines "rule" as "the whole or part of an agency statement of general or particular applicability and future effect designed to implement, interpret, or prescribe law or policy or describing the organization, procedure, or practice requirements of an agency."

63. Cooper testimony, pp. 9–10.

64. Maxim, Comment 1092.

65. Cooper testimony, p. 9.

66. Executive Order No. 13087, 3 C.F.R. 191 (1999)

67. Executive Order No. 13152, *Federal Register* 65 (2000): 26115.

68. See *Congressional Record* 44:H7255–02, H7256 (1998). Compare the floor remarks of Rep. Joel Hefley seeking to prohibit the expenditure of funds for the enforcement of Executive Order 13087 with those of Rep. Dana Rohrabacher supporting the president's action.

69. See *Employment Non-Discrimination Act of 1999*, 106th Cong., S. 1276 (1999) referred to committee. See also H.R. 2355, 106th Congress (1999) also in committee.

70. Donald Devine, "Risks of Keeping a Low Profile," *Washington Times*, August 21, 1998, p. A18.

71. Executive Order 11478, codified in *Presidential Proclamations and Executive Orders* (Office of the Federal Register).

72. See S. 1907, 106th Congress (1999) introduced by Senators Dodd and Kennedy.

73. See *Trezza v. Hartford, Inc.*, 1998 WL 912101 (S.D. N.Y. 1998); *In re Consolidated Pretrial Proceedings in the Airline Cases*, 582 F.2d 1142, 1145 (7th Cir. 1978) holding that airline policy of removing only female flight attendants after giving birth to be gender discrimination, *rev'd on other grounds*, 455 U.S. 385 (1982). But see *Bass v. Chemical Banking Corp.*, 1996 WL 374151 (S.D. N.Y. 1996) dismissing a claim because employer's policy of reduced responsibility in light of a recent birth applied to men and women alike.

74. Doyle McManus, "Clinton's Massive Invasion That Almost Was," *Los Angeles Times*, June 9, 2000, p. A1.

75. Symposium, "The Presidency: Twenty-Five Years after Watergate, Congressional Abdication: War and Spending Powers," *St. Louis University Law Journal* 43 (1999): 931. Dr. Louis Fisher notes that in a televised presidential address concerning Haiti one month later, President Clinton informed the American public of "his willingness to lead a multinational force 'to carry out the will of the United Nations.' Clinton made no mention at all of carrying out the will of Congress."

76. John C. Yoo, "The Dogs That Didn't Bark: Why Were International Legal Scholars MIA On Kosovo?" *Chicago Journal of International Law* 1 (2000): 149, 151.

77. Charles Tiefer, "Adjusting Sovereignty: Contemporary Congressional–Executive Controversies about International Organizations," *Texas International Law Journal* 35 (2000): 239, 256.

78. See *Congressional Record* 145:S3118 (daily edition March 23, 1999).

79. See generally Brien Hallett, *The Lost Art of Declaring War* (1998), suggesting that Congress anticipate war by creating a council of war that could function as a formal mechanism for carrying out its Article I functions.

80. See Symposium, 976.

81. Christopher F. Edley Jr., *Administrative Law: Rethinking Judicial Control of Bureaucracy* (New Haven, Conn.: Yale University Press, 1990), p. 4.

82. *The Federalist* No. 47 (James Madison).

83. *The Federalist* No. 51 (James Madison).

84. Douglas W. Kmiec, "Of Balkanized Empires and Cooperative Allies—A Bicentennial Essay on the Separation of Powers," *Catholic University Law Review* 37 (1987): 73.

85. Lacey, "Blocked by Congress," p. A11.

86. Ibid.

87. "Gore Pledges Another Try at Striker Replacement," *Daily Labor Report* no. 117 (Bureau of National Affairs, 1994) p. D-4 (July 17, 1994).

4. Speech and Privacy

Nadine Strossen

As other chapters in this volume make clear, the rule of law is not simply about order and regularity, but about justice as well. And central to that substantive side of the rule of law is respect for the rights of speech and privacy. To the extent that governments abuse such basic rights, they cannot claim to be operating under the rule of law. Regrettably, the Clinton administration's record in this regard leaves much to be desired.

A single essay cannot do justice to the injustices that the Clinton administration has perpetrated through its far-ranging assaults on free speech and privacy. This chapter will instead provide what Adlai Stevenson once called a "fan-dance discussion": the point of the discussion, like the point of the fan, is not to cover the subject but rather to draw attention to it. I hasten to stress that the American Civil Liberties Union (ACLU) is staunchly nonpartisan. The ACLU has never endorsed or opposed any candidate or official. The ACLU does endorse and oppose particular positions on matters involving civil liberties. From that perspective, I am not aware of any candidate or official whose overall civil liberties record is not mixed—positive on some issues, negative on others.

Thus, in fairness to Clinton, before I focus on the dark side of his civil liberties record, I should note that he has earned especially high ACLU ratings in such important areas as religious liberty and reproductive freedom.

For outstanding contributions to researching and annotating this chapter, the author thanks her assistants Amy Fallon and Kathy Davis, and her research assistants Daniel Curtin, Anna Genet, Mara Levy, Kara Miller, and Janice Purvis. For helpful comments, the author thanks members of the ACLU's Washington, D.C., office, especially Phil Gutis and Greg Nojeim.

Clinton's Mixed Civil Rights Record

In noting Clinton's positive contributions to human rights, I am deliberately omitting one important area in which he often claims—and gets—kudos: racial justice. To be sure, Clinton has staunchly opposed racial discrimination and segregation. All told, though, his administration's policies have perpetuated discrimination, subjugation, and even disenfranchisement on the basis of race. That is because one of the major sources of racial injustice today is the "War on Crime"—and, in particular, the "War on Drugs"[1]—and Clinton is one of the most militant crime and drug "warriors" we have ever seen. As one commentator observed in 1997: "The Clinton Administration is waging [the drug war] more intensely than its predecessors, having spent a record $15 billion on drug enforcement [in 1996] and added federal death penalties for so-called drug kingpins."[2] Marijuana-related arrests alone—88 percent of which are for mere possession—have risen 80 percent during the Clinton presidency, reaching a record high of 695,200 in 1997.[3]

The Clinton-championed drug policies inherently violate the whole panoply of our most cherished rights,[4] but none more than the right not to be discriminated against on the basis of race or skin color. It is bad enough that any adult should be imprisoned for voluntarily ingesting anything into his or her own body, but it is even worse when those who are imprisoned for such "consensual crimes" are disproportionately selected on the basis of their skin color—which is precisely what happens.

Consider just a few of the shocking statistics. African-Americans constitute 13 percent of the country's population and 13 percent of its drug users. In other words, as every government study confirms, African-Americans use drugs in the same proportion as members of other racial groups. Yet, when we turn from those who use drugs to those who are arrested for such use, the African-American representation jumps to 37 percent. Worse yet, when we consider those who are convicted for drug use, the African-American representation climbs still higher, to 55 percent. And when we look at the drug users who are sentenced to prison, the African-American contingent soars all the way up to 74 percent. In sum, African-Americans are 13 percent of our total drug users, but 74 percent of our imprisoned drug users.[5]

In light of such statistics, many commentators have concluded that the War on Drugs would more accurately be called the "War on the Constitution" or the "War on Racial Minorities." Our Commander in Chief in such a war can hardly claim the mantle of racial justice. As strongly as Bill Clinton may feel about civil rights and racial justice—and I am not questioning what appear to be his deep-seated commitments in these areas—he apparently feels even more strongly about being viewed as "tough on crime" and on drugs. One official's description of the Justice Department's overriding goal during the Clinton administration was "to make the president look tough on crime and worry about everything else, including civil liberties, later."[6]

In his zeal to look tough, Bill Clinton has refused to support even modest steps to correct even the most egregious examples of the racial discrimination that is endemic in the drug war. In particular, the Clinton administration rejected a recommendation of the U.S. Sentencing Commission—which can hardly be accused of being "soft on crime"—to eliminate the racially biased, 100-fold disparity between sentences meted out for crack and those meted out for powdered cocaine, which are pharmacologically identical and produce the same effect on the body. Despite the chemical identity of those two forms of cocaine, a mandatory five-year minimum sentence is now imposed for possessing five grams of crack, which is used mostly by African-Americans and Latinos, whereas the same mandatory minimum is not triggered for possession of powder cocaine until the amount rises to 500 grams. In the words of one commentator, this disparity "hammers poor blacks while treating rich whites with kid gloves."[7]

Even after such discriminatory sentences have been duly served, their racially repressive results are compounded by the widespread disenfranchisement of convicted felons. All states but four disenfranchise anyone convicted of a felony. The result is that, nationwide, a shocking 14 percent of all African-American men are stripped of the fundamental right to vote, and in some southern states that number soars to 30 percent—mostly due to our discriminatory drug laws and their discriminatory enforcement patterns.[8] In short, the Jim Crow deprivation of voting rights that the Voting Rights Act of 1965 remedied has been reinstated by the War on Drugs. How, then, can Chief Drug Warrior Clinton be viewed fairly as a civil rights champion?

Overview of Clinton's Anti–Civil Liberties Legacy

Despite Clinton's positive civil liberties accomplishments in some areas, his overall record is not good—and that is the most diplomatic way to phrase it. Many respected liberal, civil libertarian commentators have been more blunt in describing Clinton's net "contributions" concerning our precious individual rights. Such criticism cannot be dismissed as partisan sniping. For example, *Washington Post* columnist Richard Cohen concluded that Clinton's major historic legacy is that "under his presidency the civil liberties of Americans were diminished."[9] Likewise, John Heilemann wrote a cover story in *Wired* magazine that described the civil liberties record of "Big Brother Bill," to quote the title, as "breathtaking in both the breadth and depth of its awfulness."[10]

From a historical perspective, Heilemann wrote, "So atrocious is Clinton's record, it can plausibly be argued that he is the worst civil liberties president since Richard Nixon."[11] But *New York Times* columnist Anthony Lewis thought that historical comparison was unfair—unfair to Richard Nixon. In his view, we have to go back even further in history to find some fair anti-civil-liberties competition for Bill Clinton. Lewis concluded that "Bill Clinton has the worst civil liberties record of any president in at least 60 years."[12] Even that is an understatement according to another seasoned journalist—Nat Hentoff of the *Village Voice* and *Washington Post*. Hentoff has concluded that no other American president "has done so much damage to constitutional liberties as Bill Clinton."[13] Obviously, those are strong statements. Unfortunately, they are not hyperbolic. Clinton's assaults on liberty will have ongoing adverse consequences long after he leaves office.

The harsh verdicts I have quoted appeared in essays describing a long litany of specific civil liberties violations. If I had to single out one especially damaging type of abuse from this "embarrassment of riches," I would opt for the series of Clinton-championed measures that cut back on access to the courts and judicial review for many constitutional claims. In 1996, the ACLU issued a special report on those "court-stripping measures."[14] To be sure, the Republican Congress played its part in passing these measures. But they could not have been enacted or enforced without the active support of the Clinton administration, which has defended them against constitutional challenges in the courts, as well as Congress. These judicial door-closing laws will cause the greatest long-range harm to constitutional rights because they remove the ultimate safety net that our system provides for our rights: the federal courts, with their relative insulation from the majoritarian pressures that at least tempt elected officials to ignore constitutional principles.

Anthony Lewis has been a particularly persistent critic of the many new court-stripping statutes that the Clinton administration successfully promoted. In one column, Lewis put these measures in historic perspective:

> The worst aspect of [Bill Clinton's] Presidency . . . is his appalling record on constitutional rights. The Clinton years have seen, among other things, a series of measures stripping the courts of their power to protect individuals from official abuse—the power that has been the key to American freedom. There has been nothing like it since the Radical Republicans, after the Civil War, acted to keep the courts from holding the occupation of the South to constitutional standards.[15]

Clinton's Anti-Privacy Activism

One of the foremost, internationally respected experts on technology and privacy, Marc Rotenberg, the founder and executive director of the Electronic Privacy Information Center (EPIC), has assessed President Clinton's record in the following way: "Not since Richard Nixon wiretapped his political opponents has there been an administration with less regard for the privacy rights of American citizens."[16]

Widespread press and public concern about Clinton's anti-privacy policies were first triggered by the 1996 Filegate scandal. Even FBI Director Louis Freeh condemned the "egregious violations of privacy"[17] involved in that episode, in which White House officials ordered and obtained from the FBI 900 confidential personnel files of Republican appointees. At the time, the ACLU not only condemned Filegate itself but also issued a report that put the incident in context, stressing that it was part of a much larger, although much less-publicized, pattern of pervasive privacy predations by the Clinton administration.[18] In particular, this administration has constantly pushed to collect increasing categories of personal information from and about Americans for the government's ever-expanding electronic databases. The Clinton data-collection engine has extended even to personal information that most of us consider especially sensitive—medical and financial information.

Too often, these new databases have been created as part of major legislative initiatives, so they have not attracted the attention they deserve. One notable example is the 1996 welfare reform legislation, which requires all employers to collect personal information about all new employees, creating a massive new database that will include almost all of us who work—in other words, almost all of us.[19]

Another example is the Clinton health care initiative. All of the hoopla about other aspects of that ill-fated plan obscured its call for a unique national identification number and collection of medical records on every health care recipient.[20] Again, of course, that means on everyone. To be sure, the whole health care proposal went down in flames, but the Clinton administration is still supporting its data collection concept. In November 1999 the Department of Health and Human Services issued regulations that give government agents more access to our medical records.[21]

Yet one more new, nationwide Clinton-sponsored database is the "sex offender" registry. Not only did Clinton champion such a registry on the national level, he also waved the carrot of federal funding to spur similar registries in all fifty states.[22] In some especially tragic instances, these registries have ruined the lives of people who had long ago been convicted of private consensual acts that have since been decriminalized, including homosexual sex and sex with a younger teenager. In other words, one type of privacy violation—punishing private, personal relationships—has been compounded by another—telling the world about those relationships.

In addition to initiating and supporting new databases, the Clinton administration has also pushed for expanded government power to intercept our communications and snoop into our data.[23] Far from letting us pursue the potential of new communications technology to protect our privacy, the president has instead done the opposite—tried to co-opt the technology to promote government surveillance through electronic communications of all of our movements and expressions. The Clinton administration has been determined to distort the design and development of new communications technologies, from cell phones to computers, to turn them into tracking devices—tracking not only our bodies, but also our minds.

The most notorious examples are the Communications Assistance for Law Enforcement Act (CALEA) and the series of "Clipper Chip" initiatives. Those measures constitute government commandeering of cellular and computer communications, respectively, to facilitate government spying on individuals who may not even be suspected of any illicit activity. That would be analogous to the government's requiring all builders to install bugs in the walls of new homes and office buildings. As one ACLU analysis concluded, "If the Clinton administration has its way, Big Brother [will be] permanently hardwired into the country's communications infrastructure."[24] Robyn Blumner, a former ACLU leader who is now a syndicated columnist, summed up Clinton's data-gathering initiatives this way: "Clinton's willingness to abandon privacy rights puts the Filegate scandal in perspective—just another day at the White House."[25]

"Clinton vs. the First Amendment"

Clinton's anti-free-speech record was dissected in the most damning detail in a *New York Times Magazine* cover story by one of the most prominent First Amendment lawyers in the country, Floyd Abrams.[26] The title says it all: "Clinton vs. the First Amendment." The article began by describing a case whose name says it all: *ACLU v. Reno.*[27] That case culminated in the Supreme Court's landmark 1997 ruling, striking down the first federal Internet censorship law, which the Clinton administration championed. Even more telling is the fact that we now have to call that case *ACLU v. Reno I*, since Clinton subsequently championed and signed the second federal Internet censorship law, which the ACLU also promptly challenged in a case called *ACLU v. Reno II.*[28]

Floyd Abrams's article exhaustively analyzes not only Clinton's efforts to censor the Internet but also dozens of other instances in which he led or capitulated in restraints on freedom of speech and of the press. This is how Abrams summarized the overall pattern: "Time and again, the Administration has opposed serious First Amendment claims in court, acquiesced in serious First Amendment damage by legislation and ignored First Amendment limits in its own conduct. Even when the Administration has raised First Amendment concerns, it has done so haltingly and briefly."[29]

Although Abrams acknowledged several counterexamples to the Clinton administration's generally weak free-speech stances—most important, the administration's opposition to the flag-desecration constitutional amendment—his analysis showed that such pro-free-speech actions were the "exceptions."[30]

Moreover, one of the good grades—more accurately, the absence of a demerit—that Abrams awards the Clinton administration overlooks its negative record in the pertinent area. Specifically, Abrams gives positive credit to Bill Clinton on the ground that "he has said nothing as shameful about civil liberties issues as did former President George Bush in his McCarthyite attack on Michael Dukakis as a 'card-carrying member of the A.C.L.U.'"[31] That statement is literally true concerning Clinton's own public pronouncements, but it is not true concerning at least one top-level spokesperson and policy adviser on his White House staff, Rahm Emanuel. Emanuel notoriously did play the anti-ACLU card, apparently with at least the tacit blessing of the president. John Heilemann detailed this strategy in *Wired* magazine:

> In March 1996, the ACLU's press person in Washington received a call from a reporter at *U.S. News & World Report* asking for a comment on the fact that "the White House is saying that it's moderate because it opposes the ACLU on this whole list of issues." [ACLU Washington Office Director] Laura Murphy's reaction was instant: "I said, 'Oh, no, we're back to card-carrying days and George Bush, only this time the Democrat is going after us.'" When the story appeared, a quote from the White House's Rahm Emanuel seemed to confirm Murphy's fears. "We protect victims first and make criminals pay for their crimes," Emanuel declared. "That may get us in the crosshairs of the ACLU, but those are our principles."
>
> A few weeks later, . . . Murphy saw Emanuel at Ron Brown's funeral. "I went up to him and said, 'What are you doing?'" Murphy recalls. "I said, 'Lay off the ACLU.'" . . . And he said, 'Yeah, yeah, beat me, beat me—I love it when you beat up on me. Come on, say it publicly. It's good for us if you fight us.' . . . "
>
> For his part, Emanuel recalls saying no such thing to Murphy. He also insists that he sees no mileage in goading the ACLU into assailing Clinton—a claim which was undercut somewhat when another White House aide referred, unprompted, to the ACLU-baiting strategy as "the Rahm Emanuel theory of the universe."[32]

Given the foregoing facts, Floyd Abrams was overly generous toward the Clinton administration's civil liberties record when he assumed that it was untainted by ACLU-bashing. Even taking that "false positive" into account, though, his net assessment of the "Administration's entire First Amendment record" is still negative: "Sum it up this way: Lee Atwater would have admired it; Dick Morris may yet claim credit for it; and Bill Clinton should know better."[33]

Perpetuating Personal Power vs. Protecting Principles or Promoting Public Policies

The overarching theme that captures Clinton's overall civil liberties transgressions, including in the free speech and privacy areas, is that they seem animated not by ignorance of constitutional principles but rather by a brazen disregard for those principles. Accordingly, the critics of Clinton's constitutional sins—including his liberal critics—repeatedly describe those infractions with terms such as "cavalier"[34] and "blithe."[35] As Nat Hentoff put it, "There is a chilling insouciance in Clinton's elbowing the Constitution out of the way."[36] In other words, what is especially distressing is not that Clinton is wrong-headed in his thinking about constitutional rights; it is, rather, that he seems not to think about those rights at all.

What is even more distressing is that this casual disregard seems in turn to reflect not an overweening concern for the kinds of countervailing public policy goals that have motivated many other politicians to compromise the Constitution—for example, fighting Communism or crime or terrorism. Instead, Clinton's "countervailing concern" seems to be nothing more than perpetuating his own power for its own sake. Bad enough to sell your birthrights—and ours—for the proverbial mess of pottage. Even worse is selling them for the chance to go on selling them.

Again, this theme is consistently sounded by civil libertarian and liberal commentators when they deplore Clinton's anti-constitutional record. Anthony Lewis echoed Floyd Abrams in observing that Clinton's civil liberties record "is so disappointing because he knows better."[37] He added, "Clinton will not stand on principle when he thinks he might be damaged politically. In the end he is interested in only one thing: his own survival."[38] In another column, Lewis castigated Clinton's constant scapegoating of civil liberties as especially unwarranted, given the absence of any real countervailing public policy concern akin to the former Communist bogeyman:

> The Soviet threat, which used to be the excuse for shoving the Constitution aside, is gone. Even in the worst days of the Red Scare we did not strip the courts of their protective power. Why are we legislating in panic now? Why, especially, is the President indifferent to constitutional rights and their protection by the courts?[39]

Richard Cohen made the same point this way: "When it comes to political courage, Clinton has mastered only half the concept. . . . When it comes to civil liberties: he will do nothing to endanger his reelection."[40] Maureen Dowd captured the same theme with one of her trademark quips: "Clinton moved from the left wing to the right wing because what he really believes in is the West Wing."[41]

Although those perspectives seem persuasive as far as they go, they do not go far enough to explain Clinton's continued reckless disregard for constitutional rights even after he could no longer run for office and even after his political popularity had reached record levels. To my mind, that is the sorriest aspect of his sorry record—not just selling our rights for his political survival but giving away so many of our rights outright, for nothing. Here is John Heilemann's damning dissection of this pattern:

> The notion that Clinton "knows better" rests on the assumption that the president possesses principles that are independent of political calculation—and on civil liberties, at least, there exists virtually no evidence to support that assumption. It is perfectly possible that a lifetime of shameless compromise has left Clinton incapable of even identifying a civil liberty, let alone fighting for one.[42]

Congressional Coconspirators Notwithstanding, Clinton Deserves Much Blame

As noted, many of the administration's violations were not the sole responsibility of Bill Clinton or his administration. All of the legislative violations required the complicity of Congress, of course. Certainly, too many members of Congress, on both sides of the aisle, have turned a blind eye to important civil liberties, including in the areas of free speech and privacy. One illustration is the federal cybercensorship legislation referred to above. Both federal laws that suppress cyberspeech passed by overwhelming bipartisan majorities in both houses of Congress.

Notwithstanding Congress's passage of the two national Internet censorship laws—the Communications Decency Act (CDA)[43] and the Child Online Protection Act (COPA)[44]—Bill Clinton has also played essential enabling roles in the ongoing effort to "dumb down" the Internet to a level acceptable to the most intolerant parents of the most immature children. Bill Clinton did not have to sign the laws. Nor did his Justice Department have to defend the laws in court, let alone seek Supreme Court review of the unanimous lower court rulings against the first of those laws.

Neither did Clinton have to go out of his way to champion that law, even after federal judges had resoundingly repudiated it. After the first such ruling—unanimously supported by three federal judges, two of whom were Bush appointees—the president himself continued his pro-censorship pandering, declaring, "Our Constitution allows us to help parents by enforcing this act to prevent children from being exposed to objectionable material."[45]

Regarding still other anti–civil liberties legislation, Clinton's role was even more central; commentators believe that Congress would not have passed such legislation if the president had made an effort to stop it. Moreover, some of the most damaging laws were initially proposed, and consistently pushed, by Clinton himself. For these reasons, too—in addition to the sense that "he should know better"—Clinton does deserve special blame for so many of the civil liberties setbacks while he has been in office, even those in which he did have coconspirators.

One especially egregious set of civil liberties abuses was contained in the administration's own "Omnibus Counter-Terrorism Act," which the ACLU immediately denounced as the "Ominous Counter-Constitution Act."[46] It was proposed in the wake of the Oklahoma City bombing as an ostensible response to that and other instances of "terrorism." In fact, though, the legislation itself caused more damage to our cherished American way of life than any terrorism has ever done. This Clinton initiative, therefore, called to mind that sage warning by Benjamin Franklin: "Those who would give up essential liberty to purchase a little temporary safety deserve neither liberty nor safety."

Given Clinton's determination to appear tough on crime and on terrorism, that warning too often has proven prophetic throughout his presidency. The misnamed "anti-terrorism" law was staved off for a year by an ideologically broad coalition of citizens' groups—ranging from the ACLU to the Cato Institute to the NRA.[47] Ultimately, though, most of its anti-rights agenda was enacted, thanks in large measure to persistent pressure from the Clinton administration. Those civil liberties nightmares range from gutting the time-honored writ of habeas corpus, which Alexander Hamilton hailed as the greatest liberty of all,[48] to permitting sweeping, "roving" wiretaps (taps of any phone a suspect might use), to authorizing deportations on the basis of secret evidence, to outlawing association with any group that the government, at its sole discretion, might choose to brand as "terrorists."

The Clinton administration bears the brunt of the blame for all of those devastating assaults on cherished constitutional rights. Those abuses were documented and decried by Anthony Lewis in a series of columns throughout the Clinton years.[49] A quote from one such column tells the all-too-typical tale:

> The Republican Congress . . . initiated some of the attacks . . . .
> But President Clinton did not resist them as other Presidents
> have. And he proposed some of the measures trampling on
> constitutional protections. Much of the worst has happened
> [due to the Clinton-sponsored] counterterrorism . . . law. One
> [feature] had nothing to do with terrorism: a provision gutting
> the power of Federal courts to examine state criminal convic-
> tions, on writs of habeas corpus, to make sure there was no
> violation of constitutional rights. The Senate might well have
> moderated the habeas corpus provision if the President had
> put up a fight. But he broke a promise and gave way.[50]

Conclusion

Anthony Lewis sounded an important note at the end of yet another column condemning Clinton's constitutional abuses. He raised this rhetorical question about Clinton's historical legacy: "Does Bill Clinton really want to be remembered as the president who sold out habeas corpus?"[51] I would add, does Clinton really want to be remembered, more generally, as the president who sold out so many other constitutional rights?

This volume will contribute to the vital task of chronicling Clinton's record undermining the rule of law—of which his anti-rights record is so fundamental a part. That task promotes two important interrelated purposes. First, we must set the record straight—by documenting in detail the enduring damage the Clinton administration has done to our precious rights. That is an essential prerequisite to the second, more forward-looking mission: to repair that damage by taking the necessary countermeasures to restore the rule of law and the rights it secures.

Notes

1. See generally Leadership Conference on Civil Rights, Leadership Conference Education Fund, "Justice on Trial: Racial Disparities in the American Criminal Justice System," May 2000 (visited July 19, 2000) ⟨http://www.civilrights.org/policy_and _legislation/pl_issues /criminal_justice/cj_report/summary.html⟩.

2. Michael Pollan, "Opium Made Easy: One Gardner's Encounter with the War on Drugs," *Harper's Magazine*, April 1997, p. 35.

3. See "FBI Reports Marijuana Arrests Exceed Those for Violent Crime," *NORML*, October 21, 1999 (visited July 19, 2000) ⟨http://www.norml.org/news/archives/99-10-21.shtml⟩ (referring to *FBI Uniform Crime Report*, October 1999 [visited July 20, 2000] ⟨http://www.fbi.gov/ucr.htm⟩).

4. See generally Graham Boyd and Jack Hitt, "This Is Your Bill of Rights, On Drugs," *Harper's Magazine*, December 1999, p. 57.

5. American Civil Liberties Union, "Year in Civil Liberties 1999: Crime and Punishment" (visited May 31, 2000) ⟨http://www.aclu.org/library/ycl99⟩.

6. Quoted in John Heilemann, "Big Brother Bill," *Wired*, October 1996, p. 5 (visited July 20, 2000) ⟨http://www.wired.com/wired/archive/4.10/netizen.html?topic = & topic_set = ⟩.

7. Ibid., p. 3.

8. See generally Nadine Strossen, "Black America and the Right to Vote," *Intellectual Capital*, May 20, 1999 (visited July 20, 2000) ⟨http://www.intellectualcapital.com⟩.

9. Richard Cohen, "Civil Liberties: Campaign Casualty," *Washington Post*, July 11, 1996, p. A25.

10. Heilemann.

11. Ibid., p. 2.

12. Anthony Lewis, "The Clinton Mystery," *New York Times*, March 4, 1997, p. A23.

13. Nat Hentoff, "First in Damage to Constitutional Liberties," *Washington Post*, November 16, 1996, p. A25.

14. American Civil Liberties Union Special Report, "Court Stripping: Congress' Campaign to Undermine the Power of the Judiciary," June 1996 (visited July 6, 2000) ⟨http://www.aclu.org/library/ctstrip.html⟩.

15. Anthony Lewis, "Clinton's Sorriest Record," *New York Times*, October 14, 1996, p. A17.

16. Quoted in Warren P. Strobel, "Civil liberties get a reduced priority; White House actions hit from all sides," *Washington Times*, March 24, 1997, p. A1.

17. Quoted in "Requests 'without justification'; Freeh: 'FBI and I were victimized,'" *The Florida Times-Union*, June 15, 1996, p. A12.

18. See American Civil Liberties Union Report, "The President's Privacy Problems," June 27, 1996 (visited July 19, 2000) ⟨http://www.aclu.org/congress/fileltr.html⟩.

19. See American Civil Liberties Union Press Release, "Unconstitutional Welfare Bill Preys on Our Nation's Children; Measure Also Erodes Free Speech, Violates Separation of Church, State and Damages Privacy Rights," July 26, 1996 (visited July 20, 2000) ⟨http://www.aclu.org/news/n072696c.html⟩.

20. See American Civil Liberties Union Press Release, "Health-Care Bill Sacrifices Medical Privacy," August 6, 1996 (visited July 20, 2000) ⟨http://www.aclu.org/news/w080696a.html⟩.

21. See American Civil Liberties Union, "Comments on the Proposed Rule of the U.S. Department of Health and Human Services regarding Standards for Privacy of Individually Identifiable Health Information" (published *Federal Register* 64 [February 17, 2000] 59,918–60,065), (visited July 20, 2000) ⟨http://www.aclu.org/congress/1021700a.html⟩.

22. See The White House, "The Clinton-Gore Administration—A Record of Progress," April 2000 (visited July 10, 2000) ⟨http://www.whitehouse.gov/WH/Accomplishments/additional.html⟩; see also "The History of Sex Offender Registries," *The Patriot Ledger* (Quincy, MA), May 16, 1998, p. 10.

23. See American Civil Liberties Union Press Release, "ACLU Urges Congress to Put a Leash on 'Carnivore' and Other Government Snoopware Programs," July 12, 2000 (visited July 20, 2000) ⟨http://www.aclu.org/news/2000/n071200b.html⟩.

24. American Civil Liberties Union White Paper, "Big Brother in the Wires: Wiretapping in the Digital Age," March 1998 (visited July 19, 2000) ⟨http://www.aclu.org/issues/cyber/wiretap_brother.html⟩.

25. Robyn Blumner, "Under Clinton, Government Is All Ears," *The Commercial Appeal* (Memphis), August 11, 1996, p. 5B.

26. See Floyd Abrams, "Clinton vs. the First Amendment," *New York Times*, March 30, 1997, sec. 6, p. 42.

27. See *ACLU v. Reno*, 521 U.S. 844 (1997).

28. See *ACLU v. Reno*, No. 99-1324, 2000 U.S. App. LEXIS 14419 (3rd Cir. June 22, 2000), *aff'g*, 31 F. Supp. 2d 473 (E.D. Pa. 1999); see also *ACLU v. Reno*, No. 98-5591, 1998 U.S. Dist. LEXIS 18546 (E.D. Pa. November 20, 1998), granting plaintiffs' motion for preliminary injunction enjoining enforcement of the statute.

29. Abrams.

30. Ibid.

31. Ibid.

32. Heilemann.

33. Abrams.

34. See Bob Barr, "Barr, Others Force Lawsuit to Force Accurate 2000 Census," *Congressional Press Releases*, February 12, 1998.

35. See Hentoff.

36. Ibid.

37. Anthony Lewis, "Stand up for Liberty," *New York Times*, April 15, 1996, p. A15.

38. Ibid.

39. Ibid.

40. Cohen.

41. Maureen Dowd, "Clinton's Latest Stances Beyond the Pale," *San Antonio Express-News*, June 2, 1996, p. L2.

42. Heilemann.

43. 47 U.S.C.A. §223 (a)(d) (1997).

44. 47 U.S.C. §230–1 (1998).

45. Quoted in Reid Kanaley, "Supreme Court to hear arguments regarding pornography access on Internet," *Philadelphia Inquirer*, March 18, 1997.

46. American Civil Liberties Union Press Release, "ACLU Background Briefing: House to Consider Ominous Counter-Constitution Act (also known as the Omnibus Counter-Terrorism Act)," March 31, 1995 (visited July 20, 2000) ⟨http://www.aclu.org/news/n033195a.html⟩.

47. See American Civil Liberties Union Press Release, "Gun Groups, Civil Liberties Organizations Announce Opposition to Provisions of Counter-Terrorism Legislation," December 6, 1995 (visited July 19, 2000) ⟨http://www.aclu.org/news/n1206951.html⟩.

48. See generally Letter from Nadine Strossen, President, and Ira Glasser, Executive Director, American Civil Liberties Union, to William Clinton, President, United States of America, April 17, 1996 (visited July 20, 2000) ⟨http://www.aclu.org/news/n041896b.html⟩.

49. See, for example, Anthony Lewis, "Decency and Liberty," *New York Times*, February 9, 1998, p. A19; Lewis, "Menacing the Judges," *New York Times*, November 3, 1997, p. A23; and Lewis, "Running from the Law," *New York Times*, October 21, 1996, p. A17.

50. Lewis, "Clinton's Sorriest Record."

51. Anthony Lewis, "Stand up for Liberty," *New York Times*, April 15, 1996, p. A15.

5. Crime, Drugs, and Forfeiture
Timothy Lynch

President Bill Clinton once proclaimed that one of his "highest goals" in office has been to "protect and uphold the Constitution."[1] But a close examination of his official actions tells another story. Not only has he been indifferent to his obligation to uphold the Constitution, he has also positively undermined several constitutional provisions fundamental to the rule of law: the Fourth Amendment's protection against warrantless and unreasonable searches, the constitutional right to trial by jury, the Double Jeopardy Clause, and the constitutional right to due process of law. When drawn together, those assaults on our basic liberties constitute a sorry picture of disrespect that will, unfortunately, be the legacy of this administration.

The Warrant Clause

The Warrant Clause of the Fourth Amendment, specifying the conditions that must be met before officials may search a person's home or seize papers and effects, provides: "no [search] Warrants shall issue, but upon probable cause, supported by Oath or affirmation, and particularly describing the place to be searched, and the person or things to be seized." The Warrant Clause protects the citizenry from arbitrary searches by requiring law enforcement personnel to obtain judicial authorization *before* they demand entrance to any person's home. The Supreme Court described the constitutional importance of the warrant application process in *McDonald v. United States* (1948).

> The presence of a search warrant serves a high function. Absent some grave emergency, the Fourth Amendment has interposed a magistrate between the citizen and the police. This was done not to shield criminals nor to make the home a safe haven for illegal activities. It was done so that an objective mind might weigh the need to invade that privacy

in order to enforce the law. The right of privacy was deemed too precious to entrust to the discretion of those whose job is the detection and the arrest of criminals. Power is a heady thing; and history shows that the police acting on their own cannot be trusted. And so the Constitution requires a magistrate to pass on the desires of the police before they violate the privacy of the home.[2]

In asserting the power to conduct warrantless searches and warrantless drug testing, the Clinton administration has repeatedly played down the significance of the Warrant Clause.

Warrantless "National Security" Searches

The Clinton administration claims that it can bypass the Warrant Clause for "national security" purposes. In July 1994 Deputy Attorney General Jamie S. Gorelick told the House Select Committee on Intelligence that the president "has inherent authority to conduct warrantless searches for foreign intelligence purposes."[3] According to Gorelick, the president (or his attorney general) need only satisfy himself that an American is working in conjunction with a foreign power before a search can take place.

The Warrant Clause was designed to give the American people greater security than that afforded by the mere words of politicians. It requires the attorney general or other executive branch officials to make a showing of "probable cause" to a magistrate, a judicial branch official. The proponents of national security searches are hard-pressed to find any support for their position in the text or history of the Constitution. That is why they argue from the "inherent authority" of the Oval Office—a patently circular argument. The scope of such "authority" is unbounded in principle, of course. Yet the Clinton Justice Department has said that the Warrant Clause is fully applicable to murder suspects but not to persons suspected of violating the export control regulations of the federal government.[4] If the Framers had wanted to insert a national security exception to the Warrant Clause, they would have done so. They did not.

The Clinton administration's national security exception to the Warrant Clause is nothing more, of course, than an unsupported assertion of power by executive branch officials. The Nixon administration relied on similar constitutional assertions in the 1970s to rationalize "black bag" break-ins to the quarters of its political opponents.[5] The Clinton White House—even after the Filegate scandal—assured Congress, the media, and the general public that it has no intention of abusing this power.

Attorney General Reno has already signed off on the warrantless search of an American home on the basis of the dubious "inherent authority" theory.[6] The actual number of clandestine "national security" searches conducted since 1993 is known only to the White House and senior Justice Department officials.

Warrantless Searches of Public Housing

In the spring of 1994 the Chicago Public Housing Authority responded to gang violence by conducting warrantless "sweeps" of entire apartment buildings. Closets, desks, dressers, kitchen cabinets, and personal effects were examined, regardless of whether the police had probable cause to suspect particular residents of any wrongdoing. Some apartments were searched when the residents were not home. Although such searches were supported by the Clinton administration, Federal District Judge Wayne Anderson declared the Chicago sweeps unconstitutional.[7] Judge Anderson found the government's claim of "exigent circumstances" to be exaggerated since all of the sweeps occurred days after the gang-related shootings. He also noted that even in emergency situations, housing officials needed probable cause to search specific apartments. Unlike many governmental officials who fear demagogic criticism for being "soft on crime," Judge Anderson stood up for the Fourth Amendment rights of the tenants, noting that he had "sworn to uphold and defend the Constitution" and that he would not "use the power of [his] office to override it, amend it or subvert it."[8]

The White House response was swift. President Clinton publicly ordered Attorney General Reno and HUD Secretary Henry Cisneros to find a way to circumvent Judge Anderson's ruling. One month later the president announced a "constitutionally effective way" of searching public housing units. The Clinton administration would now ask tenants to sign lease provisions that would give government agents the power to search their homes without warrants.[9]

The Clinton plan was roundly criticized by lawyers and columnists for giving short shrift to the constitutional rights of the tenants.[10] A *New York Times* editorial observed that the president had "missed the point" of Judge Anderson's ruling.[11] Harvard law professors Charles Ogletree and Abbe Smith rightly condemned the Clinton proposal as an open invitation to the police to "tear up" the homes of poor people.[12]

Warrantless Drug Testing in Public Schools

The Clinton administration has defended warrantless drug testing programs in the public schools. In March 1995 the Supreme Court heard arguments on whether public school officials could drug test student athletes without a warrant or any articulable suspicion of illegal drug use. The Department of Justice sided with the school authorities, arguing that the privacy rights of individual students were outweighed by the interest of the school in deterring drug use by the student body generally.[13]

Solicitor General Drew Days, arguing for the government, claimed that the school district "could not effectively educate its students unless it undertook suspicionless drug testing as part of a broader drug-prevention program."[14] Days maintained that the Fourth Amendment's requirement of individualized suspicion would "jeopardize" the school's drug program. Justices Sandra Day O'Connor, John Paul Stevens, and David Souter expressed skepticism about that claim and pointed out that if the Supreme Court followed the Justice Department's reasoning, America's public school students might well end up receiving less constitutional protection under the Fourth Amendment than do convicted criminals under correctional supervision.[15]

The Clinton administration supports warrantless drug tests in other contexts as well. Thus, when Republican presidential candidate Robert Dole said, during the 1996 campaign, that he would subject welfare recipients to warrantless, suspicionless drug tests, President Clinton quickly followed suit with his own approval of such an initiative.[16]

The Jury Trial Clause

The Sixth Amendment provides: "In all criminal prosecutions, the accused shall enjoy the right to a speedy and public trial, by an impartial jury." The Clinton administration's fidelity to the Jury Trial Clause was tested on three occasions—all involving cases before the Supreme Court. In each case, unfortunately, President Clinton's legal team tried to weaken the jury trial guarantee.

Shifting Power from Juries to Judges

The first case was *United States v. Gaudin* (1995).[17] Michael Gaudin was accused of making false statements on Federal Housing Administration loan documents. The issue before the Supreme Court was whether the trial judge gave appropriate legal instructions to the jury. The trial judge told jurors that he had already determined that Gaudin's statements were "material" and that the only question for the jury to resolve was whether the accused had "knowingly" made false statements.

Gaudin's attorney argued that the materiality issue should have been decided by the jury, not the trial judge. The Sixth Amendment gives the accused the right to demand that a jury find him guilty of all of the elements of the crime with which he is charged. Since materiality was an essential element of the crime with which Gaudin was charged, his right to have that issue resolved by a jury was violated.

Instead of defending the Jury Trial Clause, the Clinton Justice Department urged the Supreme Court to affirm Gaudin's false statement conviction, arguing that historical and legal precedents supported the trial judge's legal instructions. The Supreme Court rejected the Clinton administration's legal position, unanimously. As Justice Antonin Scalia wrote,

> The existence of a unique historical exception to this [constitutional] principle—and an exception that reduces the power of the jury precisely when it is most important, i.e., in a prosecution not for harming another individual, but for offending against the Government itself—would be so extraordinary that the evidence for it would have to be convincing indeed. It is not so.[18]

The Court concluded that the trial judge had violated Gaudin's constitutional right to trial by jury and that the government would have to give him a new trial.

No Jury Trial for "Minor" Offenses

The second case involving the Jury Trial Clause was *Lewis v. United States* (1996).[19] Ray Lewis was a postal employee charged with two counts of obstructing the mail. Each count carried a maximum authorized prison sentence of six months. Lewis requested a jury trial, but federal prosecutors argued that because the crimes with which he was charged were only "petty offenses," he had no constitutional right to trial by jury. The magistrate sided with the prosecutors and a bench trial was held shortly thereafter. Lewis was found guilty, but he appealed the magistrate's decision denying him a jury trial.

The language of the Sixth Amendment is unambiguous. The accused is guaranteed the right to a jury trial in "all criminal prosecutions." Unfortunately, many years ago government lawyers persuaded a Supreme Court majority that a jury trial was required only for "serious" offenses. According to Supreme Court case law, a "serious" offense is a crime that carries a penalty in excess of six months' imprisonment. Over the years a number of Supreme Court justices have questioned the logic underlying the so-called petty offense doctrine. Justice Hugo Black, for example, found the "petty–serious" distinction to be utterly specious.

> The Constitution guarantees a right of trial by jury in two separate places but in neither does it hint of any difference between "petty" offenses and "serious" offenses. . . . Many years ago this Court, without the necessity of amendment pursuant to Article V, decided that "all crimes" did not mean "all crimes" but meant only "all serious crimes." . . . Such constitutional adjudication, whether framed in terms of "fundamental fairness," "balancing," or "shocking the conscience" amounts in every case to little more than judicial mutilation of our written Constitution.[20]

Instead of seizing on Justice Black's clear-eyed analysis of the constitutional text and urging the Supreme Court to correct its past mistake, the Clinton administration defended the petty offense doctrine and asked the Supreme Court to affirm Lewis's conviction.[21]

Overturning Jury Acquittals at Sentencing

The third case involving the Jury Trial Clause was *United States v. Watts* (1997).[22] Vernon Watts was arrested after police detectives discovered cocaine base in his kitchen cabinet and two loaded guns in his bedroom closet. At trial, the jury convicted Watts of drug charges but acquitted him of "using a firearm" during a drug offense. Despite Watts's acquittal on the weapons charge, the sentencing court announced that Watts had indeed possessed the guns in connection with the drug offense and that his prison sentence would be increased accordingly. Watts promptly appealed the additional prison time. The Clinton Justice Department defended the controversial sentence before the Ninth Circuit Court of Appeals, but lost. The appellate court vacated Watts's sentence, holding that "a sentencing judge may not . . . rely upon facts of which the defendant was acquitted." Undaunted, Clinton's legal team asked the Supreme Court to overturn the Ninth Circuit ruling—and to reinstate Watts's original sentence.

The legal issue in *Watts* had been festering in the federal court system for years. Ever since the Federal Sentencing Guidelines were enacted by Congress in 1984, federal courts have been engaged in "real-offense" sentencing, which basically allows a sentencing judge to consider a broad range of "relevant conduct" on the part of the defendant. As unbelievable as it may seem, our courts have been punishing individuals even after juries have found them not guilty of the conduct for which they are being punished.

The Framers of the Constitution placed the jury at the heart of our criminal justice system. They did so for a very specific reason. The Framers did not want the federal government to have the power to unilaterally brand a citizen a criminal. In America prosecutors must first persuade a jury of laymen that the accused is a criminal who must be punished. The jury's unanimous assent, after trial, to the government's indictment was to be a prerequisite to punishment.

Real-offense sentencing, however, undermines the constitutional safeguard of trial by jury in at least two ways. First, if prosecutors fail to persuade a jury of a defendant's guilt at trial, they can now ask a judge for a second opinion. That is what the federal prosecutor did in the *Watts* case. Second, by filing an indictment with a single charge, prosecutors can withhold shaky evidence on some allegations, then introduce it at the sentencing phase. If the government is able to secure a conviction on the charge set forth in the formal indictment, prosecutors can then seek "enhanced penalties" for offenses the jury never heard about. The government has a strong incentive to employ that strategy against defendants because the evidentiary standards before a sentencing judge are well below those required at trial. Prosecutors have to prove sentencing factors only by "a preponderance of the evidence" instead of by the traditionally high standard of "beyond a reasonable doubt." And because the Federal Rules of Evidence do not apply at sentencing, federal judges can add years to a defendant's sentence on the basis of flimsy hearsay evidence.

Justice Department officials defend real-offense sentencing by claiming that no person is being punished for conduct of which he has not been convicted; rather some are being punished more severely simply because of the factual circumstances surrounding the crime of which they were convicted. That is a dangerous play on words. For if the connection between trial and sentencing procedures is severed, Congress can simply manipulate the statutory maximum penalties for the thousands of offenses that are criminally prohibited. Such manipulation would effectively obviate the government's burden to prove criminal activity, beyond a reasonable doubt, before juries. Law professor Elizabeth Lear of the University of Florida observes that "under the current regime of nonconviction offense sentencing, only the judge and the prosecutor need approve the bulk of punishment decisions." Such unbridled governmental power "dislodges the jury from its crucial oversight role in the criminal justice system."[23]

The *Watts* case was a golden opportunity for President Clinton's lawyers to demonstrate the administration's commitment to an "expansive view of the Constitution and the Bill of Rights."[24] Sadly, the Justice Department once again sought the opposite, advocating a narrow reading of the Jury Trial Clause.

The Double Jeopardy Clause

The Double Jeopardy Clause provides: "nor shall any person be subject for the same offense to be twice put in jeopardy of life or limb." As Justice Hugo Black once observed, the underlying principle of the Double Jeopardy Clause was recognized long before the American Revolution.

> Fear and abhorrence of governmental power to try people twice for the same conduct is one of the oldest ideas found in western civilization. Its roots run deep into Greek and Roman times. Even in the Dark Ages, when so many other principles of justice were lost, the idea that one trial and one punishment were enough remained alive through the canon law and the teachings of early Christian writers. . . . While some writers have explained the opposition to double prosecutions by emphasizing the injustice inherent in two punishments for the same act, and others have stressed the dangers

> to the innocent from allowing the full power of the state to
> be brought against them in two trials, the basic and recurring
> theme has always simply been that it is wrong to "be brought
> into Danger for the same Offense more than once." Few
> principles have been more deeply "rooted in the traditions
> and conscience of our people."[25]

The double jeopardy principle was explicitly incorporated into the
Constitution when the Bill of Rights was ratified in 1791.

Although the Double Jeopardy Clause bars federal prosecutors
from subjecting any person to multiple prosecutions for the same
offense, the Supreme Court opened the door to double jeopardy
when it sanctioned separate prosecutions by federal and state officials for the same conduct. The Court announced its "dual sovereign" exception to the prohibition against double jeopardy in *Bartkus
v. Illinois* (1959).[26] The sharply divided (five-to-four) decision in *Bartkus* was and remains very controversial. Many legal analysts thought
the majority opinion was poorly reasoned. Indeed, 24 states have,
on their own initiative, attempted to shore up the double jeopardy
principle by prohibiting their prosecuting officials from pursuing
any defendant who has already been prosecuted by the federal
government.[27]

A president committed to vindicating the double jeopardy principle could close the Supreme Court's "dual sovereignty" loophole
with the stroke of a pen by issuing an executive order forbidding
U.S. attorneys to pursue individuals who have already been prosecuted by state authorities. To the disappointment of many civil
libertarians, President Clinton has expressed no such interest. In
fact, the Clinton Justice Department has signed off on several double
prosecutions since 1993.

The best known double prosecution in recent years involved the
federal case brought against the Los Angeles police officers who
viciously beat Rodney King in 1991. Although the Bush administration was responsible for convening a federal grand jury in the wake
of the state court acquittal, the trial did not get under way until
after President Clinton assumed office.[28] He could have—and should
have—stopped it.[29]

When columnist George Will asked Attorney General Reno about
the constitutionality of retrying the Los Angeles police officers, she

tried to absolve the Clinton administration of responsibility by invoking the *Bartkus* precedent.

> Mr. Will: As you know . . . a lot of civil libertarians, generally, are worried that this second trial constituted double jeopardy, that it violates the principle and the spirit of the principle that you should not be subject to trial twice for the same offense. Can you explain simply to our viewers why this wasn't double jeopardy?

> Ms. Reno: This wasn't double jeopardy, because you have two separate sovereigns. We addressed this issue in Miami on a number of occasions where federal authorities followed with a subsequent prosecution. And as the Supreme Court— as case law has evolved in this nation, you had two separate sovereigns, and therefore it is not double jeopardy.[30]

Reno's response, while strictly accurate, obscures the fact that the Justice Department can initiate or decline successive prosecutions at its discretion. There is a critical difference, after all, between permissible action and obligatory action. Indeed, that difference explains why the political branches of our government can be legitimately criticized for constitutional negligence with respect to their failure to desegregate the public school systems before the *Brown* decision was rendered in 1954. The fact that *Plessy v. Ferguson* (1896) had condoned separate but equal facilities did not absolve the other branches of our government of their responsibility to abide by the Constitution. Similarly, Reno cannot excuse the Clinton administration's failure to defend the Double Jeopardy Clause by throwing up her hands with a bland reference to Supreme Court case law.

The Clinton administration has not only embraced the double prosecutions that began under the Bush administration but has initiated a few of its own as well. When Lemrick Nelson was acquitted of murder charges by a jury in state court in October 1992, pressure began to build for a second trial in the federal court system. It was only a pending matter when President Clinton assumed office—a matter that required no action. The attorney general took an interest in the Nelson case, however, and the federal code was combed for possible charges.[31] Like the Los Angeles police officers involved in the King incident, Nelson was ultimately charged with violating the civil rights of the victim.[32]

The Clinton Justice Department has also sought to limit the effect of the Double Jeopardy Clause as it relates to civil forfeiture proceedings. When the United States Court of Appeals for the Sixth Circuit told a federal prosecutor that he could not constitutionally seize a drug dealer's home in a civil forfeiture proceeding *and* prosecute the dealer under federal criminal law, the Clinton administration appealed.[33] Even though there was no evidence that the home had been purchased with drug money, Solicitor General Days filed a legal brief with the Supreme Court that said the civil forfeiture action should not trigger the Double Jeopardy Clause since it could not be fairly characterized as a "punitive" measure.[34] How, one wonders, could the confiscation of someone's home *not* be punitive?

The Due Process Clause

The Due Process Clause of the Fourteenth Amendment provides: "nor shall any State deprive any person of life, liberty, or property, without due process of law." In 1995, the Supreme Court heard arguments on whether the State of Michigan could seize someone's property without having to prove any wrongdoing on the part of the property owner. President Clinton's solicitor general, Drew Days, defended the Michigan law, arguing that its provisions were not violative of the Due Process Clause.[35]

Detroit police arrested John Bennis after observing him engage in a sexual act with a prostitute in his car. After arresting and prosecuting Mr. Bennis for the crime of gross indecency, Michigan officials then instituted legal proceedings to take possession of the automobile. But since Mr. Bennis was only a joint owner of the vehicle, the other joint owner, his wife, Tina Bennis, objected to the proposed seizure. Although Mrs. Bennis did not object to the confiscation of the vehicle per se, she did insist upon compensation for her ownership interest—since she had broken no law. The lower courts held that the police did not have to prove that Mrs. Bennis had had any knowledge that the car would be used for an unlawful purpose. Mrs. Bennis appealed her case to the Supreme Court, arguing that Michigan's legal procedure deprived property owners of due process, in violation of the Fourteenth Amendment.

The forfeiture theory that the State of Michigan asserted was astonishing. If the government could take someone's property without having to prove *any* wrongdoing on the part of the property owner, businesspeople could conceivably lose airplanes, boats, and hotels simply because other people broke the law on their property. And if the Constitution does not recognize the fundamental idea of property rights—rights that can be invoked as a defense against state encroachment—the due process guarantee is rendered meaningless.[36] After all, what would be the point of a trial if the legislature could authorize the seizure of property from completely innocent people without compensation?

The Clinton administration's callousness toward individual rights was nowhere more evident than when the solicitor general urged the Supreme Court to rule in favor of the State of Michigan and against the constitutional claim of Tina Bennis. That, unfortunately, is what the Court did.

Conclusion

Protecting and upholding the Constitution has not been a "high priority goal" for President Clinton. From warrantless and unreasonable searches, to jury trial, double jeopardy, and due process, Clinton has sought to expand the power of government and to dilute the constitutional safeguards in the Bill of Rights. Indeed, it is not too much to say that Clinton has exhibited contempt for the very Constitution he took an oath to uphold. *That* is his legacy, a legacy of indifference to the rule of law.

Notes

1. Bill Clinton, "The Road Traveled, The Road Ahead: Judicial Excellence Safeguards All," *National Law Journal*, November 4, 1996.

2. *McDonald v. United States*, 335 U.S. 451, 455–56 (1948). For a fuller discussion of the Fourth Amendment's Warrant Clause, see Tracey Maclin, "The Central Meaning of the Fourth Amendment," *William and Mary Law Review* 35 (1993): 197–249; and Phyllis T. Bookspan, "Reworking the Warrant Requirement: Resuscitating the Fourth Amendment," *Vanderbilt Law Review* 44 (1991): 473–530.

3. Quoted in R. Jeffrey Smith, "Administration Backing No-Warrant Spy Searches," *Washington Post*, July 15, 1994, p. A19.

4. See Kate Martin, Testimony on behalf of the American Civil Liberties Union on Warrantless National Security Physical Searches before the House Permanent Select Committee on Intelligence, July 14, 1994, p. 17.

5. See Richard Gid Powers, *Secrecy and Power* (New York: Free Press, 1987), pp. 439–85.

6. See Benjamin Wittes, "Aldrich Ames' Legal Legacy: Surveillance Court Gets New Powers," *Legal Times*, November 7, 1994, p. 1.

7. See *Pratt v. Chicago Public Housing Authority*, 848 F. Supp. 792 (1994).

8. Ibid., 797.

9. See Guy Gugliotta, "Clinton Lets Police Raid Projects," *Washington Post*, April 17, 1994, p. A1; and Kevin G. Salwen, "White House Allows Searches Without Warrants in Public Housing," *Wall Street Journal*, April 18, 1994.

10. See, for example, Clarence Page, "For CHA Residents, a Fight to Keep Their Constitutional Rights," *Chicago Tribune*, April 13, 1994, p. 21; and Cal Thomas, "The Danger in Clinton's Desire to Waive Our Inalienable Rights," *Orlando Sentinel*, April 28, 1994, p. A17.

11. See "Gun Sweeps: No Model for Cities," editorial, *New York Times*, April 20, 1994, p. A18.

12. Charles Ogletree and Abbe Smith, "Clinton's Plan Is Misguided," *New York Times*, May 7, 1994, p. 23.

13. See Brief for the United States, *Veronica School District v. Acton*, 515 U.S. 646 (1995).

14. Ibid., 17.

15. See *Veronica School District*, 515 U.S. 646, 681 (1995) (O'Connor, J., dissenting).

16. See Robyn Blumner, "Clinton Showing Disdain for Civil Liberties," *St. Petersburg Times*, June 9, 1996, p. 4D.

17. *United States v. Gaudin*, 515 U.S. 506 (1995).

18. Ibid., 515. See also Richard Hansen, "A Ray of Hope at the End of a Bleak Term," *Champion*, January–February 1996, pp. 18–22.

19. *Lewis v. United States*, 518 U.S. 322 (1996).

20. *Baldwin v. United States*, 399 U.S. 66, 74–75 (1970) (Black, J., dissenting). See also Timothy Lynch, "Rethinking the Petty Offense Doctrine," *Kansas Journal of Law and Public Policy* 4 (1994): 7–22; and George Kaye, "Petty Offenders Have No Peers!" *University of Chicago Law Review* 26 (1959): 245–77.

21. See Brief for the United States, *Lewis*.

22. *United States v. Watts*, 519 U.S. 148 (1997).

23. Elizabeth Lear, "Is Conviction Irrelevant?" *UCLA Law Review* 40 (1993): 1237.

24. See Ruth Marcus and Joan Biskupic, "Justice White to Retire After 31 Years," *Washington Post*, March 20, 1993, p. A1 (quoting Clinton on his constitutional philosophy).

25. *Bartkus v. Illinois*, 359 U.S. 121, 151–55 (1959) (Black, J., dissenting) (citations omitted).

26. Ibid.

27. See Daniel A. Braun, "Praying to False Sovereigns: The Rule of Successive Prosecutions in the Age of Cooperative Federalism," *American Journal of Criminal Law* 20 (1992): 4, 5 n. 15.

28. See Philipp M. Gollner, "Second Trial of Officers Stirs Talk of Jeopardy," *New York Times*, February 19, 1993.

29. The federal prosecution was rightly condemned by a broad range of commentators. See William F. Buckley, "The Los Angeles Trial, in a Word, Stinks," *Houston Chronicle*, April 14, 1993, p. 10C; Alan Dershowitz, "Double Jeopardy for L.A. Cops," *San Francisco Examiner*, May 10, 1992; Charlotte Allen, "The King Cops and Double Jeopardy," *Wall Street Journal*, May 20, 1992, p. A17; and Doug Bandow, "The Risks of a Second King Trial," *Chicago Tribune*, June 23, 1992.

30. *This Week with David Brinkley*, April 18, 1993, Program no. 599, transcript, p. 4.

31. See Jan Hoffman, "A Rarely Used Law from the Civil Rights Era," *New York Times*, January 26, 1994.

32. See Joseph P. Fried, "A New Crown Hts. Trial Revisits Brooklyn Night of Murder in '91," *New York Times*, January 17, 1997, p. A1.

33. See Brief for the United States, *United States v. Ursery*, 518 U.S. 267 (1996). See also Roger Pilon, "Forfeiting Reason," *Regulation*, no. 3 (1996): 15–19.

34. Brief for the United States, *Ursery*. For another variation of this sort of one-two punch by prosecutors, see *United States v. 152 Char-Nor Manor Blvd., Chestertown, Md.*, 922 F. Supp. 1064 (1996).

35. See Brief for the United States, *Bennis v. Michigan*, 516 U.S. 442 (1996).

36. For additional background, see Roger Pilon, "Can American Asset Forfeiture Law Be Justified?" *New York Law School Law Review* 39 (1994): 311–33; Roger Pilon, "Property Rights, Takings, and a Free Society," *Harvard Journal of Law and Public Policy* 6 (1983): 165–95.

6. Property Rights and Economic Regulation

James Wootton

As the rule of law came slowly to replace the rule of man in Western nations, it was applied early on to property and economic liberty. Not that those applications were always sure or consistent— far from it. But from a practical perspective, they were the applications that were most pressing and therefore in greatest need of being secured. Religious liberty, free speech, and a wider franchise were all extremely important, to be sure, and came in time; but survival and prosperity were essential preconditions for those liberties. And survival and prosperity came to be understood as better ensured by property rights and economic liberty than by authoritarian rule. It is not surprising, therefore, that rights to property and economic liberty were fundamental for those who struggled over the centuries to secure the rule of law against authoritarian governments.[1]

As protected liberties grew more numerous, however, a certain reversal of priorities set in, especially with the rise of socialist and Marxist theories, both driven by an egalitarianism that disparaged property rights, economic liberty, and the individualism implicit in them. Throughout the West, in fact, those rights fell to a kind of second-class status during the 20th century. Even in America, where citizens enjoy significantly more economic freedom than citizens in most other countries,[2] property rights and economic liberty are not as secure today as they once were.[3] That discounting has been especially prominent in the Clinton administration, of course, with its repeated calls for more and larger redistributive and regulatory schemes; but Congress, state governments, and recent Republican administrations have played their parts as well. Today, as a result, neither the federal government nor the states sufficiently protect economic liberties or the rights of commercial enterprises—and the rule of law suffers accordingly.

99

To illustrate that conclusion, I will first define economic liberty, then outline the proper role of the federal government in protecting it. Next, I will assess briefly the performance of the Clinton administration as well as that of Congress and the states. Finally, I will propose an agenda for the next administration that will move toward restoring and safeguarding our economic liberties, which is essential if the rule of law is to be restored in its fullest sense.

Economic Liberty Defined

What is economic liberty, and what is the federal government's role in protecting it? The heart of economic liberty is, of course, the protection of the right to own private property and to engage in commerce. The Framers of the Constitution enshrined those rights in the structure of the document (especially in the limits imposed by the doctrine of enumerated powers), the Commerce Clause, the Contracts Clause, the Fifth Amendment's Takings and Due Process Clauses, and, later, in the Fourteenth Amendment. Given the prominence of private property and economic liberty in the Constitution, government is both charged with protecting those rights and limited by them. When officials fail to protect such rights, or actively violate them in pursuit of other ends, they undermine rights the Constitution's Framers regarded as fundamental.[4]

It should be clear, of course, that property rights and economic liberty go hand in hand. The right to property is not simply the right to possess, that is, but the right also to use and dispose of what we own, which is what gives property its value. In fact, the right to use property in any way we wish, consistent with respecting the equal rights of others, is the basis of economic liberty. Economic liberty ranges over our "Lives, Liberties and Estates, which I call by the general Name, *Property*," as John Locke put it.[5] When we use our labor or our property, whether for consumption or for exchange with others, we exercise our economic liberty. That liberty can be violated by private parties committing torts or crimes or breaching contracts—wrongs we create government to prevent or to rectify. But it can be violated by governments as well, by redistributive measures or regulatory excesses. Thus, abusive product liability lawsuits, to take one example, violate economic liberty by interfering with the lawful rights of firms to create and sell goods and services.

Because abuses like that often take place at the state level, it is important to define the proper role of the federal government with respect to protecting and regulating economic liberty. The Constitution plainly entrusts the federal government with the power to protect the free flow of interstate and foreign commerce. Indeed, that was the principal purpose of the Constitution's Commerce Clause and one of the principal purposes of the Constitution itself.[6] Thus, if the facts warrant it, Congress should not be shy about enacting legislation that preempts state laws that frustrate free trade among the states. Many argue, for example, that divergent state liability rules make it either inordinately expensive or essentially impossible to operate a national business.[7] In enacting appropriate legislation, however, Congress must itself be restrained by the limits inherent in the Commerce Clause: The clause was written to enable Congress to ensure the free flow of commerce among the states, not to enable it to regulate anything it wishes for any purpose it desires. Were that the case, there would have been no point in enumerating Congress's other powers since Congress could do almost anything it wanted through the Commerce Clause. Thus, just as Congress and the Executive Branch should strive to avoid burdening religion or speech, they should also avoid constitutionally unauthorized interference with property rights and economic liberties. If they fail, it falls to the courts to restrain them, which the Supreme Court is at last beginning to do again with its recent Commerce Clause jurisprudence, albeit still in very limited ways.[8]

Given that clear but limited scope of the commerce power, then, much of Congress's economic regulation should be either directional or negative, not affirmative. By directional regulation I mean, for example, regulation that might "stand behind" business self-regulation. Thus, while Congress is presently considering legislation to protect privacy on the Internet, one promising model for such legislation involves industry self-regulation, with private organizations auditing compliance with industry-generated standards, and the courts available to enforce any departures from those standards. In other ways, too, Congress can regulate—or make commerce "regular"—without employing the heavy hand we have seen so often coming out of Washington. The Framers wanted government to *ensure* the free flow of commerce, not to be a part of that commerce.

The Clinton Record

President Clinton may have said once that the era of big government is over, but an examination of his administration's record does not bear that out. During his tenure in office, a wide range of redistributive and regulatory programs has exposed a less than solicitous approach to property rights and economic liberty. Although the administration's "reinventing government" plan was ostensibly a means to lessen the economic burden of government regulation, those reductions have hardly been noticeable. On the contrary, in the matter of better protecting property rights and economic liberty—and restoring the rule of law in those areas—the administration has frequently taken positions that run counter to those interests. A few examples will suffice to illustrate the point.

Over the 20th century, property rights have been increasingly diminished as federal, state, and local regulations have restricted what owners could do with their property—not so much to protect others, as with many nuisance and environmental regulations, but to provide the public with various benefits, like below-market rental rates, wildlife habitat, scenic views, and the like. Unfortunately, the courts caved on this issue early in the century. Rather than enforce the Fifth Amendment's Takings Clause, which requires government to compensate owners when their property is taken for public use, the courts essentially distinguished "regulatory takings" from outright condemnations, saying that only if the entire property is taken, as distinct from the uses that go with it, is the owner entitled to compensation. As a result, countless owners have been all but wiped out by regulations aimed at providing the public with benefits, but have received little or nothing to compensate them for their losses. That has led in recent years, as regulations have grown more onerous, to the growth of a nationwide property rights movement and to calls on Congress for relief from such regulatory takings.

On that issue, the Clinton administration has been either absent or on the other side. Thus, when hearings were held in the House on November 3, 1993, on the Private Property Protection Act of 1993—a modest bill that called on federal agencies simply to do "takings analyses" of proposed legislation—the administration was unresponsive.[9] Then on February 10, 1995, Republicans newly in control of Congress introduced the Private Property Protection Act of 1995, a more robust bill that would have provided compensation for owners who suffered losses as a result of federal regulatory takings. Here, the administration adamantly opposed the bill.[10] Likewise, when a similar bill was later introduced in the Senate, there too the Clinton administration rose to oppose it,[11] as it has repeatedly with every other such bill that has come before the Congress.

Yet even where the courts have afforded some measure of protection for property rights, the administration has invariably been opposed. Thus, in the recent case of *City of Monterey v. Del Monte Dunes*[12]—in which the owners had been trying to use their property, in the face of government opposition, for over 17 years—the solicitor general argued before the Supreme Court that the failure of a regulation to advance *any* legitimate government purpose would not be sufficient to state a claim for a taking—this, despite 20 years of settled case law holding otherwise.[13]

In the regulatory area, here too the administration appeared to flout long-settled legal principles. Consider, for example, just a single element in its war on tobacco, which will be discussed more fully elsewhere in this volume. Before the Republican takeover of Congress in 1995, the White House had tried to get Congress to reverse the 80-year-old, uniform interpretation of successive acts that denied the Food and Drug Administration (FDA) regulatory authority over tobacco products. When that legislative effort became more doubtful after the 1994 elections, however, the FDA resorted to its rulemaking power to try to bring the reversal about, thus making an end run around Congress and raising profoundly important separation-of-powers questions. A subsequent court ruling held that the FDA lacked authority to regulate tobacco.[14]

In the antitrust area, the Clinton administration's agencies have also been extraordinarily aggressive. This is an area of the law that is fraught with uncertainty, an area in which the very idea of "the rule of law" is unsettled at best, providing antitrust agencies with added incentive to tread lightly. Yet the Clinton administration has often failed to do so. The effect of vigorous enforcement of uncertain law can only be stifling, especially in those "new economy" fields in which innovation can quickly lead to market power.[15]

The same can be said for the growth in recent years of "regulation by litigation," which has been especially destructive of the economic rights of businesses. Beginning at the state level, this litigation has spread to the federal level as well, first with the tobacco industry

103

and now with firearms and other industries. With the active support of the Clinton Justice Department, governments at all levels today are attempting to regulate politically unpopular industries without going through the normal legislative processes. To ease their task of imposing liability on those industries, they are routinely stripping businesses of long-held legal rights, making a mockery of the rule of law in the process.[16] Even Robert Reich, President Clinton's first labor secretary, recently remarked that "launching lawsuits to succeed where legislation failed may work, but at the cost of making our frail democracy even weaker."[17] Needless to say, the uncertainty such litigation engenders in industry is fundamentally contrary to the predictability that is central to the rule of law.

For all its regulatory excesses, however, the administration has also failed to regulate where it should. Yet, the fault here lies with both Congress and the administration. As discussed earlier, where the facts warrant it, Congress has authority under the Commerce Clause to ensure the free flow of commerce by preempting discriminatory state regulation. But Congress and the administration have often failed to promote and enact adequate preemptive legislation[18]—even if the administration has, to its credit, supported federal preemption in several notable court cases.[19]

Yet in agency actions and litigation positions, the administration has also sided routinely with the plaintiffs' bar to contend that state regulations are not preempted by federal law. Thus, in *Norfolk Southern Railway Co. v. Shanklin*[20] the administration argued that the Railroad Safety Act did not preempt state laws, a position the Supreme Court then rejected. Similarly, in *Lewis v. Brunswick*[21] the solicitor general argued that the Federal Boat Safety Act of 1971 did not preempt state tort suits charging manufacturers with liability for their failure to install propeller guards, despite the fact that the Coast Guard had explicitly considered and rejected requiring such guards.[22] And the Clinton FDA proposed regulations that would have allowed state product liability claims to be brought alleging injury from complicated medical devices *that had been approved by the FDA*, this despite an express preemption rule in the Medical Device Amendments of 1976.[23] The proposed regulations were withdrawn only after the industry discovered that, before they were released to anyone else, a draft of them had been given for comment to Public Citizen, Ralph Nader's public advocacy organization.[24]

Protecting Economic Liberty: An Agenda for the Next Administration

Again, those are but a few of the inroads on legal principle that have unfolded during the Clinton years, even if the abuses did not begin with the Clinton administration. If the abuses are to end, however, it is not too early to make a few suggestions about where to start. Like the preceding criticisms, this list is hardly exhaustive.

There is simply no excuse for the federal government's continuing to restrict owners in the use of their property to confer benefits on the public while leaving the costs of those benefits on the owner. If property, including the right to use property, is taken for public use, the government is obligated to compensate the owner, however lax the courts may have been in enforcing that obligation. One of the first tasks of the new administration, therefore, should be to propose legislation that would require the federal government to abide by the Constitution in this most fundamental of matters.

The next administration should also support preemptive legislation that addresses the problem of abusive litigation. Just as the Private Securities Litigation Reform Act of 1995 limited abuses by the plaintiffs' bar in the securities area,[25] and the Y2K Act addressed the danger of excessive litigation growing out of potential Y2K computer failures, so too broader legislation based on that foundation is needed to stop the growing problem of abusive litigation. Here, it is essential to recognize that tort law in general, and product liability law in particular, have long been the purview of the states. The national government has power to intervene only when state rules are impeding the flow of interstate commerce. Under those circumstances, effective legislation in this area, national and preemptive, minimizes government intrusion into daily life. Right now any state can impose its views on the entire country through its court system. Not only might that cast a shadow over economic activity across the nation but the result can be inconsistent with the national economy envisioned by the Framers.

Carefully crafted federal legislation can address the problem and still stay within the proper limits of the commerce power. Such a bill could set certain nationwide liability standards and protect our economy from the effects of abusive litigation. The bill could also enable businesses to assume that their contracts will be enforced rather than ignored arbitrarily. The net result of such reforms would be to discourage frivolous, extortionate and abusive suits, which currently plague our nation.

Another initiative for the next administration involves enacting national standards to govern Internet privacy. The Internet cries out for a limited, uniform national approach to the regulation of interstate and international commerce. Any business that ventures onto the Internet necessarily subjects itself to the laws of all 50 states. As a result, differing and inconsistent state rules can impose a significant burden on use of this national medium of commerce. Until privacy rights on the Internet are clear and predictable, e-business will be stifled unnecessarily.

The next administration should also urge Congress to enact legislation requiring federal agencies—especially employment agencies like OSHA, the NLRB, and the EEOC—to reimburse the attorneys' fees of businesses that successfully defend themselves against agency actions. Today there is little incentive for government agencies to carefully assess the often meritless enforcement actions they bring against businesses. If agencies were required to internalize the costs of their unsuccessful litigation, they would be deterred from excessive or frivolous litigation. Although the Equal Access to Justice Act currently allows fee shifting against the government in limited instances, it is an insufficient deterrent because the agencies can almost always claim that their positions were at least "substantially" justified. That standard needs to be tightened against the agencies. Moreover, if the incentive to litigate carefully is to be effective, it is imperative that the costs be borne by the agency itself rather than by the general treasury.

Those are a few reforms that would begin moving us back toward greater respect for the rule of law as it involves property rights and economic liberty. More generally, however, the next administration needs to build on the Supreme Court's recent reaffirmation of one of our first principles as a nation: "We see no reason why the Takings Clause of the Fifth Amendment, as much a part of the Bill of Rights as the First Amendment or Fourth Amendment, should be relegated to the status of a poor relation."[26] The time has come to treat property rights and economic liberty with the respect they deserve as foundations for the rule of law.

Notes

1. See generally Richard Pipes, *Property and Freedom* (New York: Alfred A. Knopf, 1999); Tom Bethell, *The Noblest Triumph: Property and Prosperity Through the Ages* (New

York: St. Martin's Press, 1998); Gottfried Dietze, *In Defense of Property* (Baltimore: Johns Hopkins Press, 1963).

2. See James Gwartney and Robert Lawson, *Economic Freedom of the World: 2000 Annual Report* (Fraser Institute, 2000) (United States ranks fourth out of 123 countries in economic freedom, on the basis of a composite ranking system).

3. See Richard A. Epstein, *Takings: Private Property and the Power of Eminent Domain* (Cambridge, Mass.: Harvard University Press, 1985); Roger Pilon, "Property Rights, Takings, and a Free Society," *Harvard Journal of Law and Public Policy* 6 (1983): 165–95.

4. See, for example, James Madison, "Property," *National Gazette*, March 29, 1792, reprinted in *The Writings of James Madison*, vol. 6, Gaillard Hunt, ed. (New York: G. P. Putnam's Sons, 1906).

5. John Locke, "The Second Treatise of Government," in *Two Treatises of Government*, Peter Laslett, ed. (New York: Mentor, 1965), para. 123. The Economic Freedom Network, originally organized by Milton Friedman and involving a host of leading economists, defines economic freedom as follows:

> The core ingredients of economic freedom are personal choice, protection of private property, and freedom of exchange. Individuals have economic freedom when: (a) their property acquired without the use of force, fraud, or theft is protected from physical invasions by others and (b) they are free to use, exchange, or give their property to another as long as their actions do not violate the identical rights of others.

Gwartney and Lawson, *Economic Freedom*, p. 5.

6. As Justice William Johnson put it in his concurrence in the first great Commerce Clause case, *Gibbons v. Ogden*, "If there was any one object riding over every other in the adoption of the constitution, it was to keep the commercial intercourse among the States free from all invidious and partial restraints." 22 U.S. 1, 231 (1824).

7. As Judge Robert Bork has urged, if the facts support it, state product liability laws *should* be preempted by federal law. Otherwise, "a state like California or Texas can impose its views of appropriate product design and the penalties for falling short on manufacturers and distributors across the nation. This is a perversion of federalism. Instead of national standards being set by the national legislature, national standards are set by the courts and juries of particular states." Letter to Newt Gingrich on H.R. 956 (February 27, 1995). See also McConnell, "Federalism: Evaluating the Founders' Design," *University of Chicago Law Review* 54 (1987): 1499.

8. See, for example, *United States v. Lopez*, 514 U.S. 549 (1995); *United States v. Morrison*, 120 S. Ct. 1740 (2000); *Jones v. United States*, 146 L.Ed.2d 886 (2000).

9. Subcommittee on Department Operations and Nutrition of the House Committee on Agriculture, *Private Property Protection Acts: Hearings on H.R. 561* before the 103rd Congress 1993.

10. Subcommittee on the Constitution of the House Committee on the Judiciary, *Protecting Private Property Rights from Regulatory Takings: Hearings on H.R. 925* before the 104th Congress 1995, statement of John R. Schmidt, Assistant Attorney General, Department of Justice.

11. Senate Committee on Environmental and Public Works, *Omnibus Property Rights Act of 1995: Hearings on S. 605* before the 104th Congress 1995, statement of John R. Schmidt, Associate Attorney General, Department of Justice.

12. 526 U.S. 687 (1999).

13. See Brief for the United States as Amicus Curiae Supporting Petitioner in Part at 21–29, *City of Monterey v. Del Monte Dunes*, 526 U.S. 687 (1999) (No. 97-1235), challenging *Agins v. City of Tiburon*, 447 U.S. 255 (1980).

14. *FDA v. Brown & Williamson Tobacco Group*, 120 S. Ct. 1291 (2000), holding that the FDA lacks authority to regulate tobacco.

15. See, for example, Wilke & Gruley, "Trustbuster Joel Klein, Once Viewed as Timid, Comes on Like a Tiger," *Wall Street Journal*, May 15, 1998. ("Mr. Klein has emerged as the most active, and the most feared, Washington regulator in a generation.")

16. Senator McConnell's *Litigation Fairness Act of 1999*, S. 1269 (106th Congress), would block this manipulative maneuver.

17. Robert B. Reich, "Don't Democrats Believe in Democracy?," *Wall Street Journal*, January 12, 2000.

18. One area in which Congress did pass such legislation was the *Y2K Act*, Pub. L. 106–37, 106th Cong. 1999, which helped counter frivolous Y2K litigation that threatened to cost more than Y2K itself cost.

19. Those cases include three from the Supreme Court's just-concluded 1999 term: *Geier v. American Honda Motor Co.*, No. 98-1811 (May 22, 2000), which held federal airbag rules to be preemptive; *Crosby v. Secretary of Administration*, No. 99-474 (June 19, 2000), which set aside Massachusetts' law barring trade with Burma; and *United States v. Locke*, No. 98-1701 (March 6, 2000), which preempted Washington State's law regulating the design and operation of oil tankers operating in interstate commerce. The administration's motivation in such cases need not be grounded in constitutional respect, of course. Indeed, agencies rarely go to court to argue that they do not have power.

20. 120 S. Ct. 1467 (2000).

21. 107 F.3d 1494 (11th Cir. 1997).

22. Propeller guards, it turns out, may cause more injuries than they prevent.

23. 21 U.S.C. § 360k(a).

24. See "Draft Device Preemption Reg Release to Public Citizen Probed by FDA," *The Gray Sheet*, p. 10 (July 6, 1998).

25. Public Law 104–67, 109 Stat. 737 (1995), codified in scattered parts of 15 U.S.C.

26. *Dolan v. City of Tigard*, 512 U.S. 374, 392 (1997).

PART III

THE CLEAREST CASES

7. Scandal, Corruption, and the Rule of Law

Fred Thompson

The importance of the rule of law cannot be overstated. In our country the rule of law is the foundation for every institution. In many countries, the chief drawback to the formation of a prosperous and civil society is the absence of the rule of law. Because of its importance, the rule of law must be properly defined. We should not dilute its importance by overuse.

The rule of law is different from, and more important than, the law itself. It is in fact the process by which a society maintains the rules that have been agreed upon, and the process by which it deals with violations of those rules. The rules must be maintained consistently, be applied evenly, and be free of corruption or undue influence. And it must be clear that this is being done. The charge of undermining the rule of law should be reserved for those whose actions are deliberate, most serious, and go to the heart of, and do harm to, our legal or political institutions or processes.

The Watergate scandal provides a good example of the distinction between laws and the rule of law. Facts were revealed in the press. Congress had hearings and further developed the facts. A special counsel, independent of the Justice Department, was brought in to investigate the matter. Individuals were prosecuted before an independent judiciary, and a president resigned. Most did not question the fact that the rule of law was alive and well and perhaps even strengthened by the time the investigation was completed. We were simply reminded once again that people in positions of power sometimes abuse that power and violate the law. And we were also reminded that we have a strong system for dealing with that problem. In other matters, from the Teapot Dome to the Iran-Contra scandals, there have been disagreements about what the outcomes should have been, as there are with almost any lawsuit, but there was never any feeling that the system had broken down.

The rule of law is especially important and most rigorously tested when those who are charged with responsibility for protecting the rule of law are alleged to have broken the law. The most critical situation occurs when the activities of the highest-ranking officials in the government are brought into question. That has happened from time to time in our history. And since it is the government itself that must investigate the accused officials, there is an inherent conflict of interest in every case. Nevertheless, I think it fair to say that in few, if any, of those cases has there ever been a serious question about whether the rule of law had been observed. That is primarily because those in the highest positions of authority—the president, the attorney general, or both—responding to the perceived demands of the citizens, would appoint an outsider to investigate such cases. Special counsels were often used long before the independent counsel statute was passed. That decision was based on the obvious, commonsense understanding that it is very difficult to prosecute one's colleagues, especially one's superior, while still appearing to be fair and objective. Some discretion has always been given the Justice Department regarding investigations of alleged wrongdoing within an administration, but the more senior the officials under investigation, the more problematic it becomes. Nevertheless, for about 200 years we have done pretty well in protecting the rule of law.

That brings us to the present and to the current administration: Travelgate, Filegate, the matters that led to President Clinton's impeachment, the failure to produce materials under subpoena, violations of the Privacy Act, the pursuit of invalid legal claims that set a precedent that arguably harmed the institution of the presidency. (President Clinton claimed executive privilege 13 times, the combined number of times of all presidents since Kennedy.) The list goes on to the point that one is tempted to conclude that there has been virtually a continuous undermining of the rule of law. No matter how egregious some of those actions were, however, I am not sure they meet the definition I have set for the rule of law. Some of the scandals did not involve the legal process. Others were investigated by an independent counsel, and the process ran its course. Still others have not, at least not yet, been proven. Finally, some involve actions that are within the limits, albeit the outer limits, of the law.

Let's just say that if those actions, or the totality of them, did not undermine the rule of law, they came close enough to raise serious and troubling concerns, especially considering that many of them were carried out by and on behalf of the person with the constitutional responsibility to faithfully execute the law.

There is one area of scandal, however, that allows us to leave ambiguity behind. It is an area in which, I believe, the facts are clear, the duties and obligations of the responsible officials are obvious, and our political and our legal processes were undermined. I refer to the campaign finance scandal emanating from the 1996 presidential election and the way in which it was handled.

Since 1973, we have had a publicly financed presidential campaign system. When candidates receive federal funding, they are required to certify that they will not raise additional campaign cash from other sources. The system is designed to protect candidates from the influence of large amounts of money. Both President Clinton and Vice President Gore signed such certifications. Having done so, however, they then proceeded to raise millions of dollars more, funneled it through the Democratic National Committee (DNC) and spent it on television ads to benefit their candidacies. The president actually sat in the White House and approved the ads, where they would run, and how often. Previously, everyone believed that such activity was illegal. However, Attorney General Janet Reno decided that this obvious circumvention of the law was legal, creating the hard money versus soft money quagmire that bedevils her and the vice president to this day.

Of course, just making such a legal determination presented her with a conflict of interest. In fact, that was one of the reasons FBI Director Louis Freeh recommended the appointment of an independent counsel. He pointed out to the attorney general that the circumvention had not even been investigated. He cited Title 18, section 371, which is a conspiracy statute I have used many times as a prosecutor. It is right on point. Section 371 prohibits a conspiracy not only to violate the law but also to "defraud the government." The underlying act does not even have to be a violation of the law. If, in order to receive federal moneys, a candidate certifies something that is not true, and that fact does not present at least grounds for investigation under section 371, we should abrogate the statute. Apparently, Louis Freeh thinks the same. But the attorney general had no problem finessing the obvious conflict of interest and turning down his recommendation that an independent counsel be appointed.

On July 8, 1997, the Committee on Governmental Affairs, which I chair, began hearings on the 1996 presidential campaign and its campaign finance abuses. Over the next four months, we saw how millions of dollars in illegal campaign contributions were funneled into the DNC. Much of that activity was coordinated by personal friends of the president or vice president. Much of the money was foreign. In fact, there was evidence that at least six of the major coordinators of illegal campaign funds had ties to the Chinese government.

On the first day of our hearings, I stated that the People's Republic of China (PRC) had tried to influence our elections with illegal campaign money. That was obvious from the classified material available to the committee, and I cleared my statement with the FBI and the CIA. Nevertheless, for the next four months, the Department of Justice (DOJ) and some Senate Democrats tried to undermine my statement.

The subsequent record speaks for itself, but the important point here is what Director Freeh was telling Attorney General Reno at about the same time. In a November 24, 1997, memo, written less than a month after our hearings concluded, Freeh told Reno of the conflict the FBI and Justice had in keeping President Clinton informed on national security matters while at the same time investigating efforts by the PRC "to gain foreign policy influence by illegally contributing foreign money to U.S. political campaigns and to the DNC through domestic conduits." The memo said that the FBI found "substantial evidence" that huge sums of money had been routed to the DNC by foreign sources as a result of the massive fundraising effort coordinated by the DNC and the White House. Freeh recommended a conspiracy investigation that would include alleged "FECA [Federal Elections Campaign Act of 1971] violations, foreign campaign contributions, telephone solicitations and a conspiracy by the PRC to bribe high-ranking U.S. political figures."

Eight months later, in a July 16, 1998, report to Reno, DOJ prosecutor Charles LaBella confirmed Freeh's concerns, saying there was reason to believe that Clinton and Gore "knew or had reason to know that foreign funds were being funneled into the DNC and

114

the reelection effort." LaBella added, "If these allegations involved anyone other than the President, Vice President, senior White House, or DNC and Clinton/Gore '96 officials, an appropriate investigation would have commenced months ago without hesitation." Finally, LaBella's memo noted the absurd catch-22 in Reno's interpretation of the independent counsel statute: it would not allow for inquiry regarding covered persons unless the evidence sought was already known to the investigators.

FBI Assistant Director Robert Bryant wrote to Freeh in 1997 that the FBI was investigating the solicitation of contributions from foreign nationals, the coordination of DNC soft money to affect the presidential race, and the solicitation of contributions on federal property. "It is difficult to understand how DOJ can dispute the contention that there 'may have' been a violation of federal law sufficient to warrant further investigation," Bryant said, adding flatly that "the Task Force is proceeding differently than it would in a 'normal' investigation" because the issue "reaches into the top levels of the White House. At various times, the task force has slowed down when the investigation began to point at a covered person."

That is the situation with which Reno was presented. I do not believe there is any real argument, legal or otherwise, for the attorney general's failure either to activate the independent counsel statute or to bring in a special counsel. Her arguments are so weak that they are not to be taken seriously. Her reasons are contrary to the adamant opinions of the head of the FBI (a former federal judge), the officer in charge of the investigation, and the principal associate deputy attorney general. And they are inconsistent with precedent within the department itself when dealing with lower-level officials accused of misconduct. Thus, the statute that some people said had a "hair trigger" when applied to lower-level officials, suddenly developed a trigger lock when applied to the president and the vice president.

The memoranda in this case are powerful and shocking documents. We see career law enforcement officials practically begging the attorney general to do the right thing. As for motivation, we know that FBI Assistant Director Bill Esposito informed Freeh that Lee Radek, DOJ's Public Integrity Section head, had told Esposito he was being pressured and that Reno's job might hang in the balance.

The memos are remarkable in several respects. First, their conclusion that the facts clearly triggered the independent counsel statute was obviously correct. Second, the attorney general had a hopeless conflict of interest that required her to call in an outsider under her discretionary authority even if she did not believe that the technicalities of the mandatory independent counsel were met. Third, honorable law enforcement officers obviously believed they were being improperly blocked in their own investigation about whether to investigate the president and vice president. Finally, the allegations in the memos of a double standard and a slowdown when the evidence pointed toward a covered person is about as serious an accusation as one can make about a department charged with the responsibility for administering justice in this country.

Thus, the record shows that the law established to deal with such scandals was not complied with when it came to the highest officials in the country. The law was not applied consistently. There was a lower threshold for activating the statute for lower-ranking officials. The country's desire for an untainted resolution of the allegations was thus thwarted. And even though the allegations involved fundamental matters that go to the heart not only of our legal but also of our political process, it appeared that the attorney general was unduly protecting high-ranking officials from the regular legal process that other citizens and public officials have to undergo. There can be no clearer example of the undermining of the rule of law. And it is of historic proportions. It will undoubtedly contribute to the cynicism and skepticism so prevalent in our society today, especially among young people. It has demoralized the Department of Justice and has disserved the public officials who should have had these matters resolved by an independent investigator long ago. It will forever be a part of this administration's legacy.

There is a lot to learn from all of this. Certainly, nowadays in Washington, the accuser is just as suspect as the accused and therefore must act responsibly if widespread public support is to be gained in this cynical age. Congress needs to reexamine its institutional role. We have demonstrated that we are no longer capable of having a bipartisan investigation in which both parties actually seek the truth and the best interests of the country.

Perhaps it is true that we have begun to rely too much on the courts and legal processes to resolve matters that are best left to the political process, because that is where such issues are ultimately resolved in a democratic society. As frustrating and disheartening as it is to see a breakdown in the rule of law, we know that in the end the American people have the final say. And we will always have the kind of government and the rule of law that we deserve.

But leaders are still responsible for reminding the American people of what is at stake. We now have peace and prosperity, and people prefer not to be bothered by Washington, which has been so disappointing in many ways. The pendulum swings, however, and when our nation faces its next crisis, and we need leadership, direction, and inspiration, who in government will the people heed if leaders abuse our most cherished institutions, including the rule of law? That, to me, is the most important issue facing us today, and how we resolve it will play a large part in determining our destiny as a nation.

PART IV

THE ABUSE OF COMMON LAW, STATUTE, AND LEGAL INSTITUTIONS

8. The War on Tobacco

Robert A. Levy

The Clinton administration did not begin the modern war on tobacco. Private and public health agencies have long urged greater regulation of the industry. And lawyers for years have sued tobacco companies on behalf of clients who claimed that the industry had caused them harm—suits that invariably failed when juries decided that companies were entitled to invoke established common law defenses like assumption of risk. Once Mr. Clinton came to power, however, his administration began working with those agencies and with its friends in the plaintiffs bar and state attorneys general offices to fashion an all-out strategy, first, to vilify big tobacco, then to plunder its coffers—while keeping the industry alive for future plundering, of course.

The stepped-up effort began at the state level, with multiple, often coordinated suits based on unprecedented theories of liability. Amounting to little more than extortion by state attorneys general and the plaintiffs bar, the effort culminated in the 1998 quarter-trillion-dollar Master Settlement Agreement (MSA), which effectively cartelized the tobacco industry. Ten months after that, Mr. Clinton's Justice Department (DOJ) decided that it wanted a share of the plunder, notwithstanding Attorney General Janet Reno's earlier declaration to Congress that she saw no legal ground for federal involvement. As a result, it is safe to say that today we have a body of "law" relating to tobacco that is far removed from anything approximating the rule of law.

The Justice Department's complaint, filed in September 1999, alleges that cigarette companies conspired since the 1950s to defraud the American public and conceal information about the effects of smoking. Specifically, DOJ contends that industry executives knowingly made false and misleading statements about whether smoking causes disease and whether nicotine is addictive. Apparently no one at DOJ realizes the irony—indeed, the unbounded hypocrisy—of the Clinton administration pursuing anyone for lying under oath.

On one hand, the Justice Department promotes its novel lawsuit to recapture smoking-related costs, supposedly wrung from the federal purse because of the tobacco industry's misbehavior. On the other hand, the same watchdog agency stands idly by while tobacco companies and state attorneys general team up to violate the antitrust laws. The multistate tobacco settlement, a cunning and deceitful bargain between the industry and the states, enables the tobacco giants to monopolize cigarette sales and foist the cost onto luckless smokers.

This essay examines DOJ's misuse of executive power: first, the department's willingness to fabricate legal theories that defy centuries of tort law; second, its refusal to enforce antitrust statutes that have been flagrantly abused by an ominous alliance of industry and government.

The "New" Tort Law: On Assumption of Risk and Causation

In its latest litigation against the tobacco industry, the federal government seeks to recover billions of dollars annually in federal health care expenditures—mostly Medicare outlays—related to smoking. DOJ's legal theory is modeled after the states' lawsuits, which were designed to replenish depleted Medicaid coffers. Like the states, the federal government argues that it can sue tobacco companies without stepping into the shoes of each smoker. To better understand that theory, and how it affects the DOJ claims, here is a quick backgrounder on the "new" tort law that animates government-sponsored litigation against cigarette makers.

For 40 years, there had been no final judgment against tobacco companies for smoking-related illnesses. That is because juries understood that we are each at liberty to consume the products we wish; but if we do so, and we are aware of the attendant risks, we assume those risks and are responsible for the consequences of our acts. At the same time that juries were laying down that basic legal principle, called assumption of risk, state Medicaid programs were coming under intense financial pressure. Under the Medicaid Act,[1] states are entitled to recover their expenditures for smoking-related illnesses, but they must follow a process known as subrogation. An insurer, like the Medicaid program, substitutes itself for the injured party and sues on his behalf. Thus the Medicaid system, as plaintiff, would have the same burden of proof that a smoker would have if he had sued directly. And, of course, the state would be subject to the same defenses that the tobacco companies could have asserted against the smoker—including the assumption-of-risk defense, which had been a consistent winner for the industry for four decades.

How then to get around assumption of risk? The states came up with a creative solution: They simply eliminated that provision of the law—and applied the new rule retroactively, as if it had been in effect decades ago when the harmful cigarettes were originally sold. Florida, Maryland, and Vermont accomplished that legerdemain by statute;[2] the other states did it by seeking equitable relief in court—that is, by asking judges to ignore conventional precepts of tort law.[3]

Bill Clinton understands the assumption-of-risk principle perfectly well. Indeed, his former Veterans Affairs secretary, Jesse Brown, invoked it when the government itself was threatened with liability for having provided millions of soldiers with cigarettes over the years. It would be "borderline absurdity" to pay for "veterans' personal choice to engage in conduct damaging to their health," he said. "If you choose to smoke, you are responsible for the consequences of your act."[4]

Evidently that principle applies only if the accused is a government agency, not a private company. Accordingly, DOJ asserts that it can recover from the tobacco industry merely because smoking injured someone protected by Medicare—even if that person, having voluntarily assumed the risk of smoking, could not recover on his own. The same tobacco company selling the same cigarettes to the same smoker, resulting in the same injury, would be liable only if the smoker is a Medicare recipient and the government is the plaintiff. Otherwise, the assumption-of-risk defense would apply. Liability hinges on the injured party's Medicare status, a happenstance utterly unrelated to any misconduct by the industry—and a legal doctrine that does not even pass the laugh test.

Also following the states' model, the federal government wants the court to ignore the traditional tort law requirement that causation be demonstrated on a smoker-by-smoker basis. Instead, DOJ wants to adduce only aggregate statistics, indicating a higher incidence of certain diseases among smokers than among nonsmokers. For example, statistics show that smokers are more likely than nonsmokers to suffer burn injuries. So tobacco companies would have to pay for many careless persons who fell asleep with a lit cigarette. Similarly, the industry will be asked to pay for persons who had heart attacks and other "smoking-related" diseases, but who never smoked. Without individualized corroborating evidence, aggregate statistics suggest liability. Only common sense dictates otherwise.

The Statutory Backdrop

To reinforce and supplement its bizarre tort theories, DOJ relies on three statutes: the Medical Care Recovery Act (MCRA),[5] the Medicare Secondary Payer Act (MSPA),[6] and the civil provisions of the Racketeer Influenced and Corrupt Organizations (RICO) act.[7] In alleging a violation of RICO, which was supposed to be invoked against organized crime, the government has stooped to what nowadays is a standard bullying tactic by plaintiffs' attorneys. This time, however, DOJ has to deal with an embarrassing admission, tucked away in the final sentence of the press release that heralded its lawsuit: "There are no pending Criminal Division investigations of the tobacco industry."[8]

After a five-year, multi-million-dollar inquiry by two dozen prosecutors and FBI agents, DOJ produced one misdemeanor plea resulting in a $100,000 fine against an obscure biotechnology company for violating a seed export law that has since been repealed.[9] The government dissected allegations that tobacco executives perjured themselves when testifying before Congress. Prosecutors plowed through documents for evidence that cigarette makers manipulated nicotine levels. Whistle-blowers and company scientists testified before grand juries. The outcome: not a single indictment of a tobacco company or industry executive.

Nonetheless, President Clinton collared his attorney general and she, somehow, conjured up a RICO claim that accused the industry of the very same infractions for which grand juries could not find probable cause. Despite consistent court rulings in union health fund cases that insurers—like Medicare—have no claim under RICO,[10] Janet Reno and her minions at DOJ included among their 116 counts against the industry all sorts of foolishness intended to ratchet up the pressure for an exorbitant financial settlement, notwithstanding the inanity of the underlying assertions. Count number three is just one example: In November 1959, the industry "did knowingly cause a press release to be sent and delivered by the U.S. mails to newspapers and news outlets. This press release contained statements attacking an article written by then-U.S. Surgeon General Leroy Burney about the hazards of smoking." There you have it—racketeering, in all its sordid detail.

DOJ's claims under the MCRA are not much better. The MCRA, passed in 1962, was intended to circumvent a 1947 Supreme Court case[11] that denied a right of recovery under the common law for government medical outlays to pay for a soldier's injuries caused by a defendant's negligence. In no instance has the MCRA ever been used to reclaim Medicare expenditures. Indeed, because MCRA was enacted three years before Medicare, it could not have been within the contemplation of Congress that Medicare costs would be recoverable. Nor is there anything in MCRA suggesting that multiple claims can be aggregated as in DOJ's suit. Nor can the government recoup from tobacco companies the costs of treating a smoker's illness when the smoker himself could make no showing that his illness was due to the companies' negligence.

As a fallback, DOJ is also claiming under the MSPA. That 1980 statute expressly covers Medicare expenditures—implicitly confirming that the earlier MCRA did not do so. But MSPA is invoked against an injured party or his private insurer, not against a tortfeasor. The purpose of the statute is to prevent an injured party from recovering twice—once from a private insurer and a second time from Medicare—or to assure that a private insurer is not let off the hook for a legitimate claim just because the claim might otherwise be covered by Medicare. MSPA has never been employed to establish liability for an injury; it was designed for cost recovery only after liability had been determined.

What Future for DOJ's Illegal Crusade?

That legal analysis is well known to the Clinton administration, which is why Attorney General Reno repeatedly rejected a federal cause of action against tobacco companies for Medicare reimbursement.[12] Commenting on the DOJ lawsuit, former Clinton aide Rahm Emanuel put it this way: "If the White House hadn't asked, [Reno] would never have looked at it again."[13] So it is politics, not law, that is driving this litigation. And what is worse, the entire scheme is cynically promoted as a way to protect the health of our children.

But it is money, not the health of children, that drives the tobacco wars. For every pack of cigarettes sold during 1998, the industry earned about 23 cents, the federal government got 24 cents, and the states averaged 36 cents.[14] Thus, even at presettlement rates, government got 60 of each 83 cents of pretax profits. In effect, federal and state governments were 72 percent stockholders in an enterprise that, according to government reports, kills more than 400,000 Americans every year.[15] No matter the incongruity, politicians are not likely to stop milking the cash cow. If fact, they struggled mightily to come up with a well-disguised plan that would guarantee the continued health of the tobacco giants. Humorist Dave Barry got it exactly right when he described the real meaning of the tobacco settlement: The industry finally admitted that its product has killed millions of Americans. Now, pursuant to the settlement, the industry will continue to kill millions of Americans—under strict governmental supervision.[16]

Here, then, is how we got to where we are today. When the big four tobacco companies signed the 1998 MSA rather than fight the states, which were rewriting centuries-old tort law, they essentially bribed the politicians, who were all too willing to be bribed.[17] That capitulation—the unprincipled surrender of the companies' right freely to market a legal product—predictably spawned President Clinton's dual assault on the industry: First, he proposed a tax hike of 55 cents per pack. Second, just in case Republicans worked up the courage to reject the higher tax, he announced federal litigation to recoup health costs allegedly connected with smoking. If Congress didn't cooperate, Clinton would simply bypass the legislature—not to mention the Constitution—and ask a federal court to exact damages in lieu of taxes. The objectives were twofold: first, to score political points against a vilified industry; second, to bail out the bankrupt Medicare system. In pursuit of those ends, anything goes—including the rule of law.

The U.S. District Court in Washington, D.C., should peremptorily dismiss Clinton's contrived litigation. Even if somehow it could be squared with time-honored principles of tort law, another "tax" on cigarettes makes no sense. It is not just the destructive effect of black markets, or the brutal regressivity of price hikes, or the inequity when 44 million adult smokers have to fork up because some retailers violate unenforced laws and sell cigarettes to one million minors. It is also the assessment by every scholar who has examined the data that existing excise taxes more than cover the social costs of smoking.[18] The uncomfortable truth is that federal and state governments have benefited handsomely from tobacco taxes, and therein lies one reason they have subsidized tobacco growers and declined to regulate cigarettes as a drug.

Our adversarial system works quite well when smokers, insurance companies, and the industry fight it out in court, applying the law dispassionately and evenhandedly. The Medicare program can recover like any other insurer; but it is not exempt from the assumption-of-risk defense—it has to prove causation smoker-by-smoker, and it must demonstrate actual damages. Under those rules, if the plaintiff can show he was defrauded, did not appreciate the risk, became addicted as a result of the industry's deception, and contracted an illness because he smoked, he may be able to prevail. But once a smoker turns 18, then he is an adult—the same adult legally allowed to sign contracts, go to war, vote, and marry—decisions no less weighty than whether to smoke. We cannot hold tobacco companies responsible for consensual adult conduct, least of all by changing the law of torts on a retroactive basis.

Meanwhile, if the health imperative is to reduce smoking among children, the remedy lies with state governments. The sale of tobacco products to youngsters is illegal in every state. Those laws need to be vigorously enforced. Retailers who violate the law should be prosecuted. Proof-of-age requirements are appropriate if administered objectively and reasonably. Vending machine sales should be prohibited in areas like arcades and schools where children are the main clientele. And if a minor is caught smoking or attempting to acquire cigarettes, his parents should be notified. Parenting is, after all, the primary responsibility of fathers and mothers, not the government.

That approach will work, and it is constitutional. By contrast, the Clinton administration is embarked on yet one more unconscionable raid on private wealth—a bald attempt to fatten the federal treasure chest without regard for individual liberty or personal responsibility.

Yet that is not the whole story. While DOJ presses its campaign to extort money from hapless tobacco companies, the Antitrust Division looks the other way as those same companies, in collaboration with state attorneys general, commit what is arguably the most egregious antitrust violation of our generation.

The Mother of All Antitrust Violations[19]

How sad and ironic that our regulators, so fervent to dismember a half-trillion-dollar software company for selling integrated products that consumers want, are so timid when it comes to challenging a collusive tobacco settlement that is bilking 45 million smokers out of a quarter of a trillion dollars. The incredible story of that scheme, and its pernicious consequences, has yet to be told.

The MSA, signed in November 1998 by the major tobacco companies and 46 state attorneys general, raises fundamental and far-reaching implications for the rule of law.[20] In effect, the MSA transforms a competitive industry into a cartel, then guards against destabilization of the cartel by erecting barriers to entry that preserve the 99 percent market dominance of the tobacco giants. Far from being victims, the big four tobacco companies are at the very center of the plot. They managed to carve out a protected market for themselves—all at the expense of smokers and tobacco companies who did not sign the agreement.

To be sure, the industry would have preferred that the settlement had not been necessary. But given the perverse legal rules under which the state Medicaid recoupment suits were unfolding, the major tobacco companies were effectively bludgeoned into negotiating with the states and the trial lawyers. Finding itself in that perilous position, the industry shrewdly bargained for something pretty close to a sweetheart deal.

Some might argue that industry executives, with a fiduciary responsibility to shareholders, should not be blamed for working out the best deal under the circumstances. Perhaps so. But the underlying question is whether the antitrust laws were violated. The answer is "yes," and fiduciary responsibility is certainly not a valid legal defense. Let there be no confusion, however; the state attorneys general and the contingency fee lawyers that they hired were the real instigating parties. The tobacco companies were unwilling participants, simply paying ransom in return for an exemption from the antitrust laws.

Whether tobacco companies on balance are helped or harmed is not the issue. What is involved here is an illegal and unconstitutional protection racket, run by the states, that imposes hundreds of billions of dollars in costs on smokers. Here is the story in a nutshell.

The MSA forces all tobacco companies—even new companies and companies that were not part of the settlement—to pay "damages," thus foreclosing meaningful price competition. Essentially, the tobacco giants have purchased (at virtually no cost to themselves) the ability to exclude competitors and thereby raise prices with impunity. Smokers, who are the principal victims, receive nothing of value. They bear the entire cost of the agreement. Nonparticipating tobacco companies, current or future, are victims too, because they are precluded from competing on a price basis by a bogus "liability" that the agreement imposes on them.

The deal works like this: Philip Morris, Reynolds, Lorillard, and Brown & Williamson knew they would have to raise prices substantially to cover their MSA obligations. Accordingly, they were concerned that smaller domestic manufacturers, importers, and new tobacco companies that did not sign the agreement would gain share-of-market by underpricing cigarettes. To guard against that likelihood, the big four and their state collaborators added three provisions to the MSA:

First, if the aggregate market share of the four majors were to decline by more than two percentage points, then their "damages" payments would decline by three times the excess over the two-percentage-point threshold.[21] Any such reduction would be charged against only those states that did not adopt a "Qualifying Statute," attached as an exhibit to the MSA.[22] Naturally, because of the risk of losing enormous sums of money, all of the states have already enacted, or will soon enact, the statute.

Second, the Qualifying Statute requires any tobacco company that did not sign the MSA to post pro rata damages—based on cigarette sales—in escrow for 25 years to offset any liability that might hereafter be assessed![23] That's right—no evidence, no trial, no verdict, no injury, just damages. In fact, because the escrow payments are nondeductible against income taxes, they are actually about one and one-half times what the majors pay per cigarette. That was the stick. Then came the carrot.

Third, if a nonsettling tobacco company agreed to participate in the MSA, the Qualifying Statute would not apply. In fact, the new participant would be allowed to increase its market share by an apparently whopping 25 percent of its 1997 level.[24] Bear in mind, however, that all of the nonsettling companies combined in 1997 had roughly one percent of the market,[25] which, under the MSA, could grow to 1.25 percent. Essentially, the dominant companies guaranteed themselves no less than 99 percent of the market in perpetuity.

How Can We Challenge the MSA?

Perhaps of equal importance, the settlement has led to massive and continuing shifts of wealth from millions of smokers to concentrated pockets of the bar. Predictably, part of that multibillion-dollar booty has started its round trip back into the political process[26]—to influence state legislators, judges, attorneys general, governors, city mayors, maybe some federal officials.

With all that money in hand, the political influence of trial lawyers will grow exponentially. Every day that passes more firmly entrenches the MSA as a fait accompli, and more tightly cements the insidious relationship between trial attorneys and their allies in the public sector. The billion-dollar spigot must be turned off before its corrupting effect on the rule of law is irreversible.

One way to turn off the spigot is to challenge the legality and constitutionality of the MSA. Without question, the MSA violates the antitrust laws and the Constitution—specifically, the Commerce Clause (Article I, section 8) and the Compacts Clause (Article I, section 10), which provides that "No State shall, without the Consent of Congress, . . . enter into any Agreement or Compact with another State." Indeed, what could be more blatant than the MSA in violating those two clauses. It is a multistate agreement, negotiated without congressional consent, which preempts key federal functions like taxation and regulation of interstate commerce. The MSA authorizes states to exercise powers they could not otherwise exercise—for example, the collection of "damages" based on sales in other states, the interstate regulation of cigarette advertising, and the exaction of penalties against out-of-state companies that do not sign the agreement.

The exercise of those powers is clearly unconstitutional—and the parties to the MSA knew it all along. That is why the MSA provides that each manufacturer expressly waives "any and all claims that the provisions of this Agreement violate state or federal constitutions."[27]

That is also why the MSA establishes a $50 million enforcement fund:[28] It will be used in part to defend against challenges to the settlement. Ironically, the fund is underwritten by smokers, who are potential claimants against the settlement.

Considering the billions of dollars in "damages" that the states are receiving, state attorneys general can hardly be expected to enforce the antitrust laws with respect to the MSA. Nor can the Clinton administration, which helped negotiate the MSA and now wants a similar federal settlement with tobacco companies.

Fortunately, there are alternatives to public sector enforcement. Injunctive relief is available in private lawsuits brought by smokers.[29] And treble damage remedies are also available under the antitrust laws to wholesalers and nonparticipating tobacco manufacturers.[30] Yes, monopolies that arise out of state action—public utilities, for example—are ordinarily exempt from private antitrust prosecution, at least when the state, as sovereign, has regulated an industry.[31] But here, because they are violating the Constitution, the states cannot be acting in their sovereign capacity.[32]

If the MSA is allowed to stand, it will create and finance a rich and powerful industry of lawyers who know how to manipulate the system and are not averse to violating the Constitution or the laws. In short, the MSA should be dismantled, the legal fees refunded, price increases canceled, and competition restored. Naturally, any challenge to the MSA will be contested by virtually all of the attorneys general, the major tobacco companies, the instant billionaires among the plaintiffs bar, and the health community. The only way litigation could possibly succeed is by mounting a coordinated effort to fight the battle both in the courtroom and in the media. That is a tall order, but the stakes are immense.

Remember that federal officials acquiesced in—indeed helped to negotiate—the multistate tobacco settlement. Then they filed baseless claims for Medicare recovery against cigarette makers. And, thus far, they have declined to prosecute the most blatant antitrust violation imaginable as tobacco companies, attorney generals, and trial lawyers collaborate to increase cigarette prices by a quarter of a trillion dollars. That increase will be paid by smokers, many of whom, so we are told, are hopelessly addicted victims of the same industry that has been granted carte blanche to break the law. Where, we must ask, is Joel Klein and his cabal of antitrust activists? In the one area in which everyone agrees that government should intervene—that is, to dismantle the barriers to entry that government itself has been responsible for erecting—the Clinton administration is curiously, and inexcusably, silent.

Notes

1. 42 U.S.C. § 1396 and 42 C.F.R. § 430.0.

2. See, for example, *Medicaid Third-Party Liability Act*, Fla. Stat. Ann. § 409.910 (1995).

3. State Medicaid recovery suits were wholly or partly dismissed in Arizona, Indiana, Iowa, Maryland, Washington, and West Virginia. Several state judges allowed the suits to proceed, but no case reached a final jury verdict.

4. Quoted in Bill McAllister, "Smoking by GIs Raises Liability Issue at the VA," *Washington Post*, April 24, 1997, p. A1.

5. 42 U.S.C. § 2651(a) (1962).

6. 42 U.S.C. § 1935y(b)(2) (1980).

7. 18 U.S.C. §§ 1861–68 (1988 ed.).

8. U.S. Department of Justice press release, "United States Sues Cigarette Companies to Recover Federal Health Care Costs," September 22, 1999.

9. John Schwartz, "U.S. Tobacco Probe Yields First Company Conviction," *Washington Post*, September 23, 1999, p. A4; Ann Davis and David S. Cloud, "Justice Agency Winds Down Tobacco Probe," *Wall Street Journal*, March 11, 1999, p. A3.

10. See, for example, Saundra Torry, "Tobacco Firms Win Suit Filed by Unions," *Washington Post*, March 19, 1999, p. A2; PRNewswire, "Reynolds Tobacco Hails Appeals Court Ruling," November 16, 1999.

11. *United States v. Standard Oil*, 332 U.S. 301 (1947).

12. See, for example, *U.S. Senate Committee on the Judiciary Hearings on Justice Department Operations*, 105th Cong., 1997 WL 210888, at *70–73 (April 30, 1997). ("[W]hat we have determined was that it was the state's cause of action and that we needed to work with the states, that the federal government does not have an independent cause of action. But I will continue to review it and see if there are new issues.")

13. Quoted in David S. Cloud, "U.S. Faces Hurdle to Recovering Tobacco Health Costs," *Wall Street Journal*, May 27, 1999, p. A28.

14. Jacob Sullum, "Vice Profits," *Reason*, May 1999.

15. See, for example, Centers for Disease Control and Prevention, *Morbidity and Mortality Weekly Report*, August 23, 1993 (418,690 Americans died in 1990 of smoking-related diseases). For a refutation of that claim, see Robert A. Levy and Rosalind B. Marimont, "Lies, Damned Lies, & 400,000 Smoking-Related Deaths," *Regulation*, vol. 21, no. 4, 1998.

16. Dave Barry, "Blowing Smoke," *Tampa Tribune*, August 10, 1997, p. 5.

17. Note the political scramble that has followed the recent $145 billion punitive damage award in the *Engle* case in Florida, which has threatened to bankrupt the entire industry. Fearful that such awards might jeopardize the ability of tobacco companies to honor their ongoing financial commitments under the 1998 MSA, several state legislatures have enacted measures to ensure that the industry can appeal the damages to a higher court. In many states, an appeal can proceed only if the appellant posts a bond. Florida rules, for example, would have required that the industry post a prohibitive 115 percent of the damage award. Accordingly, the Florida legislature

capped the bond at an affordable $100 million—not out of concern for the tobacco companies' rights, but rather to protect the state's money tree.

18. See, for example, William G. Manning, et al., "The Taxes of Sin: Do Smokers and Drinkers Pay Their Way?" *Journal of the American Medical Association*, March 17, 1989; Jane G. Gravelle and Dennis Zimmerman, *Cigarette Taxes to Fund Health Care Reform: An Economic Analysis* (Washington, D.C.: Congressional Research Service, 1994); W. Kip Viscusi, "Cigarette Taxation and the Social Consequences of Smoking," in James Poterba, ed., *Tax Policy and the Economy*, vol. 9 (Cambridge, Mass.: MIT Press, 1995).

19. Material in this and following sections is drawn in part from Thomas C. O'Brien, "Constitutional and Antitrust Violations of the Multistate Tobacco Settlement," Cato Institute Policy Analysis no. 371, May 18, 2000.

20. The full text of the Master Settlement Agreement (MSA), including exhibits, can be found at ⟨http://ash.org/setfull.html⟩.

21. MSA § IX (d)(1).

22. MSA § IX (d)(2); MSA, Exhibit T.

23. MSA, Exhibit T.

24. MSA § IX (i)(1).

25. Jeremy Bulow and Paul Klemperer, "The Tobacco Deal," *Brookings Papers on Economic Activity: Microeconomics 1998*, November 1998, p. 4, note 7.

26. See, for example, Leslie Wayne, "Trial Lawyers Pour Money into Democrats' Chests," *New York Times*, March 23, 2000, p. A1.

27. MSA, Article XV.

28. MSA § VIII (c).

29. Section 16 of the Clayton Act of 1914, 15 U.S.C. § 14, provides for injunctive relief as follows: "Any person . . . shall be entitled to sue for and have injunctive relief in any court of the United States having jurisdiction over the parties, against threatened loss or damage by a violation of the antitrust laws."

30. Section 4 of the Clayton Act of 1914, 15 U.S.C. § 14, provides for treble damages as follows: "[A]ny person who shall be injured in his business or property by reasons of anything forbidden in the antitrust laws may sue therefor in any district court of the United States in the district in which the defendant resides or is found . . . and shall recover threefold the damages by him sustained, and the cost of the suit including a reasonable attorney's fee."

31. See *Parker v. Brown*, 317 U.S. 341 (1943).

32. See *Lafayette v. Louisiana Power & Light Co.*, 435 U.S. 389, 410–13 (1978); *Ex Parte Young*, 209 U.S. 123, 159–60 (1908).

9. The War on Guns

Bill Pryor

Almost three years ago, on August 5, 1997, I visited the Cato Institute to speak at a Policy Forum with Bob Levy regarding the proposed tobacco settlement and the rule of law.[1] On that occasion, I criticized the absence of any legal basis and the unsound policy of the suits filed by many of my colleagues from other states against the tobacco industry. From the outset, my concerns involved the precedent that my colleagues sought to create and the consequences of that precedent for other industries, for the right of the people to govern themselves, and for the rule of law.[2] Unfortunately, the precedent of the government litigation against the tobacco industry has been followed by dozens of government lawsuits against the firearms industry.

Throughout the development of this new form of abusive public litigation, the Clinton administration has been more than a mere cheerleader. President Clinton, with the aid of Attorney General Janet Reno and other cabinet officials such as HUD Secretary Andrew Cuomo,[3] is the managing partner for teams of government plaintiffs. Clinton is joined by his state partners, Attorney General Richard Blumenthal of Connecticut[4] and Attorney General Eliot Spitzer of New York,[5] and big-city mayors—Marc Morial of New Orleans, Bill Campbell of Atlanta, Richard Daley of Chicago, and recently even Republican mayor Rudolph Giuliani[6] of New York, among others. Together, they have created a Clintonian framework for big government that is the antithesis of the Madisonian framework for limited government established more than two centuries ago. The Clintonian framework erodes both the separation of powers and federalism, undermines the protection of civil rights, denies individual responsibility and, if continued, will lead to a vicious cycle of futile dependence on ever-expanding government power. Nowhere is the doomed nature of this enterprise of extortion masquerading as law more apparent than in the context of the war on guns.

I will provide a contrast of the Clintonian and Madisonian frameworks, discuss the flaws of the gun litigation, and conclude with a discussion of the Madisonian response to the war on guns.

The Clintonian Framework

The Clintonian framework employs a six-step strategy. First, vilify an industry that has resisted for years abusive litigation and government regulation and that manufactures a potentially dangerous product. Scorn the industry as a band of criminals without ever mustering the courage to bring formal criminal charges. Second, pursue grandiose regulation through traditional legislative channels. Refuse to compromise, and when you predictably fail, denounce the so-called gridlock of the legislative process. Third, enlist your wealthiest and most politically active supporters, the trial bar, to create what they now call a "fourth branch of government,"[7] a phrase arrogantly appropriated by Wendell Gauthier, the trial lawyer who filed the first gun suit on behalf of the City of New Orleans. Herald their aggressive pursuit of the "public interest" through litigation while secretly negotiating lucrative contingency fee contracts, the rewards of which will bankroll your next political campaign. Fourth, unite your allies in public office, mostly Democrats, with a few liberal Republicans for the cover of bipartisanship, to pursue litigation where your legislation failed. Because there are fewer of these officials holding governorships than several years ago, seek out the last bastions of liberalism in the offices of state attorneys general and big-city mayors. Fifth, as the costs of multiple litigation and its varying results threaten to bankrupt the defendant industry, join the fray with the announcement of a proposed federal lawsuit. Sixth, settle your novel litigation with a vulnerable member of the industry, such as Smith & Wesson[8] (or in the context of tobacco, Liggett), and create incentives for an eventual settlement with the entire industry, which then achieves most of your earlier legislative goals. Secretary Cuomo calls this "death by a thousand cuts."[9]

The Madisonian Framework

The Clintonian framework stands in stark contrast to the Madisonian paradigm of limited government that has served this nation so well. Rather than vilifying an industry, the Madisonian framework

respects and promotes the innovation and opportunity of free enterprise through the protection of freedom of contract, private property,
and the free flow of interstate commerce. The Madisonian framework
promotes majoritarian compromise in the legislative process as the
sole method of lawmaking rather than using a fourth branch of
leftist bounty hunters to combine executive and judicial powers in
a new lawmaking enterprise. The Madisonian paradigm invokes
federalism, thus allowing variations in policies at state and local
levels. By contrast, the Clintonian model enlists state and local officials to create a national public policy, thus overriding the choices
of those jurisdictions that object or decline to participate, and usurping the exclusive authority of Congress to exercise its enumerated
powers to enact national laws.

The Flaws and Inevitable Failure of the Gun Litigation

The pursuit of gun control through litigation represents an attempt
to export flawed local policies and achieve national regulations that
have failed to gain the approval of Congress. Big-city mayors who
have seen crime rates explode after they imposed tight gun control
laws are attempting to blame states and local jurisdictions that have
enjoyed low crime rates with fewer regulations of firearms. Federal
officials, who have failed to enforce a myriad of national firearms
regulations, are likewise trying to shift the blame to Congress for
not enacting even more regulations.

This litigation against gun makers is an assault on fundamental
civil rights, particularly those protected by the first two amendments
in the Bill of Rights. In a republic that promotes a free society, as
opposed to a police state, one of the basic organizing principles is
that individuals have a right of self-defense and a right to acquire
the means for that defense. In the American experience, that right
is embodied in the Second Amendment, which expressly states that
"the right of the people to keep and bear arms shall not be
infringed."[10]

If successful, the firearms litigation, which is designed to coerce
a settlement agreement, not produce a final adjudication, will impair
the access to firearms for law-abiding citizens who are virtually
unrepresented in the litigation. Yet the framers of the Clintonian
paradigm evidently have no desire to hear about that civil rights
violation.

137

Less noticed, but no less dangerous, is the violation of First Amendment rights. The Clintonian war on guns began with a public relations campaign against a political advocacy group, the National Rifle Association. The Clintonians attacked the group rather than its ideas. Then they used litigation to attack the freedom of pro-gun groups to speak both in the political arena and the marketplace. The gun suits, for example, named the National Shooting Sports Foundation and the Sporting Arms and Ammunition Manufacturers Institute as defendants even though these trade associations do not manufacture firearms. Instead, they engage in First Amendment advocacy. Similarly, the gun suits challenge the advertising and marketing practices of gun manufacturers; that is, the suits seek to limit their commercial speech.

The overarching result of this new paradigm is the further erosion of individual responsibility. Rather than recognize that crimes are caused by criminals and punish those criminals in the traditional public litigation known as criminal law, the Clintonians argue that crimes are the responsibility of the firearms industry and should be addressed by a new form of public civil litigation. The Madisonian respect for individual responsibility, as embodied in the private law of torts, with its principles of proximate causation, assumption of risk, and contributory negligence, is discarded in favor of a Clintonian framework—a new public law of torts with theories of negligent marketing and design defect. The resolution of social problems, such as gun violence, is no longer primarily the responsibility of individuals in a free society; only the government allegedly can solve the problems.

Gun control through litigation, in the end, will produce only more crime. As the supply of guns diminishes and their price increases, the consumers who are most responsive to those changes—law-abiding citizens and law enforcement agencies—will become less able to combat crime. On the other hand, criminals, whose demand for firearms is highly inelastic, will become more powerful adversaries as their black market for firearms grows ever more profitable.[11] Perversely, gun control removes weapons from the hands of law-abiding citizens despite substantial evidence that violent crime declines when potential victims are permitted to possess concealed firearms.[12]

The nightmare scenario of disarmed citizens and well-armed criminals is actually playing itself out right now in Great Britain. For many years, British gun control laws have had the effect of progressively denying British citizens the means to defend themselves from criminals. The result has been crime rates much higher than in the United States.

> The overall crime rate in England and Wales is 60 percent higher than that in the United States. True, in America you're more likely to be shot to death. On the other hand, in England you're more likely to be strangled to death. But in both cases, the statistical likelihood of being murdered at all is remote, especially if you steer clear of the drug trade. When it comes to anything else, though—burglary, auto theft, armed robbery, violent assault, rape—the crime rate reaches deep in British society in ways most Americans would find virtually inconceivable.[13]

Following a further tightening of British gun laws in 1997, crime skyrocketed yet again. The *Sunday Times of London* recently reported that a surge of smuggling had introduced millions of illegal weapons into Britain, and into the hands of criminals, triggering "a rise in drive-by shootings and gangland-style executions."[14] "Criminals have maintained a steady flow of smuggled guns from eastern Europe, exhibition weapons reactivated in illegal 'factories' run by underworld dealers, and guns stolen from private collections."[15] As British criminals arm themselves, law-abiding citizens have been disarmed, with predictable effects on the likelihood of violent assault, home invasion, and the like.

When the gun control paradigm fails in the United States, as it inevitably will, guess what the Clintonians will offer as the next solution? More government. Sadly, the Clintonian framework promises a vicious cycle of failure that imposes yet more constraints on individual freedom while producing even worse results. That is why the war on guns, like the war on tobacco, is ultimately another stage of the war on freedom.

The Madisonian Response to the War on Guns

Although the Clintonian framework of regulation through litigation is dangerous and should be stopped, not all of the news on this front is bad. Indeed, there are encouraging signs that the Madisonian framework is still flexible, resilient and, one hopes, enduring. One example of the strength of the Madisonian framework is the legislative response to regulation through litigation. As a result of the gun litigation, several states, including Alabama,[16] have enacted laws to prohibit municipal suits against the firearms industry.[17] I favor broader state legislation using the model of the Litigation Fairness Act sponsored by Sen. Mitch McConnell (R–Ky.).[18] McConnell's bill prohibits governments from suing on behalf of citizens under rules that are more liberal than the rules that govern when those citizens sue on their own behalf. In addition, a handful of states, Texas, North Dakota, and Kansas, have enacted new laws to regulate the hiring of government lawyers, especially on a contingency fee basis.[19]

Another encouraging sign is the judicial response to the war on guns. In at least some quarters, apparently, there are still some judges committed to the rule of law. In Cincinnati, for example, the trial court dismissed the gun suit filed by the city as "an improper attempt to have this Court substitute its judgment for that of the legislature, something which this Court is neither inclined nor empowered to do."[20] That court reasoned, "To permit public nuisance law to be applied to the design and manufacture of lawful products would be to destroy the separate tort principles which govern those activities."[21]

The judge in the Bridgeport case found that the plaintiffs (city and mayor) had no standing, and no "statutory or common law basis to recoup their expenditures." The plaintiffs also had no "statutory authorization to initiate such claims," sought "to regulate firearms in a manner that is preempted by state law," and failed to initiate their nuisance claim in the manner required by the city's charter.[22] In an encouraging passage, the judge explains the provenance of the gun litigation:

> When conceiving the complaint in this case, the plaintiffs must have envisioned [the tobacco] settlements as the dawning of a new age of litigation during which the gun industry, liquor industry and purveyors of "junk" food would follow the tobacco industry in reimbursing government expenditures and submitting to judicial regulation. The tobacco litigation, by the states, has not succeeded in eradicating the rules of law on proximate cause, remoteness of damages and limits on justiciability. This is evidenced by a series of federal appellate decisions dismissing "me-too" cases initiated by insurers and health and welfare funds against the tobacco industries.[23]

Meanwhile, to reward Smith & Wesson for settling some of the claims against it, the Clinton administration has encouraged mayors to favor that company in purchasing police firearms. In Alabama, I have responded to that effort by reminding city officials of their obligations under Alabama law. To grant a preference to a manufacturer of firearms would violate both the competitive bid laws of my state[24] and our constitutional prohibition of exclusive grants and franchises.[25] Furthermore, effective August 1, 2000, all municipal regulation of firearms will be prohibited by a law passed by the Alabama legislature at the end of its last regular session.[26]

In the end, we also have the ultimate Madisonian response: the ballot box. Those who care about the rule of law and desire to reverse its erosion under the Clinton administration will have an opportunity in November to, as we like to say in Alabama, "send them a message."[27] Although much harm has been done to the rule of law, that damage can be reversed steadily by our efforts on all of these fronts.

Notes

1. My 1997 remarks on "The Rule of Law and the Tobacco Settlement" are available on my office's Web site, ⟨http://www.ago.state.al.us/news_speeches.cfm⟩.

2. See, for example, Bill Pryor, Editorial, "Litigators' Smoke Screen," *Wall Street Journal*, April 7, 1997, p. A14; Bill Pryor, Editorial, "The Law Is at Risk in Tobacco Suits," *New York Times*, April 27, 1997, p. E15; Bill Pryor, Editorial, "Trial Lawyers Target Rule of Law," *Atlanta Constitution*, January 13, 1999, p. A11; "Report of the Task Force on Tobacco Litigation Submitted to Governor James and Attorney General Sessions," *Cumberland Law Review* 27 (1996–97): 577; William H. Pryor Jr., "A Comparison of Abuses and Reforms of Class Actions and Multigovernment Lawsuits," *Tulane Law Review* 74 (2000): 1885. The three newspaper editorials are also available at ⟨http://www.ago.state.al.us/news_speeches.cfm⟩.

3. On Secretary Cuomo's role in the gun litigation, see Charles Babington, "U.S. Plans Role in Gun Lawsuits," *Washington Post*, December 8, 1999, p. A1.

4. Blumenthal supports both the City of Bridgeport's gun lawsuit as well as the suit filed by the State of New York. See *Attorney General's Statement on the Filing of a Lawsuit Against Gun Manufacturers by NY's Attorney General* (press release, June 27, 2000), available on line at ⟨http://www.cslnet.ctstateu.edu/attygenl/press/2000/other/guns.htm⟩.

5. Paul M. Barrett, "New York State Files Suit Against Gun Firms," *Wall Street Journal*, June 27, 2000, p. B8.

6. *Mayor Giuliani and Speaker Vallone Announce City Lawsuit Against Gun Industry* (press release, June 20, 2000), available on line at ⟨http://www.ci.nyc.ny.us/html/om/html/2000a/pr238-00.html⟩. It further appears that Mayor Giuliani is engaged in forum-shopping, hoping that U.S. District Judge Jack Weinstein will hear the case. Weinstein, a jurist noted for his receptivity to novel theories of liability, presided over

141

an earlier, private lawsuit alleging gun manufacturer liability for gunshot injuries, in which the plaintiff won. Paul Barrett, "New York City Intends to File Lawsuit Against Approximately 25 Gun Makers," *Wall Street Journal*, June 20, 2000.

7. See Douglas McCollam, "Long Shot at Gun Tort Dollars," *American Lawyer*, June 1, 1999 (describing "Gauthier's notion of the plaintiffs bar as a de facto fourth branch of government, one that achieved regulation through litigation where legislation failed"). For more recent confirmation of this trial lawyer hubris, see Adam Cohen, "Are Lawyers Running America?" *Time*, July 17, 2000. ("Ask [Richard] Scruggs if trial lawyers are trying to run America, and he doesn't bother to deny it. 'Somebody's got to do it,' he says, laughing.")

8. The HUD press release announcing the Smith & Wesson settlement includes a brief explanation of its terms. It is available on line at ⟨http://www.hud.gov/pressrel/pr00-56.html⟩.

9. Quoted in Bill McAllister, "Gun Industry Rejects Settlement Effort," *Denver Post*, February 1, 2000.

10. Nelson Lund's scholarly analyses of the Second Amendment are indispensable. Nelson Lund, "The Past and Future of the Individual's Right to Arms," *Georgia Law Review* 31 (1996): 1; Nelson Lund, "The Second Amendment, Political Liberty, and the Right to Self-Preservation," *Alabama Law Review* 39 (1987): 103.

11. I am indebted for this point to Michael I. Krauss, *Fire and Smoke: Government, Lawsuits and the Rule of Law* (Oakland, CA: Independent Institute, 2000), p. 17.

12. The work of John Lott is currently the key contribution to our understanding of this very important fact. See John R. Lott Jr., *More Guns, Less Crime: Understanding Crime and Gun-Control Laws* (Chicago: University of Chicago Press, 1998), and John R. Lott Jr. and David B. Mustard, "Crime, Deterrence, and Right-to-Carry Concealed Handguns," *Journal of Legal Studies* 26 (1997): 1. Lott has addressed the furious, and largely specious, counterattacks his work has drawn in a recent interview, Jacob Sullum and Michael W. Lynch, "Cold Comfort," *Reason*, January 2000, p. 34.

13. Mark Steyn, "In the Absence of Guns," *American Spectator*, June 2000, pp. 46–47. See also *Crime and Justice in the United States and England and Wales, 1981–96* (Bureau of Justice Statistics, U.S. Department of Justice, 1998) (reporting much higher U.K. rates of robbery, assault, burglary, and motor vehicle theft compared with the United States).

14. Jon Ungoed-Thomas, "Killings Rise as 3m Illegal Guns Flood Britain," *Sunday Times of London*, January 16, 2000.

15. Ibid. For more information from the British press on the current crime wave, see Michel S. Brown, "Results Are In for Britain—'Less Guns,' More Crime," *Medical Sentinel*, May–June 2000, p. 106.

16. Act of May 25, 2000, No. 2000–762.

17. See, for example, Alaska Stat. § 09.65.155; Ariz. Rev. Stat. Ann. § 12-714; Ark. Act. No. 951 (1999); La. Rev. Stat. Ann. § 2800.60; Mich. Act No. 265 (2000); Mont. Code Ann. § 7-1-115; Nev. Rev. Stat. § 12.107; S.C. Code § 15-73-40; S.D. H.B. 1301 (1999); Tex. Civ. Prac. & Rem. Code Ann. § 128.001.

18. See S. 1269, 106th Congress (1999).

19. Tex. Gov't Code Ann. §§ 2254.101 et seq.; N.D. Cent. Code § 54-12-08.1 (2000); Kan. Enrolled Bill No. 2627 (2000). The American Legislative Exchange Council (ALEC) has been very active on this issue. Its model "Private Attorney Retention Sunshine Act" is available on the ALEC Website, ⟨http://www.alec.org⟩.

20. *City of Cincinnati v. Beretta U.S.A. Corp.*, No. A-9902369, 1999 WL 809838 at *1 (Ohio Ct. C.P. Hamilton County, October 7, 1999).

21. Ibid. at *2.

22. *Ganim v. Smith & Wesson Corp.*, No. CV 990153198S, 1999 WL 1241909 at *2 (Conn. Super., December 10, 1999).

23. Ibid. at *4.

24. Ala. Code §§ 41-16-50 et seq. (Supp. 1999).

25. Ala. Const. art. I, § 22.

26. Act of May 25, 2000, No. 2000–762.

27. This phrase was regularly used by George Wallace, the four-term governor of Alabama. See Dan T. Carter, *The Politics of Rage* (Baton Rouge, La.: Louisiana State University Press, 1996), passim.

10. The War on Microsoft

C. Boyden Gray

Perhaps the most enduring mystery and problem with the Microsoft case is trying to understand the central point of it all. The total lack of connection between the trial and the judge's ruling on one hand and his choice of remedies on the other is only the tip of the iceberg. The recent revelation that Oracle Corporation hired a private detective to search the trash of a Microsoft-supported trade association that filed a sympathetic amicus brief at Microsoft's request tends to confirm earlier suspicions that the case represents nothing more than a successful hijacking of the government's regulatory power by Microsoft's competitors—an especially grievous abuse of the rule of law.

The "spin" put on the case by the Antitrust Division is that the case is to be a model for regulating the new economy so as to intensify innovation, the key buzzword of the case. But if there is any sector of the global marketplace that is not in need of an injection of innovation or a dose of regulation, it is the new economy of the United States, which is powering the most successful economic boom this country has ever experienced.

Whatever the Antitrust Division says about promoting innovation, that is not what the court had in mind. To the contrary, the central violation of law identified by the court is the pattern of "predatory innovation" engaged in by Microsoft. Remember that the principal legal finding by the court was that Microsoft spent too much on research and development, took too few profits, exposed its own Internet service (the Microsoft Network) to too much competition from America Online Inc. (AOL), and spent too much on promotion. The court's vision was one of punishing innovation, not unleashing it.

The Antitrust Division put together a collection of "Declarations" by academics designed to reinforce predictions of heightened innovation stemming from the breakup sought by the government. Now that the browser was dead, the antitrust chief said on a Sunday talk show, one had to search for a different competitive focus, identified by the academics as Windows Office Suite. Office Suite? What about the Internet where all the action has already migrated, or even, for that matter, Netscape Communication Corp.'s Navigator? Rumors of Navigator's death are greatly exaggerated. Indeed, the Antitrust Division seems oblivious to the fact that Navigator will replace Internet Explorer as the number one browser in January 2001 when AOL, having greatly improved Navigator by adopting all of Explorer's advantages, replaces Explorer with Navigator on its own Internet service, by far the largest such service in the world.

As far as the court was concerned, none of that is relevant. The record was closed, the government won the case, and that was that. There was no need for a hearing on remedies, which might have to take into account changes in the marketplace, because predictions on how the market will react to the proposed breakup are so speculative as to not be worth the court's time. The court will in any event retain jurisdiction and will thus have a real-world opportunity to correct things as the future unfolds.

But by what standard will the future be judged? We are left with no greater understanding about the principles that are to govern the court's future jurisdiction than we have about what triggered the lawsuit at the outset.

So what is going on? The loud self-congratulations and visible high fives by Microsoft's competitors as they all joined in taking credit for the court's unprecedented breakup suggest strongly that nothing more complicated was involved than lending the Justice Department to Microsoft's opponents. The private sector winners lost no time claiming credit, with Navigator's founder appearing on the Sunday talk shows, and Sun Microsystems, Inc.'s white paper, which had been submitted early to the Antitrust Division, finding its way into the media bearing a very eerie resemblance to the court's own findings in the case.

The temptation for special interest rent seekers to take over a regulatory regime is a well-understood problem of administrative law. Accordingly, numerous procedural protections have evolved in an attempt to preserve at least the *appearance* of fairness, if not the reality of a "level playing field." When private interests try brazenly to undermine the protections of administrative law, they usually lose, as courts are much more aggressive in pursuing procedural fairness than they are in second-guessing the merits of an agency decision, assuming all the participants had a fair shot.

The Clinton administration has abused the wide latitude that Congress and the courts have historically granted to administrative agencies on substantive issues. That may account for the recent ruling by the U.S. Court of Appeals for the District of Columbia Circuit that tries to reinvigorate the nondelegation doctrine, which questions whether there is constitutional authority for that grant of latitude. It may also account for the Supreme Court's willingness to review the D.C. Circuit case involving the Environmental Protection Agency (EPA) during the 2000–2001 term. One recent study found that EPA has lost more than half of its cases in the D.C. Circuit—a troubling trend given the deference lower courts have been required by the Supreme Court to pay to agencies. The current administration's excesses may spell the end of that generous deference, which has lasted nearly two decades.

Because of their very general and vague wording, the antitrust laws have been especially vulnerable from the beginning to special interest influence. Perhaps because of that vulnerability, revealed in the early years of Sherman Antitrust Act enforcement, the courts this century have uniformly taken the view that the antitrust laws protect competition, consumers, and the public generally, *not* competitors who must look to Section 5 of the Federal Trade Commission Act or to state law for protection from business behavior that is unfair or deceptive.

In the *Microsoft* case, however, the judge was quite generous in his allowance that Microsoft's actions had provided significant benefits to consumers and to the new economy—especially its contribution to the explosion of the World Wide Web. So what exactly was he punishing? That brings us back to the beginning. He was punishing superior innovation at the request of private competitors who could not or did not want to keep up. And when Microsoft showed that there was little support among other businessmen for this antitrust suit, frustrated competitors sought to demonize Microsoft by hiring the same private investigator who had been engaged by the Clinton White House to denigrate Kenneth Starr.

All of that is essentially lawless. One can only hope that the *Microsoft* case precedent is short-lived. We must not turn back the clock on a century of antitrust experience that warns against the danger of government interference with the marketplace at the behest of a competitor. If we do not keep that hard-earned experience in mind, our booming economy may go the way of Russia's, which is to say, nowhere.

The Justice Department's litigation against Visa International and MasterCard International Inc. is a great cause for concern. Here again, a competitor, American Express Co., has emerged to take credit for the antitrust proceeding. In addition, the Antitrust Division's highly visible communication with European competition authorities is also a source of unease. The European economy is, after all, not what one would cite as the model of a "new economy."

When antitrust enforcement migrates beyond the punishment and prevention of collusion to fix prices or divide markets, it constitutes nothing more than economic regulation without a central purpose. The experience of the bipartisan deregulation of the Ford-Carter-Reagan-Bush years, much of it spearheaded by Sen. Edward M. Kennedy (D–Mass.) and then-professor (now Supreme Court Justice) Stephen Breyer, is that pure economic regulation bears a very heavy burden of justification. Arguably, the deregulation of the '70s and '80s contributed more to the groundwork for the economic boom of the '90s than any other factor, with the exception of the successful victory against inflation by Federal Reserve Board chairmen Paul A. Volcker and Alan Greenspan.

The D.C. Circuit has played a key role in holding back the forces of re-regulation by carefully monitoring the agencies, especially the EPA, and by curbing the excesses of antitrust as exemplified by its early rulings in the *Microsoft* case itself. But there is a limit to what the courts can do. Both the White House and the Congress bear the responsibility for containing the administrative agencies and their historic vulnerability to capture by interest groups. One place to start is at the current White House. It should exercise some responsibility for antitrust policy by, among other things, giving the Treasury Department and the Council of Economic Advisers a full participatory role in the shaping of that policy, which is essentially economic in nature. If the current president exercised his responsibility to see that the laws are faithfully executed, he might very well decide that the power of the state should be exercised solely, if at all, on behalf of the public as a whole and not on behalf of a particular competitor.

Only the most arrogant of chief executives would then decide that the lawyers of the Antitrust Division can chart the future course of the economy better than the marketplace.

At the very least, Microsoft's supposed culpability for predatory innovation requires that the executive branch and the courts monitor Microsoft's profit levels and its investment in R&D and marketing. Obviously, that is not the role of government, even with a detailed, congressionally approved standard by which to regulate private sector profits. But without such a standard, such regulation is nothing more than pure politics—the very antithesis of the rule of law. If one competitor can persuade the government to regulate the level of innovation by another competitor, without regard to a legislated set of guiding principles, we will have abandoned a thousand years of Anglo-American jurisprudence.

11. Politicizing the Justice Department

Theodore B. Olson

Janet Reno has now served for more than seven years as attorney general—longer, with one exception, than any other attorney general in our history. William Wirt, who was attorney general in the early 19th century, served longer, but at a time when there was no Department of Justice (DOJ) and no FBI, DEA, INS, Bureau of Prisons, Antitrust Division, Civil Rights Division, and so forth. Those were simpler days. Remember Richard Kleindienst, Elliot Richardson, William Saxbe, Ed Levi, and Griffin Bell, each of whom served as attorney general in the 1970s? Janet Reno has served longer than all of them combined—and the rule of law is none the better for it.

Perhaps the best way to illustrate that the rule of law has suffered under the reign of Janet Reno, and that the Justice Department has been thoroughly politicized, is simply to list just a few well-publicized events that have occurred during Ms. Reno's tenure. I hasten to add that this list is hardly exhaustive, but it does give a feel for the culture that has overtaken the department during the Clinton–Reno years.

A Brief Chronicle of the Reno Years

1. February 1993: Webster Hubbell, former Hillary Rodham Clinton law partner, moves into the Department of Justice, taking over the space immediately adjacent to the attorney general's office that had been occupied for years by the assistant attorney general for the Office of Legal Counsel. According to most accounts, Webb Hubbell becomes the eyes, ears, and voice of President and Mrs. Clinton in the Department of Justice.

2. Other notable Justice Department appointees: Eleanor Acheson, assistant attorney general for policy, Hillary's roommate from Wellesley; Sheila Foster Anthony, assistant attorney general for legislative affairs, sister of Hillary's partner and friend, Vincent Foster; Anne B. Bingaman, assistant attorney general, Antitrust Division,

wife of New Mexico Senator Jeff Bingaman; Frank Hunger, assistant attorney general, Civil Division, Al Gore's brother-in-law; Kathleen Kennedy Townsend, deputy assistant attorney general, daughter of Robert Kennedy; Kent Marcus, deputy chief of staff to Janet Reno, formerly Democratic National Committee chief of staff; Robert Litt, ex-Williams and Connelly partner nominated to head the Criminal Division.

3. March 1993: Two weeks after her confirmation, Attorney General Reno fires all 93 U.S. attorneys and gives them 10 days to clean out their offices and be gone. She describes this move as a joint decision with the White House. No one suspects that it was her decision. It had been the practice to allow U.S. attorneys to serve out their four-year terms, or at least serve until a replacement was appointed and confirmed.

4. Spring 1993: The White House crudely misuses the FBI to smear, and then investigate, White House Travel Office employees. No apparent objection by Attorney General Reno, who subsequently authorizes criminal prosecution of Billy Dale, career head of the White House Travel Office. Evidence at the trial is laughable. The jury returns a "not guilty" verdict in two hours.

5. July 22, 1993: White House Deputy Counsel Vince Foster is found shot to death in Fort Marcy Park. White House Counsel Bernard Nussbaum prevents Deputy Attorney General Philip Heyman from examining Foster's office. Janet Reno does nothing. She does not insist on conducting a Department of Justice investigation. The investigation is turned over to the National Park Service. Heyman later resigns.

6. March 14, 1994: Not long after being sworn in as associate attorney general, Webb Hubbell resigns under a cloud. Attorney General Reno: "He has been a tireless crusader for justice, for doing the right thing. *I don't believe he did a thing wrong.*"

7. Fred Graham interviews Janet Reno: "On a scale of one to ten, with ten being the highest, how would you rate the criminal justice system in this country today?" Reno: "one."

8. Solicitor General files an amicus curiae brief on behalf of President Clinton in the Paula Jones case. Another amicus brief is filed claiming attorney-client privilege for Hillary Clinton's documents in possession of counsel to the president. Another brief supports a "protective function" privilege of secret service agents subpoenaed

by independent counsel Kenneth Starr, delaying his investigation for months. Numerous other questionable arguments presented to the courts. Most of those arguments are rejected by every jurist who considers them.

9. Deputy Attorney General attends a political fund-raiser, an act specifically banned by department regulations.

10. October 1997: The *Washington Post* reports that in its investigation of fund-raising abuses during the 1996 Clinton-Gore re-election campaign, Justice Department investigators had been instructed that the independent counsel law "prohibited them from looking at the activities of covered persons." According to one prosecutor, the task force was instructed not to "ask [anyone] whether a covered person committed a crime." As a result, the investigators veer away any time their investigation seems to be getting near the president, vice president, or top White House or Democratic Party officials.

11. July 1997: Laura Ingersoll, head of the fund-raising investigation (later replaced by Charles LaBella), quashes FBI efforts to search the home of Charlie Trie in Little Rock despite reports that Trie was destroying documents. Justice lawyers had refused for four months to allow agents to ask for a search warrant of Trie's home. When the search is finally approved, Ingersoll recalls the agents from Little Rock and aborts the search. FBI agent David Wehr claims that Ingersoll told him that "agents were told they were not to pursue any matter related to solicitation of funds . . . for the president . . . because that's the way the American political process works."

12. Attorney General Reno decides initially that Vice President Al Gore's telephone calls from government property to raise campaign funds were not illegal because there was "clear and convincing evidence that he was only seeking 'soft' money." According to the *Washington Post*, the DOJ task force was therefore told to stop investigating. When the *Post* and other media subsequently find proof that Gore's calls were, in fact, raising hard money, Attorney General Reno declines to seek an independent counsel investigation because she is determined that the vice president *did not know* that he was raising hard money.

13. Fall 1997: The White House turns over 44 videotapes of fund-raising coffees. The White House explains that they had not been supplied earlier to the Justice Department because the department had not subpoenaed them.

14. After the fund-raising scandal has been on the front pages of the nation's papers for months, William Safire reports that John Huang had never been interviewed, asked to testify, or required to produce any records. He also reports that after Laura Ingersoll was removed as head of the investigation for what was widely regarded as running an incompetent investigation, Attorney General Reno gave her a special commendation, praising the thoroughness of her investigation.

15. The Justice Department defends Interior Secretary Babbitt in a civil suit over his denial of an Indian casino license at the same time that the Criminal Division is investigating the same incident to determine whether to appoint an independent counsel.

16. Janet Reno declines to appoint an independent counsel to investigate relationship between Energy Secretary Hazel O'Leary and Johnny Chung, saying that she would not do so unless she had "specific and credible evidence" that a covered person had violated the law. In fact, the law requires such an appointment whenever there is "information sufficient to constitute *grounds to investigate*" whether a covered person had committed a crime.

17. Deputy Attorney General Eric Holder instructs Kenneth Starr to investigate allegations that Whitewater witness David Hale had received funds from the *American Spectator* magazine because such allegations suggest the appearance of a conflict of interest. That is the same "appearance of conflict" standard that Attorney General Reno had previously declared to be an insufficient basis on which to investigate President Clinton. Thus begins a long and expensive investigation for the *Spectator*, a magazine that had broken several of the Clinton scandal stories.

18. The Associated Press reports that the DOJ received incriminating information about fund-raising by Nora and Gene Lum concerning cash delivered by them to Commerce Secretary Ron Brown, yet waited for five years before deciding whether to prosecute. An FBI search warrant obtained in 1993 was never executed. The AP report reveals that the investigation had been stalled in 1993 by Webb Hubbell.

19. Attorney General Reno allows all issues involving claims of executive privilege to be transferred entirely to the White House, thus taking the Office of Legal Counsel and the attorney general out of the loop, despite a practice going back five presidencies that

requires a legal opinion by both the assistant attorney general and the attorney general before the president can assert executive privilege.

20. On numerous occasions, Attorney General Reno states that her decisions to not appoint an independent counsel to investigate the 1996 Clinton-Gore fund-raising abuses were based on recommendations from career prosecutors. It turns out, however, that FBI Director Louis Freeh, in writing, had strongly urged the appointment of an independent counsel. Moreover, Reno's hand-picked task force leader, Charles LaBella, told Ms. Reno that she "had no alternative but to seek an [appointment of] an independent prosecutor." Even the Criminal Division's Robert Litt, described as a Democratic Party loyalist and "friend of Bill," twice urged that an independent counsel be appointed to investigate whether Vice President Gore lied to FBI agents in connection with his fund-raising. The current head of the fund-raising task force is also urging a special counsel to investigate those matters. Attorney General Reno has rejected every one of those recommendations from the top, experienced, career prosecutors in charge of the investigations.

21. July 30, 1998: The *Washington Post* reports that DOJ officials debriefed Secret Service officials after their grand jury testimony in the Starr investigation and that the gist of that testimony was circulated to the Clinton defense team.

22. Despite Al Gore's attendance at a lengthy and detailed meeting during which the solicitation of hard money was discussed (according to notes relative to such discussion by his chief of staff and several other witnesses), Attorney General Reno rejects for the third time the appointment of an independent counsel, concluding that "there is no evidence that [Gore] heard the statements or understood their implications."

23. February 22, 1999: The *Washington Post* reports that, as President Clinton's impeachment trial begins in the Senate, Attorney General Reno sends Kenneth Starr a letter informing him that the department is opening an investigation of him with respect to his handling of the Monica Lewinsky matter and "potentially unethical contacts with [lawyers pursuing the] Paula Jones' sexual harassment suit against Clinton."

24. 1997: The Justice Department repeatedly declines FBI requests for access to Wen Ho Lee's government computer in Los Alamos. When the FBI finally is allowed to access the computer—after getting

permission from Dr. Lee to do so—the agents find evidence of the transfer of highly secret "legacy" codes for American warheads. The DOJ then declines to approve either a search of Dr. Lee's home or an application for court approval to do so. When the home computer is finally checked, it shows the transfer to an unsecured computer of files containing millions of lines of highly classified, immensely sensitive, computer code. Given the most recent developments in the case, however, it is now unclear whether DOJ botched the investigation from the start or whether it should never have pressed the investigation from the start.

25. The Justice Department strikes a settlement with John Huang: he pleads guilty to raising $7,500 illegally and is sentenced to one year's probation. Other fund-raising officials are charged with minor crimes unrelated to or highly peripheral to the Clinton-Gore fundraising efforts.

26. Former Watergate prosecutor Henry Ruth and Harvard professor Alan Stone report that the DOJ's internal evaluation of the department's role in the Waco tragedy was a "whitewash," "clearly written to vindicate the attorney general."

27. The Justice Department forwards to the president a pardon report concerning 16 convicted Puerto Rican terrorists despite strong and unanimous opposition from the FBI, the Bureau of Prisons, and the U.S. attorneys in Illinois and Connecticut. According to *New York Times* reporter David Johnston, the format of the report "suggested a diversity of views within law enforcement agencies that did not exist." August 27, 1999: *New York Times* reporter Neil Lewis subsequently reports that "the Justice Department took extraordinary steps to enhance the chances for clemency" for the Puerto Rican terrorists "after receiving . . . expressions of interest from the White House." The application for clemency was processed by the department even though the terrorists did not personally submit applications.

28. The Department of Justice files a brief in the Supreme Court arguing in support of racial preferences in the state of Hawaii. The state had denied the right to vote in certain elections to persons who were not related to a specially defined class of native Hawaiians. The Supreme Court later finds the practice to be a clear violation of the 15th Amendment.

29. 1997: Attorney General Reno tells the Senate Judiciary Committee that there is no legal basis on which the federal government

can sue tobacco companies. January 1999: President Clinton announces in his State of the Union Address that he has instructed the Department of Justice to sue the tobacco companies. October 1999: The suit is filed.

30. June 1998: After the Defense Department leaks information from Linda Tripp's confidential personnel files to *New Yorker* reporter Jane Mayer following a meeting between Mayer and former White House aide Harold Ickes, the Defense Department inspector general conducts an investigation that is turned over to the Department of Justice. After two years of silence, the Department of Justice announces that it is dropping the matter.

31. May 11, 2000: The Justice Department removes Bob Gorence, the lead prosecutor in the Wen Ho Lee case, replacing him with someone to be selected by Washington. Dr. Lee's defense counsel responds: "This is good news for Dr. Lee, as Mr. Gorence was an experienced prosecutor." June 19, 2000: Mr. Gorence is replaced with a prosecutor with "no background in nuclear issues or national security matters."

32. Four years after the fact, reports surface that FBI Deputy Director William Esposito was told by Justice Official Lee Radek, early in the 1996 fund-raising investigation, that Radek "was under a lot of pressure not to go forward with the investigation because Reno's job 'might hang in the balance.'" Another memo reveals that early in the probe the Justice Department tried to avoid using FBI agents to do investigative work, relying instead on Commerce Department investigators.

33. May 10, 2000: The *New York Times*, a source clearly not part of any vast right-wing conspiracy, declares in a lead editorial, "Attorney General Janet Reno has consistently failed to enforce the law against top Clinton Administration officials. . . . She has an uncanny instinct for ignoring or misreading the evidence and the law when top officials are credibly accused of misconduct."

Conclusion

Again, the list is hardly exhaustive. From published sources alone, there is much more to tell. When the Clinton–Reno Justice Department is seriously investigated, if it ever is, and the full story is told, there is every indication that we will be stunned—if we are not stunned already—by what we learn. But if the department remains in the control of the same people who have been running it for the past seven years, we will probably never learn the full story. As President Carter's attorney general, Griffin Bell, was quoted as having said recently in an article in the *National Review*, "if you want to clean house, it would be better to have a Republican. Then you can change everybody."

12. The Imperial President Abroad

John C. Yoo

Aside from getting himself impeached, President Clinton's most signal impact on the Constitution, and the rule of law it embraces, will have been in the area of foreign affairs.[1] As his domestic agenda met with frustration in a Republican Congress, President Clinton exercised the powers of the imperial presidency to the utmost in the area in which those powers are already at their height—in our dealings with foreign nations. Unfortunately, the record of the administration has not been a happy one, in light of its costs to the Constitution and the American legal system. On a series of different international relations matters, such as war, international institutions, and treaties, President Clinton has accelerated disturbing trends in foreign policy that undermine notions of democratic accountability and respect for the rule of law.

In one respect, those questions involve struggles between the executive and legislative branches that go back to the beginnings of the Republic. It was, after all, Alexander Hamilton and James Madison who staked out the initial positions on presidential power in foreign affairs in response to President Washington's Neutrality Proclamation. Our debates over war powers—whether the president may act unilaterally to bring the nation into hostilities—or over the treaty power would sound a familiar ring to the ears of the framing generation. Nonetheless, in those areas, the administration has taken foreign affairs decisions with little regard for the law or even for its own previous legal arguments.

From a different perspective, however, the Clinton administration's actions pose new, difficult challenges for constitutional government that we have not seen before and that the Framers could not have anticipated. In particular, the Clinton administration has rushed to embrace multilateralism—by which I mean cooperation with other nations under the aegis of formal international agreements and institutions—without due consideration to notions of

American sovereignty. In areas such as war and arms control, President Clinton has sought to delegate governmental power to international institutions to achieve dubious foreign policy goals. It appears that this administration has the distinction of being the first to transfer public power outside of the American governmental system. This unprecedented delegation of authority undermines American constitutional norms of democratic accountability, and it threatens to create international institutions in which the problems of the American administrative state would only be compounded, but on a vaster scale.

As I will argue, the administration has played fast and loose with the law to avoid making decisions for which the American people could hold the executive branch accountable. I will illustrate the administration's cavalier attitude toward the rule of law by discussing two significant areas, war powers and arms control, that have been at the center of the Clinton administration's foreign policy.

Waging War

The War Power

When it comes to using the American military, no president in recent times has had a quicker trigger finger. In March 1999, for example, President Clinton ordered 31,000 American servicemen and women to engage in air operations against Serbia to prevent the "ethnic cleansing" of Albanians living in Kosovo. As part of an operation sponsored by the North Atlantic Treaty Organization (NATO), 7,000 American ground troops then entered Kosovo on June 10, 1999, after NATO bombing had forced Serbia to withdraw its forces. Now, more than a year later, those ground troops remain, to keep the peace and to foster the construction of a new nation in Kosovo, often in dangerous circumstances.

Although broader in scale and destructiveness, President Clinton's Kosovo operation followed a pattern set by similar military interventions over the last eight years. In 1993, Clinton expanded the goals of the 28,000 American troops in Somalia, originally deployed by President Bush for humanitarian reasons, but then withdrew them after the deaths of soldiers in combat. In 1994, he sent 16,000 American troops to Haiti, under the auspices of the United Nations, to oversee its transition to democratic government. In December 1995, Clinton ordered 20,000 American ground troops to implement a

U.N.-brokered peace plan in Bosnia, another former province of the former Yugoslavia. In the summer of 1998, he used cruise missiles to hit suspected terrorist targets in Sudan and Afghanistan. American warplanes continue to enforce a no-fly zone in Iraq, and on occasion American cruise missiles and bombs have attacked Iraqi military assets. During the last eight years, American troops have participated in U.N. peacekeeping missions in dangerous places such as Macedonia and Rwanda.

In none of those cases did Congress provide authorization for the Clinton administration's decision to use force abroad. In the case of Kosovo, for example, the House of Representatives passed a resolution by 424 to 1 that declared its support for American troops, but refused to authorize the use of force. The House of Representatives rejected, by a vote of 427 to 2, a joint resolution declaring war on the Federal Republic of Yugoslavia. It also rejected, by a tie 213–213 vote, a Senate resolution authorizing the use of force. The House also defeated, by a 290 to 139 vote, a concurrent resolution that would have required the president to remove all American troops from Yugoslavia operations. Instead, the House passed a bill that barred the use of any funds for the deployment of American forces in Yugoslavia without specific congressional authorization,[2] which the Senate refused to enact. Later, Congress as a whole doubled the administration's request for emergency funding for Yugoslav war operations, to the tune of $11.8 billion, but without authorizing the war. President Clinton responded by deploying even more aircraft and combat ground troops to the region to support deep strike operations in the Yugoslav theater of operations.

Rather than rely on congressional approval, the president has justified those interventions more often on the need to uphold our obligations to the United Nations or NATO. Although on several occasions Congress refused to authorize the use of force, President Clinton argued that he had the sole constitutional power as commander in chief to send American servicemen and women into harm's way. Although he signaled that he would welcome congressional support, he also made clear that he would act without it. President Clinton further refused to acknowledge the binding effect of the War Powers Resolution, which requires the president to remove troops from combat environments within 60 days unless Congress gives its approval. The Clinton administration's use of the military in several long-term interventions has rendered the War Powers Resolution a dead letter.

Kosovo may represent a significant theoretical shift in the nature of the American way of war, one that the Clinton administration has accelerated if not set in motion. During the Reagan and Bush administrations, the United States often intervened unilaterally, quickly, and generally in pursuit of purely American interests. American invasions in Grenada and Panama, for example, occurred without any significant multilateral participation, were executed within the 60-day War Powers Resolution period, and did not receive Security Council approval. Intervention during the Clinton years—though still significantly American in force structure, military organization, and political leadership—has been anything but unilateral. In Bosnia and Kosovo, American forces participate as part of an international military structure, sometimes under foreign command. Military operations are no longer short. Deployments in Haiti and Bosnia have proceeded for years rather than weeks. Most likely, American troops will be stationed in Kosovo for years, not months.

Under the Clinton administration, the goals of war have changed as well. During the Cold War, the United States engaged the military primarily in nation-state to nation-state conflicts, in which the goal was both military and political victory. Under President Clinton, however, the nation has become involved more often in what is known as "low-intensity conflict" in which civilian leaders have employed military force for more diffuse objects, such as rebuilding nations, enforcing international peace or the status quo, and imposing costs on a hostile regime that fall short of total military and political victory. As a result, the administration has used troops not to achieve total victory or to contain the spread of Soviet influence but to achieve more limited goals—such as maintaining stability in the international order—whose long-term benefits for American security are unclear.

In pursuit of those objectives, the Clinton administration has given those types of interventions a new, and potentially significant, legal twist. Under the Clinton approach, the approval of the U.N. or other international organizations has become the foundation on which justifications for intervention are built. In sending troops to Haiti and Bosnia, for example, President Clinton expressly relied on the need to carry out U.N. Security Council resolutions, not on domestic legal mandates.[3] Although he could not rely on the Security Council for approval of the Kosovo bombings, President Clinton still justified the intervention by appealing to our NATO obligations.[4] As he declared when announcing the bombing campaign, "America has a responsibility to stand with our allies when they are trying to save innocent lives and preserve peace, freedom, and stability in Europe." Although the Clinton administration has yet to fully explain the legal significance of international authorization, it may believe that the president's authority to interpret and execute treaty commitments may buttress his constitutional authority to send American troops abroad. At the level of domestic law, however, the Clinton administration's refusal to seek affirmative congressional authorization for its conduct may have been consistent with historical practice, but it is still open to constitutional question.

Those deployments have several implications for constitutionalism and the rule of law. First, the interventions call for long-term, sustained (if low-intensity) hostilities that run counter to the express terms of the War Powers Resolution. In Kosovo, President Clinton committed 31,000 troops to an air war that lasted 79 days, well in excess of the limitations of the War Powers Resolution. He then sent 7,000 more troops for a long-lasting ground deployment in Kosovo itself. Congress never declared war, nor did it issue any kind of statutory authorization. Although Congress provided funding for the war and expressed its support for the troops, critics of presidential warmaking authority have never accepted such actions as sufficient legislative authorization for military hostilities. President Clinton's use of ground troops in Bosnia is about to enter its fifth year. Personally, I have maintained that the president has broader unilateral discretion to initiate hostilities than many academics and congressional Democrats had once argued. I do not find the violation of the War Powers Resolution to be as troubling as those critics once did—critics who fell remarkably silent during the Kosovo conflict. I believe that the Constitution—through the Commander in Chief and Executive Power Clauses—provides the president with the constitutional authority to use force abroad, subject to congressional control over the purse.[5]

That approach, however, has not been the Clinton administration's previously considered view. During the Haiti intervention, for example, the Clinton administration acknowledged the force of the War

Powers Resolution and read its "overriding interest" as "preventing the United States from being engaged, without express congressional authorization, in major, prolonged conflicts such as the wars in Vietnam and Korea, rather than to prohibit the President from using or threatening to use troops to achieve important diplomatic objectives where the risk of sustained military conflict was negligible."[6] In Haiti, for example, the administration's lawyers argued that the intervention did not implicate Congress's power to declare war because the "nature, scope, and duration of the deployment were not consistent with the conclusion that the event was a 'war'" within the constitutional meaning of the word, especially since American troops did not engage in extreme uses of forces, such as a bombardment.

What is disturbing for the rule of law is the administration's direct contradiction of its own announced principles, clearly for political purposes. According to the administration's own justification for the Haiti intervention, the NATO bombing of Kosovo was a "war" within the constitutional definition of the word. American forces engaged in a foreign deployment in which they engaged in the "extreme use of force," without the consent of the nation's rulers, where American lives were (and continue to be) at risk. Kosovo involved more than the "the risk of sustained military conflict"— American planes actually attacked for a prolonged period the civilian targets and military forces of another sovereign nation. Yet, Congress never gave its affirmative consent to the Kosovo operation. Further, Kosovo violated the time limits of the War Powers Resolution, which the administration previously had acknowledged as binding. Even though presidents from Nixon through Bush had never acknowledged the resolution's constitutionality, they generally respected its expression of legislative preference by keeping military interventions within the 60-day clock. President Clinton not only flagrantly disregarded the resolution, his administration never attempted to justify the need to violate its terms.

In Kosovo, the administration clearly contradicted itself. That was put on clear display when Rep. Tom Campbell (R–Calif.) and others sued in federal court seeking a declaration that Kosovo was an unconstitutional war. The administration compounded its lack of respect for the law by failing to issue *any* public legal explanation for the use of force in Kosovo—seeming to believe that silence would cure any constitutional errors. Whether one believes that the Constitution grants the power to decide to use force to the president or to Congress, one cannot help but find troubling the administration's cavalier disregard for its own previously announced constitutional principles. In areas such as foreign affairs and the separation of powers, in which the courts exercise judicial review only sparingly, the executive branch has an important duty in establishing and maintaining constitutional precedent that may guide the interaction of the branches. In Kosovo, the Clinton administration ignored its obligation on this score in favor of achieving its short-term political goals abroad. And if one agrees with Rep. Campbell, many of his formerly vocal Democratic colleagues, and many legal academics that Congress must authorize all offensive uses of force, then President Clinton's Kosovo operation clearly violated both the War Powers Resolution and the Constitution.

Multilateral Engagements

War powers questions to one side, President Clinton's military adventures raise a second legal and political difficulty—their unprecedented reliance on multilateral cooperation. To be sure, the record of postwar interventions provides other examples of American military participation in international organizations. Both the Korean and Persian Gulf conflicts received the authorization of the U.N. Security Council. Because of the strategic imperatives involved, however, it seems safe to conclude that Security Council refusal to authorize the use of force would not have prevented the United States from intervening in either situation, even if U.N. approval may have been necessary for purposes of international opinion. In the recent Clinton administration actions, however, one has the impression that without U.N. or NATO approval, the United States was unlikely to have intervened.

In fact, the recent rise in cooperation with international organizations is not just for the sake of window dressing. In many other areas, such as the environment, crime, or arms control, problems that were once viewed as wholly within the powers of individual nations to address have become international in scope. The Clinton administration appears to believe that developing solutions to these problems may require multilateral action to be fully comprehensive and effective. Correspondingly, Clinton's international policy initiatives rely on new forms of cooperation that include multiple parties, that create independent international organizations, and that pierce the veil of the nation-state and seek to regulate individual private conduct. But globalization and its attendant effects place new stresses on our domestic constitutional and political system. Novel forms of international cooperation increasingly call for the transfer of rule-making authority to international organizations that lack American openness and accountability. Collective action may require the United States to vest legal authority in institutions and individuals who are free from the legal and political controls that apply to American officers and institutions. Further, participation in multilateral action may alter domestic decisionmaking processes on foreign policy because of the need to comply with international obligations.

Events in Kosovo serve as a prime example of the conflict between the administration's reliance on international cooperation and the demands of our domestic legal system. Kosovo presented problems of regional and even international significance. Historically, the Balkans have been a tinderbox for broader European wars. Restoring international peace and stability in the wake of these wars has required the United States to expend lives and resources. American and European policymakers feared that conduct that would once have been considered domestic only in nature now threatened to cause wider disruptions to European security. Serbia's course of repression, for example, produced a stream of refugees that might destabilize neighboring countries, and ultimately our European allies. Widespread human rights violations not only offended European and international norms but might even have provoked intervention by regional powers, raising the possibility of conflict between greater powers and even NATO allies.

Responses to this transnational problem required a multilateral solution, it was argued. No individual European nation had the military or political wherewithal to attack Serbia to end its aggression. It was equally unlikely that the United States would unilaterally intervene so far from home in a nation with close cultural and historical ties with its former Cold War enemy, especially where its direct national interests were hard to define. Operating through the multilateral structure of NATO, therefore, allowed member nations to gather their collective resources to address the common security risk posed by events in Kosovo. Multilateralism allowed the NATO nations, particularly the United States, to submerge the identification of any single nation's interest as dominant in the operation. NATO presented a less threatening front to nations like Russia that sympathized with Serbia and might have feared an intervention so close to its own borders. Multilateralism allowed the NATO allies to share the risks and burdens of delicate and difficult tasks such as nation-building, a job no one nation may have had the determination and resources to handle. Thus, Kosovo signaled the transformation of NATO from a defensive alliance whose primary goals were to contain Soviet expansionism and to promote European reconstruction to a multilateral organization that now engaged in proactive operations to preempt threats to regional security.

Although multilateralism may confer certain short-run benefits, it is not clear whether it makes for good American national security policy over the long term. Using international organizations to achieve security ends might amount to warmaking by committee. As apparently happened in Kosovo, NATO's unanimous consent requirement essentially allowed those member nations most reluctant to use force to dictate the alliance's rules of engagement. Differing goals among the NATO nations may lead to a diffusion of war aims, as some nations may have wanted merely to convince Serbia to return to negotiations while other countries may have wanted to drive Serbia out of Kosovo. Confusion or disagreement over war aims may lead to ineffective strategic or tactical choices or to an imbalance between military means and political ends. That effect may only be compounded when one of the aims of an intervention is to prove the political unity of the alliance itself. Political leaders may prove even less willing to undertake necessary military measures if those actions cause dissension with an alliance that is concerned about the appearance of solidarity.

Further, a multilateral organization itself might have interests, or at least decisionmaking values, separate from those of its members. For example, officers of international organizations might be more likely to respect international law, which gives such organizations their legal status and powers, than American military and political leaders, who might be willing to tolerate violations of international law in the course of achieving national security goals. International organizations such as NATO also might seek new missions that sustain or expand their power and existence; we certainly know this has been the case with domestic administrative agencies. It may be no mistake that Kosovo resulted in transforming NATO from a purely defensive alliance against a disappearing foe into a regional security arrangement that now acts out-of-area. A growing divergence between the goals not just of other NATO or U.N. members and those of the United States, but between those of the international organizations and of the United States, should give even more pause to American policymakers who see multilateral cooperation as the future of war.

Kosovo raises yet a third constitutional question of no small significance—the effect of this new multilateralism on the Constitution's structures that ensure democratic accountability, a subject yet to receive sustained scrutiny. Clinton-style international cooperation requires the transfer of legal authority over American citizens to entities outside the control of the federal government and, ultimately, the people. During the Kosovo air war, for example, overall command remained with General Wesley K. Clark, who served both as NATO's Supreme Allied Commander in Europe (SACEUR) and as commander in chief of the U.S. European Command. Clark's dual roles meant that strategic command of U.S. forces rested in the hands of an American general. American troops, however, could serve under Clark's non-American theater commanders, such as British General Michael Jackson, who commanded the 16,000 NATO troops stationed in Macedonia during the air war and then led the NATO ground forces that have essentially occupied Kosovo. In other deployments ordered by President Clinton, such as those in Somalia and Bosnia, American forces attacked military targets at the instruction of non-U.S. commanders acting under the authority either of NATO or the U.N.[7]

It seems that President Clinton's willingness to send American troops into combat under non-U.S. officers is for the most part unprecedented. American experience in modern alliance warfare suggests that although the political branches have allowed the transfer only of certain levels of command to non-U.S. officers, they have reserved most forms of command—especially at the tactical level—solely for American military officers. Only American officers have exercised the authority to both coerce and discipline American units and troops.[8] Postwar conflicts do not appear to have changed this practice. Although the United Nations Charter called for the creation of a U.N. military force composed of national units placed at the Security Council's policy, strategic, and operational command, the ideal of an international military force died with the advent of the Cold War. In the two large-scale military conflicts sanctioned by the U.N., the Korean War and the Persian Gulf War, American generals exercised strategic command over the allied military, while American officers maintained operational and tactical command over American troops. As purely American interventions, the use of force in places such as Vietnam, Grenada, and Panama did not raise questions of multilateral command.

But interventions in Bosnia, Somalia, and now Kosovo have changed that practice. Responding to congressional efforts to stop the new policy, the Clinton administration has claimed a broad constitutional power in the president to delegate military command authority to any person.[9] According to the administration, the president's commander-in-chief power allows him to select whomever he believes necessary for military success. Because "U.N. peacekeeping missions involve multilateral arrangements that require delicate and complex accommodations of a variety of interests and concerns, including those of the nations that provide troops or resources," the administration argues, a mission's success may depend on the commander's nationality or on the "degree to which the operation is perceived as a U.N. activity" and not that solely of the United States.

That position has serious constitutional and policy defects. First, the administration's legal justification for its recent multilateral command policy fails to account for the Constitution's limitation on the delegation of federal power outside of the national government.[10] Although the Supreme Court has recognized that the Constitution allows Congress to transfer some of its lawmaking power to the executive branch, and though the president has broad discretion to delegate authority to his subordinates within the executive branch, the Constitution nowhere permits the president, the treatymakers, or Congress to delegate federal power completely outside of the national government. In fact, placing American troops under foreign command runs counter to recent cases of the Supreme Court, which have held that the Constitution requires that only officers of the United States may exercise substantial federal authority.[11]

That law of conservation of federal power prevents the national government, as a whole, from concealing or confusing the lines of governmental authority and responsibility by transferring power outside of it. When only U.S. officers exercise federal power under federal law, the people may hold the actions of the government accountable. Allowing the transfer of command authority to non-U.S. officers threatens that basic principle of government accountability. International or foreign officials have no obligation to pursue American policy, they do not take an oath to uphold the Constitution, nor can any American official hold them responsible for their deeds.

Transfer of command authority to foreign commanders also has the effect of cutting Congress and the public out of the policy debate over the use of force. Although, as a formal matter, the president has plenary control over the military as commander in chief, Congress has other informal methods for overseeing and regulating the armed forces. It not only maintains lines of communication to officers in the services, it can also employ oversight hearings and make use of the press to gather information and influence national security policy. If the president delegates command authority over American troops entirely outside of the federal government, however, neither Congress nor the public can determine whether foreign or international commanders are exercising their authority according to American standards, nor can they enforce their policy wishes through the usual legal or political methods available when power is delegated within the executive branch. Independent of the executive branch, foreign commanders need not obey presidential directives, need not follow American laws and regulations, and cannot be removed or disciplined by the president. If Congress or the people disagree with military policy, or they disapprove of the execution of a military operation, they have no political avenue to oversee the officials who are in command. They cannot demand that the president remove an official for incompetence, failure to obey orders, or disagreement over policy.

Second, the lack of formal authority over foreign commanders may increase the possibility that the pursuit of U.S. national interests will take a back seat to coalition goals. Any exercise of federal authority by a person who is not a member of the executive branch, and thus is not removable by the president, keeps the president from fully controlling the implementation of national policy.[12] Once the president delegates authority to a foreign commander he cannot issue orders to that commander backed up by the threat of removal and discipline, as he could to an American officer, even though that foreign official may issue directives to subordinate American soldiers. Although they may exercise the power of life and death over American soldiers, foreign commanders may hold very different allegiances and interests from those of U.S. officers. Foreign commanders, for example, may have different attitudes toward tactical strategies, about acceptable casualty rates, and about the amount of violence to use. As the Clinton administration has noted, however, the independence of such foreign commanders from American control is the very raison d'être of international enforcement actions. One of the main purposes of multilateralism is to create the impression that a military operation represents the policy of a neutral international organization, not simply that of the world's remaining superpower. It seems, however, that indulging the appearance of multilateralism makes it almost inevitable that foreign commanders will pursue goals that deviate from pure American interests.

Arms Control

The constitutional problems wrought by the Clinton administration in the context of multilateral military operations are compounded when it comes to international agreements. In attempting to address various international problems, President Clinton has focused America's diplomatic efforts again on multilateral solutions. Those solutions sometimes rely on new international institutions that exert regulatory authority over the activities of many nations. Further, those agreements may seek to regulate the private conduct of citizens within nation-states, versus the actions of the nation-states themselves. As is the case with military multilateralism, these new forms of international cooperation will require the United States to transfer authority outside of the federal government and hence outside of the control of the Constitution. The Clinton administration has ignored the accompanying constitutional problems in order to reach these types of agreements, which may be of doubtful national security value.

Arms control sits at the heart of these developments. Earlier arms control agreements had sought to place numerical limits on certain types of weapons, such as nuclear missiles, or on the deployment and use of different classes of forces. New Clinton-era agreements, most notably the Chemical Weapons Convention (CWC), have a different goal in mind. They seek to impose absolute bans not just on use but on the development and production of weapons as well. The ease with which such weapons can be manufactured and concealed, however, poses novel difficulties for a verification regime. Such weapons often can be created by dual-use facilities that can double as civilian sites engaged in the legitimate production of chemicals and pharmaceuticals. Furthermore, the multilateral nature of the treaties requires a verification regime that allows multiple state parties with disparate resources to measure compliance. In contrast, earlier arms control agreements, such as nuclear weapons treaties between the United States and the Soviet Union, forced the parties to rely on their own national technical means of verification to ensure compliance.

To overcome those challenges, the CWC has adopted the most intrusive verification mechanism yet seen in an international agreement. It requires state parties to provide annual, detailed reports on facilities that might produce chemical weapons; it subjects sites involved in the chemical industry to on-site inspections; and it allows state parties to demand "challenge" inspections of any location in another party's jurisdiction. The CWC creates a new international organization, the Organization for the Prohibition of Chemical Weapons, to monitor compliance with the treaty and to conduct inspections. This new organization, not national authorities, conducts on-site searches; and it, not the federal government, decides which chemicals are banned and cannot be produced. Nations interested in improving the effectiveness of other arms control regimes are likely to demand similar verification mechanisms, and we can see similar developments occurring in other areas of international regulation, such as the environment.

It is the intrusiveness of those verification procedures that produces difficulties under American constitutional law. CWC inspections may violate the Fourth Amendment's restriction on unreasonable searches and seizures and they may raise Fifth Amendment takings issues should international inspectors steal trade secrets. Putting those serious issues to one side, however, the CWC provides another example of the Clinton administration's unfortunate willingness to delegate governmental authority to entities outside of the control of the Constitution. The CWC's signal innovation in the area of verification is its creation of an independent international agency

172

for the execution of routine and challenge inspections. The CWC is a watershed in the development of arms control because of its reliance on its own verification methods rather than on national governments. That has the effect of rendering national governments transparent to international law in its ability to reach through the state into the lives of private citizens. Traditional international agreements usually place obligations on the national governments of state parties, which then assume the responsibility of enforcing treaty terms on their citizens. The CWC seeks to sidestep national governments in conducting inspections of private facilities and locations. Members of the new CWC international organization, not American officials, choose the American sites to be inspected according to standards that they develop. International inspectors conduct the searches, accompanied by American officers only in an observer capacity. Members of the international organization are not accountable to any American official; they are not appointed or elected by American officials; they cannot be removed by American officials; and they do not take orders from any American official.

Although perhaps desirable from the perspective of international policy, it is precisely that independence and neutrality that produces constitutional problems. Vesting verification in an impartial international organization may build assurance and trust, but it also creates tensions with fundamental constitutional principles of government accountability and popular sovereignty. Two constitutional provisions—the Appointments Clause and the Executive Power Clause—promote those values, and it is those clauses that pose obstacles for the future of international agreements like the CWC. Recent Supreme Court decisions interpreting those clauses indicate that individuals who exercise significant federal authority must be appointed as officers of the U.S. government. The requirement that all officers of the United States undergo appointment and be subject to presidential control renders all who exercise national power answerable to the people's elected representatives, who ultimately are responsible to the people themselves. Efforts to vest federal power in officials who do not undergo appointment according to constitutional requirements and who are not subject to presidential control come into conflict with constitutional principles of government accountability.

Turning first to the Appointments Clause, the Constitution establishes procedures for the creation and the filling of offices within the federal government. Under Article II, section 2, clause 2 of the Constitution, the president

> shall nominate, and by and with the Advice and Consent of the Senate, shall appoint Ambassadors, other public Ministers and Consuls, Judges of the supreme Court, and all other Officers of the United States, whose Appointments are not herein otherwise provided for, and which shall be established by Law: but the Congress may by Law vest the Appointment of such inferior Officers, as they think proper, in the President alone, in the Courts of Law, or in the Heads of Departments.[13]

At first, one might think that the Appointments Clause is but an anachronism from the 18th century. In a series of recent cases, however, the Supreme Court has identified a broad principle of government accountability underlying the clause. According to the Court, the Appointments Clause pursues two goals. First, the clause prevents Congress from arrogating to itself the power to appoint federal officials who enforce federal law. Thus, in *Buckley v. Valeo*, the 1976 case that struck down parts of the federal campaign spending laws, the Court declared that the Appointments Clause prohibited Congress from appointing members of the Federal Elections Commission.[14] In *Morrison v. Olson*, the 1987 case that upheld the independent counsel law, the Court permitted Congress to vest the appointment of the independent counsel in the federal courts, so long as the president retained ultimate removal authority over the counsel.[15] In *Printz v. United States*, the 1997 case that invalidated the Brady handgun law's background checks, the Court emphasized that Congress could not vest federal power in officials who were not removable by the president.[16] Allowing Congress to vest executive power outside of the executive branch, the Court wrote, would undermine the independence and effectiveness of the presidency.[17]

Second, the Appointments Clause embraces broader concerns about the scope of national power and those who exercise it. If the clause, for example, were limited only to certain types of federal officials, such as cabinet officers, then it would still permit the delegation of authority to officers outside the federal government. The Supreme Court, however, has answered this question by declaring that anyone who exercises significant federal authority must undergo the process outlined in Article II, section 2 of the Constitution.[18] By requiring the appointment of such officials, the Constitution prevents the national government from blurring the lines of responsibility between the people and their agents. It ensures that anyone who wields the power of the state be appointed by, and therefore be controlled by, democratically elected officials, who themselves are monitored and controlled by the people. As Chief Justice Rehnquist wrote for the Court in a 1991 case, "The Clause is a bulwark against one branch aggrandizing its power at the expense of another branch, but it is more: it preserves another aspect of the Constitution's structural integrity by preventing the diffusion of the appointment power."[19]

In divining this principle from the Appointments Clause, the Court has been guided by the original understanding of the provision and the history of its drafting and adoption. Historical evidence—too detailed to review here—suggests that the Framers sought to provide for the appointment of government officials in a manner that was open and accountable to the public.[20] Shaped by their revolutionary experience with Great Britain, the Framers wanted to avoid the diversion of public authority to individuals who were not accountable to the electorate but instead were appointed by a distant government in which the affected citizens had no representation. "Those who framed our Constitution," the Court observed in a recent Appointments Clause case, "addressed these concerns by carefully husbanding the appointment power to limit its diffusion."[21] With a centralized appointment process, the people would know whom to turn to when the government acted improperly. "By limiting the appointment power," the Court has said, the Framers "could ensure that those who wielded it were accountable to political force and the will of the people."[22]

Two other structural elements of the Constitution reinforce the Appointments Clause's promotion of government accountability. First, the Constitution creates a unitary executive branch that requires that all officials who enforce federal law remain subject to the president, who is the only member of the government elected by the entire nation. A vigorous debate continues in legal circles, between "formalists" and "functionalists," about how far Congress may go in shaping the organization and powers of the presidency.[23] Formalists believe that the Constitution creates only three types of government power—executive, legislative, and judicial—that are to be exercised by the three branches suited to those powers. Functionalists are willing to provide more flexibility to the political branches

175

in arranging, allocating, and sharing government powers. This division in academia mirrors confusion in the Supreme Court's recent separation of powers cases, which have wavered between formalist[24] and functionalist approaches.[25]

An effort to transfer power outside of the federal government, however, raises constitutional difficulties under either theory of the separation of powers. A formalist would argue that the power to execute federal laws, such as conducting searches or enforcing treaty provisions, belongs to the executive. Therefore, those powers can be exercised only by the president or those removable by him—in other words, members of the executive branch. But a functionalist, too, would object, because the leading functionalist case—*Morrison v. Olson*—held that the president ultimately must have removal authority over all officers who execute federal law, even if the Court recognized that Congress possessed some power to condition the removal power.[26] Further, functionalists believe that the strict separation of powers can be relaxed only to further other governmental values such as public accountability, which is undermined by the transfer of federal authority outside of the national government.

Second, a separate but related constitutional principle, known as the nondelegation doctrine, also enforces accountability in government. Ever since the New Deal, the Supreme Court has permitted the legislature to delegate significant administrative and rulemaking powers to the executive branch.[27] According to the nondelegation doctrine, however, Congress may not delegate such authority without providing intelligible guidelines and standards for its use.[28] Such standards prevent Congress from wholly abdicating its constitutional responsibility to formulate policy, and they ensure that Congress will remain responsible to the electorate for its legislative decisions. The nondelegation doctrine also seeks to preclude the executive branch from exercising lawmaking power without standards both to guide its discretion and to review its performance. And it prevents Congress and the president from colluding in transferring public policymaking authority to those who are insulated from the electorate. Delegating authority outside of the national government overrides those safeguards because Congress cannot enforce its standards through the usual legal and political methods that are used to oversee the administrative state. Such delegation also undermines the public-regarding nature of federal power and risks the capture of government policy by private interests. Because of those concerns, the Court in the New Deal period struck down laws that attempted to delegate to private industry the power to promulgate regulatory codes and standards.[29]

Those principles of government accountability, and their expression in the Supreme Court's modern reading of the Appointments Clause and other provisions, create significant difficulties for the Clinton administration's experiments in multilateralism. Simply put, new regulatory treaties such as the Chemical Weapons Convention require the vesting of federal power in officials who are not members of, or responsible to, the federal government. Members of the new international organizations are not appointed pursuant to the Appointments Clause, are not members of the executive branch, and are not removable by the president. Their decisions about where, why, and how to search a location within the United States are not made by officers of the United States, nor are their choices and methods subject to review by American officials. Within the borders of the United States, they operate with the authority of federal law behind them—it is illegal, for example, for facility owners to interfere with the CWC's inspectors' freedom of access. No legally enforceable criteria constrain the officials in their selection of locations to search; in fact, some of the searches are conducted at random. Finally, they are immune from the ultimate check on government action that is provided by the national political process. Congress cannot use its oversight or funding powers to affect CWC inspections, nor can public criticism succeed in changing an inspection policy over which the president has no control.

Despite those constitutional difficulties, the Clinton administration went forward in seeking Senate ratification of the CWC. Achieving arms control objectives through a multilateral setting was believed to be more important than respecting the Constitution's limitations on the delegation of power and its restrictions on the use of power against American citizens. That should come as no surprise because the Clinton administration was merely adopting the same disregard for constitutional principles that it displays in the case of international military operations. Indeed, the administration's record on both arms control and military intervention demonstrates an unfortunate willingness to trust multilateral solutions that delegate power over American citizens to international organizations.

Those are only the first steps toward what might be called an international administrative state. Clinton-style multilateralism bears many of the hallmarks of our domestic administrative state: reliance on bureaucracies that are independent of the political process; unchecked delegations of power to those bureaucracies; and the idea that social welfare can be stabilized and enhanced by the proactive regulation of such bureaucracies. And it suffers from many of the same problems, not the least of which is the lack of democratic accountability, as I have argued. But while mimicking in some respects the New Deal administrative state, the Clinton administration's new multilateralism is much worse. Unlike domestic administrative agencies, international organizations rest completely outside of the American political process and enjoy no place within our constitutional separation of powers. They are under no obligation to respect American law or political values; they are not subject to congressional oversight; and they are not limited by American-style judicial review, the primary method we have to corral our administrative state.

The establishment of an international administrative state may be President Clinton's longest-lasting legacy in foreign affairs. It certainly represents his most extensive use of the powers of the imperial presidency to ignore constitutional limitations on government, all in the service of his foreign policy goals. It is too soon to tell whether the achievement of those goals will bring about tangible improvements to American national security, but we have some experience in predicting that the costs to constitutional government of delegating power outside of the government will not be small. It will be up to the next president to decide whether to allow those developments to continue, or to restore the rule of law in foreign affairs.

Notes

1. For a fuller treatment of some of these issues, see John C. Yoo, "Kosovo, War Powers, and the Multilateral Future," *University of Pennsylvania Law Review* 148 (2000): 1673; John C. Yoo, "The Dogs That Didn't Bark: Why Were International Legal Scholars MIA on Kosovo?" *Chicago Journal of International Law* 1 (2000): 149; John C. Yoo, "The New Sovereignty and the Old Constitution: The Chemical Weapons Convention and the Appointments Clause," *Constitutional Commentary* 15 (1998): 87.

2. H.R. 1569, 106th Congress (1999).

3. See, for example, President's News Conference, Pub. Papers (August 3, 1994) (Haiti); Remarks and Exchange with Reporters, Pub. Papers (February 6, 1994) (Bosnia); Letter to Congressional Leaders on Bosnia, Pub. Papers (September 1, 1995) (Bosnia).

4. Address to the Nation on Airstrikes against Serbian Targets in the Federal Republic of Yugoslavia (Serbia and Montenegro), *Weekly Compilation of Presidential Documents* 35 (March 24, 1999): 516.

5. See John C. Yoo, "The Continuation of Politics by Other Means: The Original Understanding of War Powers," *California Law Review* 84 (1996): 167.

6. Letter from Walter Dellinger, Assistant Attorney General, to Senator Dole et al., Deployment of United States Armed Forces into Haiti, September 27, 1994.

7. See Yoo, "Kosovo, War Powers."

8. Ibid.

9. Memorandum for Alan J. Kreczko, Special Assistant to the President and Legal Adviser to the National Security Council, Placing of United States Armed Forces Under United Nations Operational or Tactical Control, May 8, 1996, ⟨http://www.usdoj.gov/olc/mem_ops.html⟩.

10. See generally Yoo, "The New Sovereignty."

11. See *Buckley v. Valeo*, 424 U.S. 1 (1976); *Ryder v. United States*, 115 S. Ct. 2031, 2035 (1991).

12. See Steven G. Calabresi and Saikrishna B. Prakash, "The President's Power to Execute the Laws," *Yale Law Journal* 104 (1994): 593–99.

13. U.S. Constitution, Article II, § 2, cl. 2.

14. Ibid.

15. *Morrison v. Olson*, 487 U.S. 654 (1988).

16. *Printz v. United States*, 117 S. Ct. 2365 (1997). See also *Edmond v. United States*, 117 S. Ct. 1573 (1997).

17. *Printz*, 117 S. Ct. at 2378.

18. *Buckley v. Valeo*, 424 U.S. 1, 126 (1976).

19. *Ryder v. United States*, 115 S. Ct. 2031, 2035 (1991) (quotes and citations removed).

20. See Yoo, "The New Sovereignty," 105–11.

21. *Freytag v. Commissioner*, 501 U.S. 868 (1991).

22. Ibid., 884. See also *Weiss v. United States*, 114 S. Ct. 752, 757 (1994).

23. See, for example, Martin S. Flaherty, "The Most Dangerous Branch," *Yale Law Journal* 105 (1996): 1725; Steven G. Calabresi and Saikrishna B. Prakash, "The President's Power to Execute the Laws," *Yale Law Journal* 104 (1994): 541; Lawrence Lessig and Cass R. Sunstein, "The President and the Administration," *Columbia Law Review* 94 (1994): 1.

24. *INS v. Chadha*, 462 U.S. 919 (1983) (invalidating legislative veto); *Bowsher v. Synar*, 478 U.S. 714 (1986) (invalidating Gramm-Rudman-Hollings budget deficit legislation); *Metropolitan Washington Airports Authority v. Citizens for the Abatement of Airport Noise*, 501 U.S. 252 (1991); *Plaut v. Spendthrift Farm, Inc.*, 115 S. Ct. 1447 (1995).

25. *Morrison v. Olson*, 487 U.S. 654 (1988); *Mistretta v. United States*, 488 U.S. 361 (1989).

26. *Morrison*, 487 U.S. 692.

27. See *Yakus v. United States*, 321 U.S. 414 (1944).

28. See, for example, *Mistretta v. United States*, 488 U.S. 361 (1988).

29. *Carter v. Carter Coal Co.*, 298 U.S. 238 (1936); *A.L.A. Schechter Poultry Corp. v. United States*, 295 U.S. 495 (1935). See also *Larkin v. Grendel's Den*, 459 U.S. 116 (1982).

PART V

THE GUARDIANS OF LAW FAIL

13. The Political Parties

Daniel E. Troy

Historians and political scientists will debate for years why the political parties allowed the Clinton administration to run roughshod over the rule of law. I hope that this preliminary look at the parties' reaction to the Clinton administration will illuminate some of the difficulties both parties face when confronting a politically popular president who, during a period of prosperity, repeatedly flouts the law.

To begin with a hypothetical, imagine that a young refugee from Pinochet's Chile had fled to the United States and appealed to the Reagan administration for assistance. President Reagan, instead of helping the refugee who had escaped the dictatorship, instructed his Justice Department to extradite the refugee to Chile. The Justice Department obtained a warrant to search for weapons in the refugee's temporary U.S. home and, when executing the warrant, seized the refugee, flashing weaponry appropriate to the liberation of Grenada. Would the Democrats have sat by quietly while the Reagan administration seized the refugee? Would the Republicans have formed a solid block united behind the president? The answers speak for themselves. Accordingly, we must ask how and why the laws have changed for President Clinton.

The Clinton administration, more than any other, has used government power to serve private interests. At the same time, the administration has claimed that the private matters of the president and his administration are immune from public scrutiny. Administration officials from Agriculture Secretary Mike Espy[1] to Associate Attorney General Webster Hubbell[2] to Commerce Secretary Ron Brown[3]

The author gratefully acknowledges the invaluable assistance of Michael Dimino, Harvard Law School, '01, in drafting this paper, and the helpful comments of Gil and Tevi Troy, Roger Pilon, Alex Azar, and Harold Furtchgott-Roth, as well as the input of David Tell.

to Energy Secretary Hazel O'Leary[4] and beyond have been accused of benefiting from private deals while working in the administration. Hubbell and others were found guilty. Repeatedly, however, investigations were hampered because the administration—which is charged with faithfully executing the laws—persisted in delaying and obstructing justice.

Perhaps the most brazen claim of presidential immunity was argued by the president in *Clinton v. Jones*.[5] Clinton argued that the woman who accused him of sexually harassing and assaulting[6] her should have to wait to sue him until the end of his presidency because allowing the suit to proceed would distract him from his presidential duties. The Supreme Court handily rejected the president's argument—unanimously. Although President Nixon had been accorded immunity for official actions,[7] President Clinton was the first president to claim immunity for conduct wholly outside his official capacity. By asserting that his office immunized him from suit, Clinton seems implicitly to have adopted President Nixon's startling remark that "when the president does it, that means that it is not illegal."

Defining the Problem: How Have the Parties Failed?

Time and again, both parties watched members of the Clinton administration, from the president on down, ignore governing law with only the most transparent of excuses. To take but two examples, consider Al Gore's claim that there is "no controlling legal authority"[8] on raising soft money inside of the White House, and President Clinton's preposterous argument that whether he acted illegally "depends on what the definition of 'is' is."

At other times the Clinton administration violated the law without even providing an excuse—for example, when Linda Tripp's personnel records were released in blatant violation of the Privacy Act,[9] or when Bill Clinton adopted an executive order (later held illegal by a court) barring the government from doing business with companies employing strikebreakers.[10] My purpose here is not to provide a comprehensive list of occasions on which the Clinton administration violated the law. Rather, it is to present a few examples of *how* the political parties acquiesced to the administration's abuses of power and to suggest *why* they failed to control this president.

How Did the Democratic Party Fail?

Nearly all Democrats consistently supported President Clinton. They defended him most famously and vigorously during the impeachment process. Even such a respected senator as former astronaut John Glenn degenerated into rank partisanship.[11] No Clinton administration wrongdoing—lying about Whitewater or Travelgate, violating campaign finance laws by accepting illegal foreign money, lying about his dalliance with Ms. Lewinsky, or seizing Elián Gonzalez at gunpoint—led congressional Democrats to stop defending the president. It was only welfare reform[12] that spurred any resignations "on principle" from the administration.[13]

Although Democratic politicians rallied around the president, liberal commentators were aghast. As Richard Cohen,[14] Nat Hentoff,[15] and Nadine Strossen[16] noted, not even President Clinton's "appalling record on constitutional rights"[17] caused congressional Democrats to cease supporting this administration. Hentoff went so far as to say that *"[n]o American president . . . has done so much damage to constitutional liberties as Bill Clinton. . . ."*[18] Nadine Strossen detailed some of the instances in which President Clinton has "elbow[ed] the Constitution out of the way."[19]

It bears repeating that those charges come most ardently from liberals—not from the Democrats in Congress—and examples of such criticisms abound. Those who most treasure the Constitution's protections are the ones most betrayed by President Clinton. Floyd Abrams has noted the administration's disregard for the Constitution, finding that "[t]ime and again, the administration has opposed serious First Amendment claims in court, acquiesced in serious First Amendment damage by legislation and ignored First Amendment limits in its own conduct."[20] In short, "Bill Clinton should know better."[21]

John Heilemann of *Wired* disagrees, but not in a way that should give comfort to the president. He notes that "the notion that Clinton 'knows better' rests on the assumption that the President possesses principles that are independent of political calculation—and on civil liberties, at least, there exists virtually no evidence to support this assumption."[22] Heilemann concluded that "a lifetime of shameless compromise has left Clinton incapable of even identifying a civil liberty, let alone fighting for one."[23] President Clinton's "blatant disregard for civil liberties" is "breathtaking in both the breadth and the depth of its awfulness,"[24] but congressional Democrats continue to support him.

Although there are many examples of the Democrats' acquiescence and ardent defense of the Clinton administration's lawlessness, the prime example, which will be debated throughout the ages, arose over impeachment. Historians will long compare the Republican Party's performance during Watergate with the Democratic Party's performance during President Clinton's impeachment trial. As is well known, in 1974, Richard Nixon, who had won the electoral votes of forty-nine states less than two years before, was forced from office without even a vote on impeachment. Yet, in 1998, a Democratic president, who had never commanded even a majority vote of the American people and who had cost his party its decades-long monopoly in the House of Representatives, easily survived a Senate impeachment trial.

There are several important differences, of course, between Nixon's era and Clinton's era. First, the economy was different. President Nixon presided over a recession and a time of inflation while President Clinton presided over an economic boom. Second, President Nixon conducted an unpopular and costly war, whereas President Clinton engaged in foreign adventurism that was largely bloodless. Finally, the behavior of the presidential parties in the two cases was quite different.

The Republicans were never united in supporting President Nixon. Representative William Cohen, for example, notably refused to support the administration. And the ranking Republican on the Senate Judiciary Committee, Howard Baker, continually pressured President Nixon by asking, "What did the president know and when did he know it?"

The disclosure of President Nixon's smoking-gun tape of June 23, 1972—his conversation with aide H. R. Haldeman—announced the president's malfeasance to the nation. Immediately, almost all of the Republican support for the president vanished, and Nixon's August 9, 1974, resignation became inevitable. In fact, a contingent of four Republican members of Congress, led by Representative John Rhodes, visited the White House and convinced Nixon to resign.

The contrast with the Democrats' reaction to Bill Clinton could not be starker. Clinton all but admitted committing several felonies. Notwithstanding his betrayal of his supporters—he repeatedly told them for months that he "did not have sexual relations with that woman"—the overwhelming majority of Democrats lined up to defend the president even before any hearings were held.[25] Not only did Clinton keep most of the Democratic support, but immediately after he was impeached, more than 100 congressional Democrats trooped to the White House for a photo opportunity with the president. It was there that Vice President Al Gore announced that history will remember Bill Clinton as "one of America's greatest presidents."[26]

But it is not just the congressional wings of the two parties that behaved differently during the two crises. Nixon's Justice Department, unlike Clinton's, was the site of a revolt against the president. The attorney general resigned, Nixon fired the deputy attorney general, and Solicitor General Robert H. Bork stepped in (at considerable risk to his career) to stem a massive exodus from the department. The new attorney general promised to appoint a new special prosecutor. Shortly thereafter Leon Jaworski took charge of the investigation.

By contrast, Attorney General Janet Reno has stood as a barrier against any investigation of President Clinton's campaign irregularities. The *Washington Post* and *New York Times* routinely attack her for her unwillingness to hold the administration to account.[27] And certainly the *Wall Street Journal* has demonstrated time and again that Janet Reno's Justice Department has ignored evidence that the president's illegal fund-raising put the national interest in jeopardy.[28] Instead of acting on the evidence and investigating the allegations fully, Reno regularly "insists that the 8,000-pound campaign-finance gorilla is no big deal."[29]

Apart from the investigations into campaign financing, the Justice Department's independence and integrity have been questioned in several contexts.[30] Although the attorney general has steadfastly maintained that she is independent of the administration, her actions indicate otherwise. As an example, in 1997 Reno told Congress that there was no legal ground for a suit against the tobacco companies. The next year, after the president indicated his desire to bring a suit against the tobacco companies, Reno decided there was a basis for action after all.[31] Rather than admit, as she might have, that the president, as the nation's chief executive, plays a role in the decisions of the Justice Department, Reno claimed that her decision was not political.[32]

The reflexive defense of the Clinton administration by the Democrats on Capitol Hill has led more than one lifelong Democrat (but not many more) to quit the party in disgust. Henry Ruth, a Democrat and Watergate special prosecutor, said that the Democratic Party's principles during the Clinton administration had given way to "pure political expediency. They [Democrats] have turned the impeachment inquiry into a sporting event in which the only object is to win."[33]

Similarly, Jerome Zeifman, a self-described lifelong Democrat and chief counsel of the House Judiciary Committee at the time of the Nixon impeachment inquiry, concluded that House Democrats should have voted for impeachment. Zeifman found that the president's only defense was to "attack Kenneth Starr" and "declare war on Congress itself by charging . . . Republicans with partisanship and 'unfairness.'" Zeifman concluded that the president's defense was itself "indefensible," "shameful," and that it "betrayed the trust of both the country and the Democratic Party."[34]

Ruth predicted in 1998 that the Democratic Party would eventually "rebel against a presidency that rejects individual responsibility and has no ideal higher than the lowest common denominator."[35] Such repudiation has yet to come.

How Did the Republican Party Fail?

Despite controlling both houses of Congress for the past six of the Clinton administration's eight years, Republicans repeatedly watched the president evade the law. For much of the past eight years, though, this failure was not for lack of trying to summon outrage among the public. Indeed, it may be that their constant tone of outrage desensitized the public and prejudiced public opinion against them. Like the boy who cried wolf too often, their credibility was gone by the time the wolf had eaten the sheep. Thus, in contrast to the sins of the Democrats, which were ones of active collaboration and commission, the Republicans often—but not always—challenged the Clinton administration's lawlessness, at least until after the impeachment battle was over, when they essentially gave up.

Ineffective Challenges. Again and again, the Republicans' attempts to investigate the administration's wrongdoing were thwarted by partisan Democratic tactics and ineffectual Republican tactics. One example of the Republicans' failure was their inability to hold the administration accountable for its "systematic laundering of foreign money."[36] Thus, despite a Senate report identifying Chinese connections among six of the individuals investigated for campaign finance irregularities, the Department of Justice refused to appoint an independent counsel. Instead, Justice claimed that it would investigate on its own, but it initiated few prosecutions.[37] And when the violators were prosecuted, they were frequently let off with a slap on the wrist.

Republicans also failed to adequately challenge the invasions of privacy of individual Republicans. The State Department's personnel files of Bush administration employees were supposedly investigated "by mistake."[38] The president had no explanation for why the FBI files on hundreds of Republican appointees were sent to the White House.[39] The Privacy Act violation with respect to Linda Tripp could not have been clearer, but the offenders were let off with no more than a mild rebuke from Defense Secretary William Cohen.[40]

In fairness, Republicans, like everyone else, have been overwhelmed by the many times the Clinton administration obstructed attempts to investigate questionable activity. Even liberal *Wall Street Journal* writer Al Hunt, for example, described the First Lady's "stonewalling" about her Arkansas finances, and wrote that her "short interviews with the news magazines typified the 'modified limited hangout route'"[41] considered by President Nixon during Watergate. The news media even coined a new phrase: Clinton fatigue.

Executive privilege was repeatedly asserted (sometimes successfully, most often not) to avoid or stall inquiries about everything from Agriculture Secretary Espy's misdeeds[42] to the operation of the First Lady's Health Care Task Force[43] to the role of the Secret Service in facilitating the president's marital infidelity.[44] Yet Republicans repeatedly allowed Clinton administration witnesses to get away with the mantra, "I don't recall"—the same response that Watergate defendants gave to investigators 27 years ago, albeit unsuccessfully.[45] Indeed, FBI Director Louis Freeh implicitly compared this administration's stonewalling to the actions of La Cosa Nostra. When asked "if he's ever seen a case where so many witnesses fled the country or took the Fifth Amendment . . . . Mr. Freeh replied, 'I spent about sixteen years doing organized crime cases in New York City, and many people were frequently unavailable.'"[46]

Of course, it is up to the executive branch, not Congress, to enforce the law. And the Republican Congress's inability to hold Clinton accountable illustrates the difficulty of rooting out a corrupt executive under our system, especially if the president is willing to go to extraordinary lengths to cover up his misdeeds, such as suborning perjury. Still, congressional Republicans themselves must (and will) be held accountable because everything that took place was on their watch. Congress has an oversight role, and the Republicans, who controlled both houses of Congress, were supposed to exercise that oversight.

Plainly, the Republicans most egregious failure was their inability to convince the American people that their reasons for pressing impeachment were not partisan. However, in many ways, impeachment, to quote the *Weekly Standard*, was the Republicans' "finest hour."[47] One may criticize the tactics of those who take a principled position and lose, but one cannot assail their courage, morality, or commitment to principle.[48]

Republican Acquiescence. Far harder to understand are the many occasions the congressional Republicans allowed the administration to violate the law—indeed, to invade congressional prerogatives—without putting up much of a fight. To illustrate, the Republicans allowed the president to continue to grant preferences to minorities despite a Supreme Court holding that such preferences are unconstitutional.[49] Republicans also allowed the president to violate the treaty-making provisions of the Constitution through his unilateral continuance of the ABM treaty following the disintegration of the Soviet Union.[50]

Again, through his disregard for the Vacancies Act,[51] the president has repeatedly bypassed the Senate's constitutional role in confirming nominees.[52] The most glaring example of the president's actions in this regard was his appointment of Bill Lann Lee to head the Civil Rights Division of the Justice Department. Lee has held the post since December 1997, even though the Senate has never approved his appointment.[53] By law, Lee should have left his post after 120 days.[54]

More than a century ago, Congress anticipated the problem of vacancies in office and passed the Vacancies Act. As D.C. Circuit Judge Ray Randolph wrote, "from the beginning Congress limited how long the president's designee could serve."[55] President Clinton, however, has ignored that clear limitation, and Republicans have said little or nothing about it. In fact, Lee's appointment on an acting basis was praised by, among others, Senator Orrin Hatch,[56] chairman of the Senate Judiciary Committee. Despite the fact that Lee's tenure has now lasted eight times the statutory maximum, Congress has not yet demanded Mr. Lee's removal.

Congressional Republicans also failed to protect their own interests when they relied on the Supreme Court rather than fighting the Clinton administration on whether the use of statistical sampling in the census was constitutional, despite a textual requirement that there be an "actual Enumeration."[57] Later, the Supreme Court vindicated that principle by a vote of 5 to 4.[58] The Republicans' failure to fight on that issue is especially discouraging. For one thing, the future of the Republicans' control of the House is directly at stake in the battle. If the Clinton administration were allowed to manipulate the census figures as it proposed, the Republicans would almost certainly lose the House. One would not expect the Clinton administration to manipulate the figures to help the Republicans. Moreover, the Republicans have on their side a clear provision of the Constitution. Nonetheless, even on this political life-or-death issue, the Republicans ran from the fight.

In sum, the Republicans, through ineffectiveness or acquiescence, let through a great deal of lawlessness. The question is, why?

Examining the Causes of Failure: Why Did the Parties Lapse?

Why Did the Democrats Fail?

At least five reasons begin to explain the Democrats' support for the Clinton administration.

Party Loyalty. There is a story about a Chicago politician who, when asked about his support for a colleague's proposal, responded, "If he's right, I'll support him because he's right. If he's wrong, I'll support him because he's a Democrat." That story goes far toward explaining why the Democrats stood by Bill Clinton.

Partisanship. After three terms of Republican presidents, the Democrats were reluctant to reject one of their own. Also not to be underestimated was the Democrats' intense desire to prevent their opponents from winning. Often it seemed as if the Democrats were rallying behind Bill Clinton simply to deprive the Republicans of a victory. Thus, as the *Wall Street Journal* noted, the Democrats "allow[ed] the likes of Barney Frank, Maxine Waters and Hollywood weathervanes to make the party complicit in the Clinton strategy of contempt, obstruction and stonewall."[59]

Moderate Democrats nervous about retaining the president in office were quiet, and even those, such as Joseph Lieberman and Daniel Patrick Moynihan, who spoke against the president's misdeeds, ultimately fell in line. In the words of author Peggy Noonan, "[t]he Democrats in Congress now are like the young Chuck Colson, partisan, ruthless, and tough."[60] Rather than judge the guilt or innocence of the president, the impeachment trial was, as the *Wall Street Journal* put it, "a poll-driven jury nullification, with Senate Democrats in the role of the O. J. [Simpson] jury."[61]

Abortion. Still, the question is, why the unyielding support? I believe a key factor is that the Left was simply unwilling to abandon a pro-choice president. The attitude of Democrats was perhaps best summarized by former *Time* magazine correspondent Nina Burleigh, when she said that she would be happy to give Bill Clinton oral sex "just to thank him for keeping abortion legal."[62]

Sex über Alles. A variation on that explanation is the view associated with author David Frum and *National Review On-line* columnist Jonah Goldberg. They contend that the Democrats' intense defense of Clinton was due to their support for "the central dogma of the baby boomers: the belief that sex, so long as it's consensual, ought never to be subject to moral scrutiny at all."[63] Goldberg contended that, for "the cultural Left in the 1990s . . . [s]exuality has become the linchpin of human identity ."[64] David Frum noted that sexual freedom has been "the one issue on which [Clinton] has defied the polls and staked out a principled position regardless of political risk."[65]

Goldberg wrote that supporters of the president "cannot condemn him without condemning great chunks of their own lives; . . . if their man's actions are seriously wrong, then their own approximations of their man's actions might be adjudged wrong, too."[66] For liberals, Goldberg concluded, the solution has been to celebrate the president as "a sex-rights Rosa Parks."[67]

Thirst for Power. *Wall Street Journal* columnist Paul Gigot offered a different explanation for the Democrats' support of the president: the thirst for power. Henry Hyde, chairman of the House Judiciary Committee, agreed, saying that "[t]he attraction of power" was the reason Democrats never supported the impeachment inquiry. Gigot noted that the Democrats' "moral high-mindedness" had disappeared in the wake of Clinton. "In covering for Bill Clinton, the left has shown that what it really cares about now is power. Democrats have excused campaign-finance violations because 'everybody does it,' perjury because 'it's just about sex,' and trashing an individual civil-rights plaintiff because Mr. Clinton is good on civil-rights in general."[68]

Gigot added that the Democrats obstructed the impeachment "even as those same Democrats decried 'partisanship.' It's as if Pamela Anderson Lee denounced cosmetic surgery."[69] In pursuit of power, Democrats sold their souls to the interests of Bill Clinton.[70] Or, as the *New Republic* put it, Bill Clinton "turned the Democratic Party into his private political machine."[71]

Why Did the Republicans Fail?

Perhaps more perplexing is why the Republicans, in the majority, were unable to counter the repeated lawlessness of the Clinton administration. Many reasons account for the inability and the unwillingness of the Republican Party to successfully uphold the rule of law against Clinton's assault on it. Among the key factors are inexperience at congressional leadership, fear of losing control of Congress after having finally won it back, and sheer frustration at the overwhelming number of scandals and the public's evident weariness and toleration of them. After losing seats during the 1998 election and then losing the impeachment effort when the Senate failed to convict, congressional Republicans largely gave up the fight.

Gingrich and the Government Shutdown. The congressional elections in 1994 brought Republican majorities to both the House and the Senate for the first time since the Republicans lost the House in 1954. The resounding rejection of the Clinton health care plan and acceptance of the Republicans' "Contract with America" led the 104th Congress to conclude that the public would support them in conflicts with an administration that was even then mired in scandal.

But almost immediately after the first 100 days, a sense of "What do we do now?" began to pervade the Republican caucus. An iconoclastic Newt Gingrich turned out to be a historic deliverer but not an effective legislative tactician. Republican hubris after the 1994 election crested in December 1995 with the budget debacle and the government shutdown, for which the Republicans were blamed. Then, as Gigot put it, Republicans "internalized the Clinton critique of their own 'extremism' and have been wandering aimless and fearful ever since."[72] Failing to overcome the spin of Clinton and the press, the Republicans lost faith in their ability to rally the public against the administration.

Republicans also had a hard time finding leaders who were capable of successfully challenging the administration. In particular, according to Gigot, Gingrich's "lack of political focus" as House speaker led to "the worst of all possible politics: The appearance of doing too much while doing nothing at all."[73] Moreover, Gingrich was handicapped by his own background, by his inability to fight the reprimand and fine the House imposed for alleged financial irregularities, and by his own adulterous affair, which eventually became public.

Other Republicans, including Kenneth Starr, were too easily demonized by the administration. The Clinton administration "put the prosecutor on trial," an "assault on Mr. Starr [that] succeeded spectacularly."[74] Starr was even compared to Hitler.[75] Yet the too-courtly Starr, trained for the more formal processes of the law and hobbled by Judge Norma Holloway Johnson's constant efforts to plug alleged leaks, failed to fight back. And Republicans, sensing Starr's unpopularity, failed to defend him.

Inexperience of Congressional Republicans. The Republicans' inexperience in congressional leadership also cost them dearly. The Republican leadership lost control of the House to the moderates (probably out of fear that their slim majority would slip away in the next election). In the process, party discipline disappeared. The Republican Party embraced no agenda. In winning, it came to resemble Franklin Roosevelt's New Deal coalition: an amalgam of individuals with little in common.

Even so, had the Republicans picked a fight on principle instead of on matters initially related to the president's personal life, they might have been on more solid ground.[76] But Republicans failed to hold oversight hearings to expose the Clinton administration's misdeeds. The Republicans conducted no hearings like those of the Watergate Committee of 25 years ago. There were no effective hearings on the administration's repeated stonewalling of the Whitewater investigation or its use of the IRS to investigate conservative organizations. Moreover, apart from the highly successful hearings on the need for IRS reform (although not on the political abuse of the IRS), Republicans often seemed not to know how to conduct effective hearings.

Republicans would call hearings when they should not have done so.[77] They would allow Democrats to seize control of those hearings, often through superior staff work. Frequently, the Republican members would not even bother to show up at hearings. When they did, many were unprepared. A myriad of stories are told by Republican-friendly witnesses about going undefended after being attacked by Democrats.

In sum, Republicans often did not know how to wield the reins of power in the House and Senate. There were some notable exceptions of course, such as Senator Jon Kyl's brilliant outfoxing of the administration on the Comprehensive Test Ban Treaty. But Kyl's success only highlighted what might have been.

Republican Naïveté. Republicans were also often naïve. Take Senator Fred Thompson, chairman of the Senate Governmental Affairs Committee, a formidable talent with experience as a Watergate investigator. Thompson undertook hearings into the Chinese campaign contributions as if his Democratic colleagues were going to join him in an objective search for the truth. Unfortunately, despite his being an experienced Washington lawyer, a media favorite, and a Hollywood star, Thompson was repeatedly thwarted by the intensely partisan actions of Senator Glenn, among others. Like many other Republicans, Thompson failed to realize until it was too late that the Democratic Party had changed, and so had the times.

Repeated Republican Overreactions. Republicans also diminished their credibility by frequently overreacting to the Clinton administration. As is often said, Clinton was lucky in his enemies. Republican moralism led to tone deafness.

Almost from the start of his presidential campaign, Clinton's casual approach to morality and law infuriated the Republicans. Many of them could not understand why the public did not react the same way. The Republicans failed to communicate what they thought was so egregious about Bill Clinton. At the same time, many Clinton critics were constantly upset about one or another Clintonian outrage. Gradually, the public tuned out, and they could not be tuned back in again, no matter what Clinton did.

195

Republicans were simply too far ahead of public opinion. They never communicated to mainstream Americans why Bill Clinton's repeated violations of the law warranted removal from office. To paraphrase Bob Dole from the 1996 campaign, the Republicans never understood Americans' lack of outrage. Accordingly, by the time flagrant events occurred, such as the mysterious appearance of the Rose Law Firm billing records in the White House residence, Clinton's Republican critics had lost their ability to rally the public.

Fear of Risk. Having finally won back the House, the Republicans often seemed unwilling to risk losing it again by challenging the Clinton administration's lawlessness if it may have seemed politically incorrect to do so. Thus, congressional Republicans were unwilling to make an issue of the president's refusal to implement the *Adarand* decision barring affirmative action. (In fact, Republicans reauthorized clearly unconstitutional racial preferences, as in the transportation bill of 1998.[78]) The fear of seeming politically incorrect also explains the Republicans' failure to fight on the census, and their humiliating reversal on the attempt to cut off funding for the administration's baseless lawsuit against the tobacco companies.

Tactical Mistake in the Run-Up to Impeachment. Republicans may also have made an important tactical error in the run-up to the impeachment battle. Once the impeachment hearings began, it certainly seemed as if the Democrats were determined from the start to make impeachment a "food fight,"[79] destined to soil everyone alike. Early in the process, however, it did seem as if the Republicans might have been able to reach an agreement with House Democrats, some of whom felt pressured to do something about Clinton's overt violations of law. Such an agreement might have persuaded some Democrats to cooperate with the Republicans, and could have given the impeachment inquiry at least a semblance of bipartisanship.

Thus, when House Democrats pushed early on for a quick resolution to the impeachment proceedings, the Republicans could have and perhaps should have obliged. They might have lost the vote, of course. But a quick bipartisan vote for impeachment would have constituted a decisive rejection of the president's unlawfulness. Prolonging the proceedings did not make them more impartial. It paralyzed the government. And it enabled the Democrats to attack the Republicans from both sides. Democrats complained that the proceedings were unnecessarily long and that the president was being subjected to a "trial" without a record or witnesses on his behalf. Of course, that demonstrates how difficult it would have been for the Republicans to gain Democratic support for any disciplinary action, but early procedural concessions might have persuaded some Democrats to support impeachment.

There never was a true trial, of course. The main witness that the House Judiciary Committee called was Judge Kenneth Starr, the independent counsel. The House never did lay out the story in the words of the participants. A quarter of a century earlier, by contrast, the Senate Watergate Committee told the story over a seven-month period by having the participants themselves testify.

Losing Effective Control of the House. A six-seat majority in the House, which is what the Republicans currently hold, enables a party to elect a speaker, but little else—at least without strong party discipline. The Republicans never exercised such party discipline. Moderate and liberal Republicans, not the House leadership, called many of the shots.

Although the 104th and 106th Congresses accomplished some things, the 105th was more open to the charge of being a do-nothing Congress. One reason was its overreliance on the "six-year itch." Congressional Republicans thought that doing as little as possible would lead to a huge increase in Republican members, enabling them to work their will during the 106th Congress. Obviously, that was not to be. For the first time since the mid-1800s, the party of a president who had been in office for six years actually gained seats. Democratic House members ran better without the president than they had two years earlier when they relied on his coattails. The narrow majority in the 106th Congress, plus the failure to win the impeachment battle, has caused many Republicans to conclude that fighting the Clinton administration's lawlessness is futile.

Unfavorable Media. Republicans face obstacles to good public relations, to be sure, the principal one being an unfriendly media. As many have demonstrated, favorable publicity is harder to obtain when, "the viewpoints of most in the media coincide with those of dedicated, active liberals."[80] Not only do most reporters personally favor liberal positions, but this bias changes the impact of news stories.[81] "[A] journalist's approach to a story invariably reflects his opinions."[82] As a result, Democrats have "a band of journalists who

defend the president at practically every turn, who disparage virtually his every accuser, and who treat almost every criticism of his
administration as a threat to enlightened government,"[83] wrote Jay
Nordlinger in the *Weekly Standard*.

The reporters' natural inclination to favor Democrats is a function
in part of the differing ideologies of the two parties. Republicans
often push for government to do nothing or at least less, while
Democrats tout government activism. Such activism makes for sexy
stories involving new initiatives. By contrast, Republican calls for
private initiatives often sound like indifference to the plight of the
poor—hence, the wisdom, perhaps, of George W. Bush's emphasis
on "compassionate conservatism."

But the Clinton scandal raised the stakes to new levels. The media
loved it. It had interesting players. It was getting great audiences.
The media became key participants in the struggle. But they wanted
the story to have a happy ending. The *New York Times*'s Maureen
Dowd exemplified the reaction of the national press which, having
viciously attacked Bill Clinton, turned on Starr even more angrily
once impeachment and removal from office seemed possible.[84]

Prosperity. Even if Democrats had not been as united as they were
against the Republicans and impeachment, the country's economic
prosperity made impeachment more difficult. As Al Hunt, who
usually defended Clinton, admitted, "President Clinton's high public standing, even in the face of scandal, is a result of the booming
economy."[85] A number of Republicans were reluctant to rock the
boat and risk disrupting the economic growth the country was expe-
riencing. They did not want to be accused of attacking the person
who many in the public and the media credited for the prosperity,
even if the real authors of our recent prosperity were Ronald Reagan,
George Bush, and Alan Greenspan.[86]

The Public's Nonjudgmentalism. As Allan Bloom pointed out in *The
Closing of the American Mind*, the last "sin" remaining in American
public life is to judge another person's morality or behavior—particularly his sexual behavior. Bloom wrote about the indignant tone
with which the term "judgmental" is wielded today. American culture has become so coarse that many Americans seem to have been
more amused than disgusted by Clinton's sexual behavior.[87]

Those problems, which fed on each other, caused the Republicans
to descend into frustration and paralysis. Ultimately, they became

convinced that they could not beat this administration. The belief became a self-fulfilling prophecy, which was confirmed and compounded when Republicans valiantly tried, but failed, to "kill the king," so to speak.

After years of the Clinton administration's intransigence, which led to public apathy, Republican enthusiasm for enforcing the rule of law understandably dissipated. Even an idealistic political party cannot be expected to challenge a president when polls constantly show a majority of Americans supporting him and opposing his removal from office. Thus, the weary and cowed Republicans largely gave up, contenting themselves to the occasional outburst, which was inevitably dismissed by the Left as partisan.

Why This Is a Problem—Responsibilities of Parties

As the 2000 election approaches, the scandals of the Clinton years blend into one for the public, the media, and the Republicans, resulting in profound "scandal fatigue." Neither the Republicans nor anyone else can keep all of Clinton's offenses straight. The country, and particularly the political parties, have been "narcotized"[88] by the many scandals associated with this administration.[89]

That situation is unhealthy because one of the traditional functions of political parties in this country has been to defend the rule of law by elevating principle over person. Parties are supposed to articulate principles around which people can organize politically and rally to promote those principles. Healthy political parties are not controlled by, and do not serve the interests of, any one person. As we see in other nations, and have occasionally seen in our own, movements or institutions that rely too heavily on any one person are fraught with peril and inevitably face a crisis—at a minimum, when that individual passes from the scene. Parties should reflect principles, not personalities.

William Saletan, writing in the *New Republic*, recognized the threat Bill Clinton's dominance poses for the Democratic Party. Pleading for Democrats to adopt an agenda beyond preserving a Clinton "legacy," Saletan flogged "Clinton's narcissistic presidency" as risking his party's future.[90] "A Democratic Party synonymous with Clinton and Gore will be wiped out when Clinton and Gore meet a big problem they can't solve," he wrote, adding that the Democratic

Party will "die" unless it ceases to be Clinton's "private political machine."[91]

The idea that political parties are guardians of law may sound peculiar to political scientists like Anthony Downs, who conceived of parties simply as "loosely formed group[s] of men who cooperate chiefly in an effort to get some of their number elected to office."[92] Yet even if parties are viewed more narrowly—as providing the electorate with cues about how to vote (and party identification is still the most accurate vote-predicting mechanism available to political scientists[93])—they need an identity that transcends that of their individual members.

That conclusion is not new. In fact, Downs himself suggested that parties are properly viewed not as loose coalitions, but as "a team of men seeking to control the governing apparatus by gaining office."[94] When viewed in that way, the party represents at least some ideals, because "each member of the team has exactly the same goals as every other."[95] Party ideologies assist voters by helping them "make [their] voting decision[s] without knowing about every policy specifically."[96]

At approximately the same time that Downs was writing, political scientist E. E. Schattschneider chided the parties for not involving the public in politics. Schattschneider's solution was to have the parties take positions on issues so that voters could identify with a party.[97]

Unfortunately, that does not seem to have happened to any great extent. Indeed, modern "[p]olitical campaigns are largely candidate focused and candidate driven."[98] The failure of congressional Republicans and Democrats to bring Clinton to heel will likely cause the 2000 election to be a referendum on the policies and presidency of a man who is constitutionally barred from running in the election. The danger is not only that that distracts from the larger issues— and the principles at issue, in particular—but that it also threatens to destroy any semblance of identity the parties might claim. And a politics of personality is unhealthy for any nation.

Conclusion

The uncomfortable truth is that both parties failed to control President Clinton because, at bottom, the American people did not care enough to ensure that he be controlled. Votes were cast against the president and for the president, but it seems that too few voters cast their ballots for the valiant defenders of the Constitution.[99] In fact, Judge Starr's experience suggests that challenging a popular president, on principle, during a period of prosperity, may bring more condemnation than praise. With such incentives, it is little wonder that members of Congress would rather discuss anything but the Clinton administration's assault on the rule of law and the Constitution.

Notes

1. See Review & Outlook, "Espy's World," *Wall Street Journal*, October 5, 1994, reprinted in *Whitewater: The Impeachment and Trial of William Jefferson Clinton* 2 (1996): 16–17, noting that Espy argued that the act banning officials from taking gratuities from meat and poultry interests "didn't apply to him."

2. See generally Review & Outlook, "Who is Mochitar Riady?," *Wall Street Journal*, March 1, 1996, reprinted in *Whitewater: The Impeachment and Trial of William Jefferson Clinton* 2 (1996): 282–84.

3. See Review & Outlook, "Presumption of Rascality," *Wall Street Journal*, March 1, 1994, reprinted in *Whitewater: The Impeachment and Trial of William Jefferson Clinton* 1 (1994): 193, 194.

4. See Sharon Walsh, "Early Concerns Over O'Leary's Travel," *New York Times*, February 5, 1996, p. A19.

5. 520 U.S. 681 (1997).

6. Ms. Jones alleged, inter alia, an unconsented touching, that is, a battery.

7. See *Nixon v. Fitzgerald*, 457 U.S. 731 (1982).

8. Editorial, "Donor Maintenance," *Washington Post*, September 4, 1997, p. A18.

9. 5 U.S.C. § 552a.

10. See *Chamber of Commerce v. Reich*, 74 F.3d 1322 (D.C. Cir. 1996).

11. See, for example, Review & Outlook, "Second Term Stall," *Wall Street Journal*, February 11, 1997, reprinted in *Whitewater: The Impeachment and Trial of William Jefferson Clinton* 3 (1997): 307, 310, noting that "normally thoughtful Democrats such as Senator Glenn" should not support "partisan defensiveness."

12. See generally "HHS Official Resigns in Protest of Decision to Sign Welfare Bill," *Washington Post*, August 18, 1996, p. A18.

13. Deputy Attorney General Philip B. Heymann resigned amid conflicts within the administration, but he did not resign in protest; his resignation letter cited differences in "operational and management styles." Ana Puga, "Reno Deputy Resigns, Cites Poor 'Chemistry,' " *Boston Globe*, January 28, 1994, p. 1.

14. See, for example, Richard Cohen, "Who Is Bill Clinton?" *Denver Post*, March 2, 1999, p. B-7.

15. See, for example, Nat Hentoff, "Just Between You, Your Doctor, and the Police," *Washington Post*, November 1, 1997, p. A21, opining that "civil liberties are of no apparent interest to the Clinton administration."

16. See Nadine Strossen, "A.C.L.U. on Privacy," Letters to the Editor, *New York Times*, July 11, 1996, p. A22.

17. Anthony Lewis, "Abroad at Home; Clinton's Sorriest Record," *New York Times*, October 14, 1996, p. A17.

18. Nat Hentoff, "First in Damage to Constitutional Liberties," *Washington Post*, November 16, 1996, p. A25 (emphasis added).

19. Ibid.

20. Floyd Abrams, "Clinton vs. the First Amendment," *New York Times*, March 30, 1997, sec. 6, p. 42.

21. Ibid.

22. John Heilemann, "Big Brother Bill," *Wired* (October 1996), at ⟨http://www.wired.com/wired/archive/4.10/netizen_pr.html⟩, visited July 13, 2000.

23. Ibid.

24. Ibid.

25. See, for example, *Whitewater: The Impeachment and Trial of William Jefferson Clinton* 5 (1999): 2, noting that Democrats thought impeachment too harsh for a "private mistake."

26. Susan Baer, "President Vows to Stay 'Until the Last Hour,'" *Baltimore Sun*, December 20, 1998, p. 1A.

27. See, for example, "Donor Maintenance," 8, noting that the facts of Vice President Gore's fund-raising scandal do not support Attorney General Reno's reasons for not appointing an independent counsel; Editorial, "Mr. Freeh's Truth Grenade," *New York Times*, December 3, 1997, p. A34, noting Attorney General Reno's "persistent blindness to the conflict of interest this case [1996 White House fund-raising] presents to her and the Justice Department."

28. See Review & Outlook, "Try Again," *Wall Street Journal*, March 6, 1998, reprinted in *Whitewater: The Impeachment and Trial of William Jefferson Clinton* 4 (1998): 283, 285. See also, for example, Review & Outlook, "Clinton's Charlie Horse," *Wall Street Journal*, October 27, 1997, reprinted in *Whitewater: The Impeachment and Trial of William Jefferson Clinton* 4 (1998): 86–88.

29. Review & Outlook, "Democrats and Coverups," *Wall Street Journal*, May 12, 1998, reprinted in *Whitewater: The Impeachment and Trial of William Jefferson Clinton* 4 (1998): 383, 384–85.

30. See Chapter 11 of this volume, "Politicizing the Justice Department," by Theodore B. Olson.

31. See Byron York, "Restoring Justice," *National Review*, June 5, 2000, p. 43.

32. Ibid.

33. Henry Ruth, "Clinton Has Corrupted His Party's Soul," *Wall Street Journal*, December 8, 1998, reprinted in *Whitewater: The Impeachment and Trial of William Jefferson Clinton* 5 (1999): 194, 195.

34. Jerome M. Zeifman, "To Save the Party, Democrats Must Vote to Impeach," *Wall Street Journal*, October 6, 1998, reprinted in *Whitewater: The Impeachment and Trial of William Jefferson Clinton* 5 (1999): 70, 70–72.

35. Ruth, 5:198.

36. Robert Dole, "The Election Was Decided by Early 1996," *Wall Street Journal*, January 15, 1998, reprinted in *Whitewater: The Impeachment and Trial of William Jefferson Clinton* 4 (1998): 177, 182.

37. See Review & Outlook, "Try Again", 4:283.

38. Review & Outlook, "Honest Mistake No. 99," *Wall Street Journal*, June 12, 1996, reprinted in *Whitewater: The Impeachment and Trial of William Jefferson Clinton* 2 (1996): 398, 399.

39. Ibid., 2:398.

40. See Robert L. Jackson, "Pentagon Officials Violated Tripp's Privacy, Report Says," *Los Angeles Times*, May 26, 2000, p. A11.

41. Albert R. Hunt, "Whitewater and the Battle of Stalingrad," *Wall Street Journal*, March 17, 1994, reprinted in *Whitewater: The Impeachment and Trial of William Jefferson Clinton* 1 (1994): 266, 266–67, accord William S. Cohen, "Bunker Mentality," *Wall Street Journal*, March 11, 1994, reprinted in *Whitewater: The Impeachment and Trial of William Jefferson Clinton* 1 (1994): 233.

42. See *In re: Sealed Case*, 121 F.3d 729 (D.C. Cir. 1997).

43. See *Association of American Physicians and Surgeons v. Clinton*, 997 F.2d 898 (D.C. Cir. 1993).

44. See Katharine Q. Seelyes, "The Presidency Has Its Privileges," *New York Times*, September 19, 1999, sec. 4, p. 3.

45. See Tom Shales, "Watergate Redux," *Washington Post*, June 17, 1982, p. D1.

46. Review & Outlook, "Demonizing Starr," *Wall Street Journal*, November 19, 1998, reprinted in *Whitewater: The Impeachment and Trial of William Jefferson Clinton* 5 (1999): 151, 153.

47. William Kristol and Robert Kagan, "The Senate Republicans' Finest Hour," *Weekly Standard*, October 25, 1999, p. 11.

48. That can be said of House Republicans, not of Senate Republicans. See especially the account of David Shippers, *Sell Out: The Inside Story of President Clinton's Impeachment* (Regnery Publishing, Inc., Washington, DC, 2000).

49. See *Adarand Constructors, Inc. v. Peña*, 515 U.S. 200 (1995).

50. See Troy, "Lip Service," *National Review*, August 3, 1998, p. 34.

51. 5 U.S.C. §§ 3345–3349.

52. See U.S. Constitution, Art. II, § 2, stating that the president "shall nominate, and by and with the Advice and Consent of the Senate, shall appoint Ambassadors, other public Ministers and Consuls, Judges of the supreme Court, and all other Officers of the United States."

53. See John F. Harris and Helen Dewar, "President Bypasses Congress, Appoints Lee on 'Acting' Basis," *Washington Post*, December 16, 1997, p. A1.

54. See 5 U.S.C. § 3348; "Clinton Justice Appointment Was Violation, Agency Says," *New York Times*, January 18, 1998, pp. 1–23. Cf. *Doolin Security Savings Bank, F.S.B. v. Office of Thrift Supervision*, 139 F.3d 203, 208 (1998), stating that the 120-day limit on making recess appointments runs during the tenure of a temporary appointee.

55. See *Doolin*, at 210.

56. See Harris and Dewar, "President Bypasses Congress."

57. U.S. Constitution, Art. I, § 2.

58. See *Department of Commerce v. United States House of Representatives*, 525 U.S. 316 (1999).

59. Review & Outlook, "The Democrats String Along," *Wall Street Journal*, December 2, 1998, reprinted in *Whitewater: The Impeachment and Trial of William Jefferson Clinton* 5 (1999): 175, 176.

60. Peggy Noonan, "The Good Guys Finally Won," *Wall Street Journal*, December 21, 1998, reprinted in *Whitewater: The Impeachment and Trial of William Jefferson Clinton* 5 (1999): 251, 253.

61. Review & Outlook, "Faust's Democrats," *Wall Street Journal*, February 11, 1999, reprinted in *Whitewater: The Impeachment and Trial of William Jefferson Clinton* 5 (1999):

385, 387; see also David Tell, "Jury Nullification in the Senate," *Weekly Standard*, January 25, 1999, p. 7.

62. See Valley and State, "Writer won't apologize for remark about Clinton," *Arizona Republic*, July 16, 1998, p. B6.

63. David Frum, "A Generation on Trial," *Weekly Standard*, February 16, 1998, p. 19.

64. Jonah Goldberg, "Who Is Really 'Obsessed by Sex'?" *National Review*, November 23, 1998.

65. Frum, "Generation on Trial."

66. Ibid.

67. Goldberg, "Obsessed by Sex."

68. Paul A. Gigot, "Clinton Wins, If You Call This Winning," *Wall Street Journal*, February 5, 1999, reprinted in *Whitewater: The Impeachment and Trial of William Jefferson Clinton* 5 (1999) 365, 366.

69. Paul A. Gigot, "Hyde on His Mistakes—and Ours," *Wall Street Journal*, February 12, 1999, reprinted in *Whitewater: The Impeachment and Trial of William Jefferson Clinton* 5 (1999): 394, 395.

70. See David Tell, "Our Parties and Our President," *Weekly Standard*, December 28, 1998, p. 7.

71. William Saletan, "Party of One," *New Republic*, April 3, 2000, p. 18.

72. Gigot, "Clinton Wins," 5:367.

73. Ibid., 5:134.

74. Review & Outlook, "Demonizing Starr," 5:151, 153.

75. See Review & Outlook, "Dumpster Politics," *Wall Street Journal*, March 6, 1998, reprinted in *Whitewater: The Impeachment and Trial of William Jefferson Clinton* 4 (1998): 286, 286.

76. See generally Troy, "Lip Service."

77. See generally Daniel E. Troy, "The GOP's Hearing Loss," *American Spectator*, November 1999, p. 34.

78. *Congressional Record* 144:51,481–96 (1998). Five Republicans voted for the bill, which was enough to tip the balance. See "Senate Refuses to End Set-Asides in Awarding Highway Contracts," *St. Louis Post Dispatch*, March 7, 1998, p. 2.

79. Paul A. Gigot, "Hillary's Advice: Impeachment Has Its Uses," *Wall Street Journal*, September 11, 1998 reprinted in *Whitewater: The Impeachment and Trial of William Jefferson Clinton* 4 (1998): 531, 533.

80. L. Brent Bozell III and Brent H. Baker, *And That's the Way It Is(n't): A Reference Guide to Media Bias* (Media Research Center: Alexandria, VA, 1990), p. 53.

81. See generally L. Brent Bozell III, "How About a Media Culpa?," *Wall Street Journal*, August 20, 1998, reprinted in *Whitewater: The Impeachment and Trial of William Jefferson Clinton* 5 (1999): 9.

82. Bozell and Baker, *And That's the Way It Is(n't)*, p. 1. Bozell and Baker grant that media bias may not be "a conscious attempt to distort the news. [Instead, i]t stems from the fact that most members of the media elite have little contact with conservatives and make little effort to understand the conservative viewpoint." Ibid., p. 3.

83. Jay Nordlinger, "Clinton's Courtier Press," *Weekly Standard*, April 6, 1998, p. 26.

84. Compare, for example, Maureen Dowd, "1,000 Points of Lust," *New York Times*, April 8, 1998, p. A19, with Maureen Dowd, "Lighten Up, Baby!" *New York Times*, June 13, 1999, sec. 4, p. 17.

85. Albert R. Hunt, "The Clinton Legacy That Could Have Been," *Wall Street Journal*, December 3, 1998, reprinted in *Whitewater: The Impeachment and Trial of William Jefferson Clinton* 5 (1999): 183, 184.

86. See Richard W. Stevenson, "Inside the Head of the Fed," *New York Times*, November 15, 1998, sec. 3, p. 1 ("Mr. Clinton's place in history will owe much to Mr. Greenspan's stewardship of the economy over the last six years and how well the economy holds up over the next two. Some would argue, in fact, that Mr. Clinton's political survival this year was due in large part to the contentment that the prosperous Greenspan era has induced in the electorate."); see generally Gretchen Morgenson, "Hail to the Fed Chief (for Now, at Least)," *New York Times*, January 5, 2000, p. C1.

87. Goldberg, "Obsessed by Sex."

88. Telephone conversation with David Tell, opinion editor of the *Weekly Standard*, June 20, 2000, Washington, D.C.

89. David Frum similarly notes that "[t]he Clinton scandals long ago exhausted our capacity for astonishment," in "A Generation on Trial."

90. Saletan, "Party of One."

91. Ibid.

92. Anthony Downs, *An Economic Theory of Democracy* (Harper: New York, 1957), p. 25.

93. See Abramson, Aldrich, and Rhode, *Change and Continuity in the 1996 Election* (Congressional Quarterly Press: Washington, DC, 1997).

94. Downs, *Economic Theory of Democracy*, p. 25 (emphasis added).

95. Ibid.

96. Ibid., p. 113.

97. See generally E. E. Schattschneider, *The Semisovereign People: A Realist's View of Democracy in America* (Holt, Rinehart and Winston: New York, 1960).

98. *Nixon v. Shrink Missouri Government PAC*, 120 S. Ct. 897, 919–20 (2000) (Thomas, J., dissenting). See, for example, Samuel Kernell, *Going Public: New Strategies of Presidential Leadership*, 3d ed. (Congressional Quarterly Press: Washington, DC, 1997).

99. The 1974 election is illustrative in this respect. The Democrats picked up gains because of the country's disgust with Richard Nixon. Nobody suggests that the public was so pleased with Senator Sam Ervin and his cronies that they rewarded them with Democratic votes.

14. The Bar and the Legal Academy
Ronald D. Rotunda

It is common for liberal columnists to criticize Republican presidents and for conservative columnists to criticize Democratic presidents. That complaining and carping is part of the political landscape. With President Clinton, however, things are different: liberal columnists have included this Democratic administration among their targets. Until I began this essay I did not fully appreciate what has happened during Mr. Clinton's tenure because the organized bar and the legal academy, where my attention has been largely focused, have been relatively less vocal in their disapproval.

Yet if the rule of law is at issue in so much of what the Clinton administration has done, as others in this volume have argued, that relative silence is no small matter. Where have the guardians of the rule of law been?

As for the columnists, consider, for example, liberal Nat Hentoff's comments a year into Mr. Clinton's second term. He charged that "civil liberties are of no apparent interest to the Clinton Administration." To make sure that no one misunderstood his assessment, he added, "The president has eroded habeas corpus, among other civil liberties. Is there no limit to his disdain for the Constitution?"[1] That kind of denunciation is not often hurled at any president, Republican or Democrat, particularly when the organized bar, representing practicing lawyers, and the academy, representing law professors, have been relatively silent in criticizing the administration's civil liberties record. One would think that those interested professionally in preserving the rule of law would be concerned that a series of independent counsel and the president's own Department of Justice have been quite active in investigating this president, his vice president, and many of his cabinet officials.

Here is another columnist to the same effect:

> He [Vice President Gore] was part of the team that sold access and demeaned the White House in an unseemly

money chase. And, in reading the recently released interview
with the Justice official, his pathetic description of the White
House coffees—they were shakedowns, pure and simple—
underscores what a pernicious system this is.[2]

Lest you think I am repeating a scolding from a dyed-in-the-wool
Clinton-hater, note that I have just quoted from liberal icon Al Hunt,
a vocal and consistent supporter of the Clinton administration. In
his article he was *praising* Janet Reno and *defending* her decision not to
appoint a special counsel to investigate what Hunt calls "campaign
finance irregularities." Yes, that is what Clinton *supporters* say in
justifying the administration.

The Scandals

The Clinton years have witnessed a long series of administration
scandals. To catalogue them is well beyond the scope of this essay.
Instead, I will briefly review the responses of the legal academy and
the organized bar to some of the more important issues. That job is
a lot easier because the general response of both has typically been
silence—when it has not been support.

The Office of Independent Counsel

When Janet Reno was first appointed attorney general she went
to court several times to seek judicial appointment of independent
counsel to investigate the president and several of his cabinet members. Later, however, when it appeared that her job might be in
jeopardy,[3] she seemed never to be able to find enough evidence to
justify appointment of additional counsel.[4]

If there is one constant during the Clinton years, it is that the
president, his wife, and many of his closest supporters have never
shied from public attacks on the bona fides of their critics, especially
Independent Counsel Kenneth Starr, the one chosen to investigate
the president himself. In Starr's case, they have constantly accused
his Office of Independent Counsel (OIC) of illegal leaking, partisanship, and abuse of prosecutorial powers. The charges have not held
up in court,[5] but that has not prevented them from being made,
repeated, and repeated again.

It is unusual for a high government official who is the subject of
an investigation to attack the bona fides of the counsel appointed
to conduct the investigation. For example, neither Attorney General

Edwin Meese nor his personal attorney ever attacked the people investigating him, even though the independent counsel was a member of the other political party. In fact, it has been typical for the independent counsel to be a member of the opposing political party.[6]

Attorney General Reno has responded to the president's attacks on Judge Starr in an unusual way. If she had actually believed that Judge Starr ever acted unethically she could simply have fired him, because the law makes clear that the attorney general may terminate the independent counsel for cause. Instead, at various times she went to court to *expand* the OIC's jurisdiction (even over Judge Starr's objection)[7] to include Travelgate, Filegate, and the Monica Lewinsky perjury scandal.[8]

When the president, her boss, attacked Judge Starr, Ms. Reno did not defend Starr. If she thought that the OIC or any of its attorneys were acting improperly in investigating President Clinton, she should have fired him, not expanded his jurisdiction.

By contrast, consider the March 1998 statement by a bipartisan group of former attorneys general, written to rebut the attacks on the integrity of the independent counsel. Although it received little media attention at the time, the statement was extraordinary. It said, in part:

> As former attorneys general, we are concerned that the severity of the attacks on Independent Counsel Kenneth Starr and his office by high government officials and attorneys representing their particular interests, among others, appear to have the improper purpose of influencing and impeding an ongoing criminal investigation and intimidating possible jurors, witnesses and even investigators. We believe it is significant that Mr. Starr's investigative mandate has been sanctioned by the Attorney General of the United States and the Special Division of the United States Court of Appeals for the District of Columbia.
>
> Further, Mr. Starr is effectively prevented from defending himself and his staff because of the legal requirements of confidentiality and the practical limitations necessitated by the ongoing investigations.
>
> As former attorneys general, we know Mr. Starr to be an individual of the highest personal and professional integrity. As a judge on the United States Court of Appeals for the District of Columbia and Solicitor General of the United

States, he exhibited exemplary judgment and commitment to the highest ethical standards and the rule of law.

We believe any independent counsel, including Mr. Starr, should be allowed to carry out his or her duties without harassment by government officials and members of the bar.[9]

The former attorneys general released that statement shortly after the *New York Times* had reported President Clinton's plan to frustrate the investigation of him: "One White House official was blunt about the strategy, calling the coordinated hostilities 'part of our continuing campaign to destroy Ken Starr.'"[10] And what was Janet Reno's response? The sound of silence, complete and utter silence. She said nothing to defend the person to whom she kept sending more business.

Joining her silence, however, were the American Bar Association (ABA) and the established bar in general. One wonders, would Attorney General Elliot Richardson and the ABA have sat in silence if President Nixon had announced a continuing campaign to destroy Archibald Cox?

The legal academy, however, was not silent. Instead, many law professors joined in the attacks on Judge Starr.[11] The contrast was thus striking: former attorneys general defended Judge Starr; the current attorney general was silent, as was the bar; the legal academy attacked him. What did law professors know that four former U.S. attorneys general of both parties did not know?

The Impeachment Debate

I now turn briefly to the time when the House and Senate were considering impeaching the president, given his apparent misrepresentations under oath before Judge Susan Webber Wright in a civil case and before a grand jury.[12] Many of the president's supporters, particularly in academia, argued that the president really did not perjure himself and that the Lewinsky scandal was just about sex. (For the record, the impeachment referral and the House impeachment focused on repeated perjuries, witness tampering, suborning, and obstruction of justice, not sex.)[13]

The ABA, as one prominent ABA-watcher noted, "has uttered not a single syllable of criticism of the president—who is, after all, a lawyer—for repeatedly lying under oath, hiding evidence, coaching witnesses, and sitting in rapt and approving silence while his lawyer misled a federal judge."[14] Recall that President Clinton's own lawyer described the president's testimony under oath as "evasive, incomplete, misleading—even maddening."[15] That lawyer was *defending* the president.

Unlike the ABA, the legal academy was more than silent: for the most part, it sided vocally with the president and claimed that it was inappropriate to impeach a government official for "private perjury," although Congress, only a few years earlier, had removed a federal judge for "private perjury."[16] In fact, some 430 law professors signed an open letter to the Speaker of the House claiming that *even if* the president violated federal criminal law and committed perjury, that should not lead to his impeachment.[17] One law professor trumpeted, correctly but tendentiously, that there was "widespread agreement among scholars that even if President Clinton has committed acts that are impeachable offenses, the House has discretion to choose not to impeach him."[18] Even impeachable offenses, these academicians argued, do not merit impeachment. Perjury, in their view, is just not that important, although it is a crime that shields all other criminal acts from public scrutiny. Those 430 law professors joined 400 historians in supporting the president.

Academia did not speak with one voice of course. It seldom does. In response, nearly 100 academicians and former government officials took the opposing view, warning that this president "has taken great pains and used government resources, including White House personnel and the Secret Service, to see that the laws are not faithfully executed."[19] Nonetheless, a clear majority of the academic community opposed impeachment, even if the crimes committed were impeachable. Academicians who seldom cherished the intent of the Framers—referring to them often as "dead white males"—now professed to be very interested in their intent, which they claimed supported their views.[20]

The role of the ABA with respect to the very existence of the independent counsel law speaks volumes. For a quarter of a century the ABA had supported the independent counsel law. The ABA supported the law when it was used to investigate President Reagan, to investigate Attorney General Meese, and to investigate President Bush. In early 1999, however, at the ABA mid-year meeting, just after the law had been used to investigate President Clinton, the ABA did an about-face, urging Congress not to reenact the law "in any form."[21]

The ABA Honorees

During the summer of 1999, Judge Susan Webber Wright held the president in contempt of court because of "the clarity with which his falsehoods are revealed by the record. . . ."[22] Shortly after that the ABA honored President Clinton by asking him to address its annual convention.

Even the *Washington Post*, often sympathetic to Clinton, called the ABA's decision "an odd choice."[23] The *Post* did not mince words: "inviting a perjurer to speak to a professional association of attorneys is a move that could not be better calculated to entrench the larger public's contempt for lawyers as people who twist the truth for selfish ends."[24] The *Post* relied on Judge Wright's opinion that found that the president lied under oath.[25]

The ABA also invited former Associate Attorney General Webster Hubbell to grace its annual convention. As the ABA noted in one of its publications, Mr. Hubbell earlier had pled guilty and had spent 18 months in prison for defrauding his law partners.[26]

At least President Clinton is a lawyer and Webster Hubbell is a disbarred lawyer. One cannot say that of Susan McDougal, a convicted felon, who spoke at the ABA's July 2000 annual convention in New York City. Ms. McDougal joined other ABA speakers, including Supreme Court Justices Ruth Bader Ginsburg, Stephen Breyer, and John Paul Stevens, and Secretary of State Madeleine Albright.

The ABA issued this press release regarding Ms. McDougal:

> *Luncheon with Susan McDougal*—Join the ABA Criminal Justice Section's Committee on Women in Criminal Justice for a special luncheon presentation featuring Whitewater defendant Susan McDougal. Ms. McDougal is noted for her involvement with the Whitewater prosecution conducted by Independent Counsel Kenneth Starr, and was incarcerated for her refusal to testify before the Whitewater grad [sic] jury. Since her release, Ms. McDougal dedicated herself to issues concerning incarcerated women. Luncheon tickets are $35 per person.

Note the expression "noted for her involvement with the Whitewater prosecution." One might say that Professor Archibald Cox was "noted for his involvement in the Watergate prosecution." Professor Cox was involved as a prosecutor, however, not as a felon. Ms. McDougal was not just "involved." She is a convicted defendant who served prison time. Her peers on an Arkansas jury found her guilty of crimes related to the Whitewater scandal. Later, a federal judge found her in contempt of court. She is not a lawyer, not even a disbarred one. Why did the ABA honor her with an invitation to speak? Should the Securities and Exchange Commission or the Business Law Section of the ABA invite Ivan Boesky or Michael Milken to address its staff?[27]

How did Ms. McDougal enlighten the ABA? In her remarks she attacked the grand jury system: "There is *no redeeming value to the grand jury system* because a prosecutor with no honor will turn the system to his benefit."[28] Then she attacked the prosecutor: "I went to jail because Starr was the most dishonorable and despicable person I had ever seen in my life."[29] She forgot to mention the jury, which found her guilty, and the judge, who found her in contempt.

The ABA could have had a different perspective if it had invited the man whom President Clinton appointed to head the FBI. When Judge Starr left his position as independent counsel, FBI Director Louis Freeh wrote to Starr, saying that he and his colleagues at the FBI "have been continuously impressed with your integrity and professionalism. You have always respected the truth and have never engaged in any misleading or evasive conduct or practice."[30]

After Judge Wright held the president in contempt, Mr. Clinton did not appeal or otherwise contest the contempt order, and he paid the $90,686 fine she had assessed. But Judge Wright also referred the matter to the Arkansas Supreme Court's Committee on Professional Conduct for review and for any action it deemed appropriate. Subsequently, the Arkansas Supreme Court ordered the state's Professional Conduct Committee to look into the matter.[31] The committee recommended that the president be disbarred for "lying under oath before a federal judge in a sexual-harassment lawsuit deposition and obstructing justice."[32] The matter now awaits trial.

The question of a sitting president's disbarment—President Nixon was disbarred, but that was after he resigned the presidency—has given rise to commentary in the press by legal ethics academicians. The academic commentary is divided. Alan Dershowitz of Harvard thinks it "preposterous" that the disciplinary prosecutor seeks to hold against the president the fact that he failed to challenge Judge Wright's 1999 contempt charge, did not appeal it, and paid the $90,000 fine without challenge. "I've never heard of such a situation where such an order would become res judicata. Even if he did lie for purposes of contempt, [President Clinton's lawyers] can argue that the criteria for disbarment are different."[33] Others argue that the disciplinary prosecutor has developed a strong case.[34]

The Arkansas bar has proposed to disbar President Clinton for his misrepresentations, under oath, and that case is now in the state courts. What I find particularly interesting is the reaction of the ABA to the proposed legal discipline of the president. Various people have written on the disbarment issue, and at least one of them, a Mr. David M. Bresnahan, cited the *ABA Standards for Imposing Lawyer Sanctions*.[35] WorldNetDaily, an Internet newspaper that published that article, described Mr. Bresnahan as "an investigative journalist for WorldNetDaily.com." Mr. Bresnahan's article was titled, *Should Clinton be barred? ABA guidelines say president should lose law license*.[36] Although the ABA standards do support the argument for permanent disbarment, the ABA promptly dissociated itself from the article in which Mr. Bresnahan quoted from the ABA standards. The ABA quickly responded that, although

> *these quotes may be accurate*, he makes it appear as if the Arkansas Committee on Professional Conduct and the Arkansas Supreme Court are required to apply the Standards. Such is not the case. The Arkansas Supreme Court has not adopted the ABA Sanctions Standards, which are simply a theoretical framework to assist jurisdictions in ensuring consistency in the imposition of disciplinary sanctions. The Arkansas Supreme Court *has adopted criteria* to be used for determining sanctions that are *similar to the framework provided in the ABA Standards*, but it has not adopted the ABA Standards as a whole.[37]

Note that there is no claim that the quotations from the ABA standards are incorrect. It even turns out that Arkansas has adopted standards "similar to" the ABA recommended framework. One can debate what amount of discipline would be appropriate, but that is not the point. Rather, the ABA was very swift to distance itself from an article that *correctly* quoted the ABA standards and concluded that they recommended disbarment—a conclusion that the ABA does not claim is unreasonable or unfair.[38] I do not suggest that the ABA seek blood or be vindictive regarding the president's legal problems. No one can or should take pleasure at another's misfortune. But the established bar, in contrast to its role regarding President Nixon's bar problems a quarter of a century ago, now seeks to emphasize its noninvolvement.

Beyond the Scandals

I turn now from the scandals that have marked the Clinton administration to a few more conventional legal matters. Here too the bar and the legal academy could have risen to defend the rule of law, but they failed to do so, or failed to do so with sufficient force to address the matter. And here too we are left with the question, who will defend the rule of law if those most directly involved with the law will not?

Death Penalty

President Clinton has long supported the death penalty. As governor he sent people to their deaths. Now, his administration has raised the question of whether some defendants on death row are innocent. The president is right to propose DNA testing to protect those who may have been wrongly convicted. If capital punishment is to deter future murders, it can do so only if the system convicts guilty people. Yet DNA testing was not invented yesterday.[39] Where have the president and the Justice Department been during the last eight years?

One of President Clinton's last acts as governor was to sign the death warrant for a mentally retarded, African-American defendant with the mind of a five-year-old. The man probably did not understand that the state of Arkansas was about to execute him. He chose pecan pie for his last meal and then asked the prison guards to save him a slice so he could eat it later, *after* his execution. For over 1,000 years it has been the common law rule that the state should not execute the mentally retarded. With this execution, however, the legal academy was silent. There were "[n]o panels of Ivy League law professors with Alan Dershowitz screaming for due process."[40]

Although federal law authorizes capital punishment, the federal government has not imposed the death penalty in nearly 40 years. On August 5, 2000, a federal inmate was scheduled to be executed, but his lawyers applied for clemency, and President Clinton stayed the execution until December 12, 2000.[41] Hence, the president will not decide on clemency until *after* the November presidential election.[42] For those who might conclude that the president has a political motive,[43] the White House response is to blame the Justice Department, asserting that it had failed to complete the new clemency procedures in time. However, the Justice Department insists that "the draft procedures were sent to the White House this past spring but weren't taken up by the White House lawyers until last month."[44] Whom should one believe? One would think that the bar, which has opposed the death penalty, would raise questions if it appeared that the president was playing politics with the condemned on death row, but it has raised no objection.

Free Speech

The Clinton administration's string of defeats in the free speech area is remarkable. In 1996, in *Denver Area Educational Telecommunications Consortium, Inc. v. FCC*,[45] the Supreme Court declared unconstitutional two sections of the Cable Television Consumer Protection and Competition Act of 1992. Congress overrode President Bush's veto of that legislation, but President Clinton supported the law and his solicitor general unsuccessfully defended it before the Supreme Court. Then in *Reno v. ACLU*,[46] the Court also invalidated crucial sections of the Communications Decency Act of 1996, another law that the administration supported. Here the Court said, broadly, that the First Amendment protects cyberspace just as it protects physical space.

The effort to restrict the Internet is a matter of special concern to me. I have worked with several of the emerging democracies of the former Soviet Union. The Internet is a tool that allows anyone to distribute what any Communist would call "insidious democratic propaganda." The word "insidious" is apt: it means "menacing" or "threatening." Information about democracy is always threatening to dictators. In fact, information in general is threatening to dictators, which is why photocopy machines in the U.S.S.R. were often kept behind locked doors.

In *Greater New Orleans Broadcast Association v. United States*,[47] the Clinton Justice Department defended a federal law that prevented radio and television stations from advertising private casino gambling, stations that were located in a state in which such gambling is legal. Thus, the law forbid the communication of truthful information in an effort to affect, mold, and change the actions of those

216

who heard the information. The Court invalidated that attack on commercial free speech. As Justice Thomas noted in his opinion concurring in the judgment, the government should not be able "to keep legal users of a product or service ignorant in order to manipulate their choices in the marketplace."

In *United States v. Playboy Entertainment Group, Inc.,*[48] the Court invalidated section 505 of the Telecommunications Act of 1996, another law that the Clinton administration embraced and defended. The law provides that cable television operators offering channels "primarily dedicated to sexually-oriented programming" must "fully scramble or otherwise fully block" those channels or must limit their transmission to hours when children are unlikely to be viewing.[49] As the Court put it, "for two-thirds of the day no household in those service areas could receive the programming, whether or not the household or the viewer wanted to do so." And the Court went on to note that the empirical evidence showed that parents did not appear to be all that interested in the purported protections the law afforded.[50]

Given the importance of the First Amendment in our legal system, one would expect to find substantial opposition to the efforts just listed. For had those efforts succeeded, our speech rights would have been increasingly diminished. To be sure, the ACLU was there to speak up. But one searches in vain to find substantial, much less sustained, opposition from the organized bar. Here again, it is as if this administration gets a free ride, even when it goes after our most fundamental principles.

Privacy and the Fourth Amendment

Flash back to the spring of 1994, during the first term of the Clinton presidency: the Chicago Housing Authority responded to gang violence by conducting warrantless searches of entire apartment buildings. Those searches were called "sweeps" because of their thoroughness: closets, desks, dressers, kitchen cabinets, and personal effects were examined even if the police had no probable cause to suspect particular tenants of any criminal wrongdoing. Police searched some apartments when the residents were not at home. Plaintiffs sued and a federal judge ruled that the "sweeps" violated the Fourth Amendment as applied to the states through the Fourteenth Amendment. The federal judge enjoined further sweeps.[51]

In response, President Clinton ordered Attorney General Reno to find a way to allow such sweeps. Within one month, he presented a proposal. The White House plan would require tenants, as a condition of being allowed in federally subsidized public housing, to sign leases with a clause whereby the tenants agree to searches that do not comply with the mandate of the Fourth Amendment. President Clinton said,

> There are many rights that our laws and our Constitution guarantee to every citizen, but victims have certain rights that we are letting slip away. They include the right to go out to the playground, and the right to sit by an open window, the right to walk to the corner without fear of gunfire, the right to go to school safely in the morning and the right to celebrate your 10th birthday without coming home to bloodshed and terror.[52]

Acting Associate Attorney General Bill Bryson said, "I think that there certainly are circumstances in which it is legitimate to have in the lease a provision . . . which would allow for administrative inspection for firearms."[53] Attorney General Janet Reno added her support, along with Housing Secretary Henry Cisneros.[54] One way to protect the residents is to supply an adequate number of police to patrol and protect. Perhaps another way, the unconstitutional way, is to ignore the Fourth Amendment.

The constitutional issue should not have been difficult. A federal court had already held that such sweeps, executed without search warrants or probable cause, were blatant violations of the Fourth Amendment.[55] Seven years earlier, the Supreme Court had held that Congress could not constitutionally use its spending power to cause a citizen to give up his constitutional rights.[56]

Organizations like the ACLU and the NRA opposed President Clinton's proposal.[57] Although some academicians also opposed it,[58] others claimed it might be constitutional.[59] A Westlaw search of newspapers and the media shows that the organized bar was silent. There was no official protest of this proposed violation of the privacy rights of the poorest of Americans.

If President Clinton, a former law professor, and Attorney General Reno are correct, why stop with the Fourth Amendment? Could the government require housing tenants to waive their rights against self-incrimination under the Fifth Amendment, or their right to a jury trial in a criminal case? Could the government force its contracting parties to waive their rights of free speech? The right against cruel and unusual punishment? In none of those cases is there any true "waiver," because a waiver is a voluntary relinquishment of a known right. Here, the government is conditioning benefits on the recipients' giving up constitutional rights.[60]

The proposal finally died on its own, but the effort to undercut important privacy protections would not die an only child. Health and Human Services Secretary Donna Shalala later informed Congress that proposed new federal regulations to protect medical records would exempt law enforcement from the tougher privacy standards. Law enforcement personnel could search through those records without a warrant and without a patient's permission or knowledge. As Nat Hentoff said, "under the Clinton-Shalala approach to shredding privacy, any intelligence agent can order a health care provider—and anyone who pays for health care—to hand over confidential health records. All the agent has to say is that the records are 'needed for a lawful purpose.'"[61]

More recently, privacy groups have objected to Federal Communications Commission proposals that would impose new requirements on telecommunications companies. The new rules would require cellular companies to supply to the FBI, without a warrant, the location of cellular phone users, any digits dialed such as credit card numbers, and "packet-mode communications," which contain both the phone numbers involved in the call and the voice content of the phone calls.[62] One's cell phone would also serve as a tracking device for the government.

In July 2000, the FBI, in an effort to monitor e-mails, disclosed a new software program dubbed "Carnivore," so named because it can search millions of e-mails per second to get at the meat of what it really wants. Carnivore analyzes every snippet of data traffic to determine if it should record the data for the police. Said a former computer-crimes prosecutor, "It's the electronic equivalent of listening to everyone's phone calls to see if it's the phone call you should be monitoring."[63] The FBI secures a search warrant before using Carnivore, but the search warrant is served on the Internet service provider (ISP), not the person whose e-mail is the subject of the wiretap. In at least one instance, the ISP had to install older software on its system because its updated software was not compatible with

Carnivore. That, in turn, led to a crash of the system, which knocked out access to some of the ISP's customers.[64]

The response of Attorney General Reno? She said that she did not know about Carnivore until it was in the newspapers. "FBI officials were shocked" to learn that, the *Wall Street Journal* reported, because the "FBI's cyber-technology section briefed Reno aides and top Justice Department officials more than a year ago, before the program began."[65] If her denials are true, it leads one to wonder who really is in charge of the Justice Department.

Shortly after Ms. Reno protested her ignorance, the White House proposed legislation making it easier for the Justice Department to eavesdrop on e-mail and other Internet communications. For example, the proposed law would allow the FBI to seek a search warrant two days *after* it had received Internet data and traced transmission. First would come the search; then the warrant.[66]

Here again one finds little opposition from the bar or the legal academy. As with the scandals, one wants to know, where is the outrage?

The English Language and the Clinton Presidency

English was not my parents' native tongue, which may be why they taught me the importance of learning and respecting the language. I thought that I understood English, but I find that even a dictionary will not help me understand the new English.

We know that the president uses words in a way that ordinary people do not always understand. Recall that during his grand jury testimony he debated the definition of "is." Whatever causes such verbal machinations must be akin to a virus that is airborne, for it has affected others in the administration. Attorney General Reno, for example, has defended her decision not to follow her own regulations and appoint a special counsel to investigate Vice President Gore's alleged fund-raising irregularities by claiming that the fund-raising scheme was not a "conspiracy"; instead, it was more a "loose enterprise."[67]

Justice Department lawyers recently examined Gore about alleged campaign financing violations. In the course of questioning Gore, Robert J. Conrad, head of the Justice Department task force investigating 1996 fund-raising abuses, noted that Gore had previously described the His Lai Temple event both as "community outreach" and as a "political event" with "financing people" present. Mr. Conrad then asked, "Having said those two fairly different things, knowing that you are under oath today, can you tell me what you knew about the His Lai Temple event and when you knew it?" The vice president's response,

> *You* expressed the opinion earlier that community outreach and finance-related are two very different things. That is *your* opinion. That is not necessarily a fact.[68]

The legal academy has done more than merely go along with such verbal machinations. It basks in them. The academic community has been the hotbed of political correctness and speech codes, even after courts have invalidated such codes following student challenges.[69]

For its part, the organized bar has sought to make lawyers subject to legal discipline for uttering politically incorrect speech. Under ABA rules, enacted during the Clinton years, if two lawyers are representing a client and discussing tax policy, and one says "We should reform welfare because some of its recipients are lazy," he has violated the ABA rules because he has manifested "by words" an indication of bias on the basis of socioeconomic status. If the other lawyer responds, "You're just saying that because you are a short, fat, hillbilly, neo-Nazi," he is in the clear because those epithets are not part of the forbidden litany.[70]

Conclusion

During the Clinton presidency, in the face of sustained assaults on elementary principles central to the rule of law, the organized bar and the legal academy have generally been more quiescent than active, more sluggish than energetic. Despite the need to be vigilant in the face of such assaults, no matter who is president, the bar and the academy have been largely silent. And it is not as if we were not warned about this president. One is reminded of the evaluation of the Reverend Jesse Jackson, who said of the president in 1992, "I can maybe work with him but I know now who he is, what he is. There is nothing this man won't do. He is immune to shame. Move past all the nice posturing and get really down in there in him, you find absolutely nothing . . . nothing but an appetite."[71] Not even the frank assessment of Senator Bob Kerrey, a member of the president's own party, stirred the bar or the academy: "Clinton's an unusually good liar. Unusually good."[72]

Why were even some Democratic politicians vocal in criticizing their president while the bar and the legal academy were silent? Professor Susan Estrich of the University of Southern California Law School offers one answer. Legal journalist Stuart Taylor asked her if she was conceding that her position and the views of other feminists were inconsistent insofar as they supported Anita Hill's claims against Justice Clarence Thomas but opposed Paula Jones' claims against President Clinton. Her candid response—"You believe in principle, I believe in politics."[73]

Notes

1. Nat Hentoff, "Just Between You, Your Doctor, and the Police," *Washington Post*, November 1, 1997, p. A21, accessed on 1997 Westlaw 14710457.

2. Albert R. Hunt, "Janet Reno: Narrow and Naïve, but Honest," *Wall Street Journal*, June 29, 2000, p. A27, col. 6. A few days before this column appeared, we learned that Robert J. Conrad Jr., the head of the Department of Justice task force investigating the 1996 fundraising scandals, urged Attorney General Reno to appoint an outside investigator to consider whether Vice President Gore was untruthful in answering questions from Justice Department officials. His recommendation followed the earlier, similar recommendations of Charles LaBella, another Justice Department official, and Louis J. Freeh, the FBI Director. Charles Babington and George Lardner Jr., "Gore Issues Fund Probe Transcript," *Washington Post*, June 24, 2000, p. A1, col. 6.

LaBella wrote: "The contortions the [Department of Justice] has gone through to avoid investigating these allegations are apparent." George Lardner Jr., "Memos: Reno Was Warned: Freeh, Others Saw Conflict in Campaign Probe," *Washington Post*, June 7, 2000, p. A1, col. 1.

3. See, for example, "FBI Memo Quotes Justice Official on Campaign Probe 'Pressure,'" *Washington Post*, May 19, 2000, p. A9, accessed on 2000 Westlaw 1960756; George Lardner Jr., "Public Integrity Chief, GOP Clash on Probes; Use of Independent Counsel Law at Issue," *Washington Post*, May 25, 2000, p. A35, accessed on 2000 Westlaw 19610919. ("Confronted with a December 9, 1996, memo by FBI Director Louis J. Freeh, quoting Freeh's top deputy, [Lee] Radek [head of the Justice Department's Public Integrity Section] denied that he would ever have said that he and his unit were under a lot of pressure 'because the attorney general's job might hang in the balance (or words to that effect).' At the same time, he said he had no recollection of the conversation.") Editorial, "Truth and Consequences," *Wall Street Journal*, May 24, 2000, p. A26, accessed on 2000 Westlaw-WSJ 3030485.

4. *Morrison v. Olson*, 487 U.S. 654, 108 S. Ct. 2597, 101 L.Ed.2d 569 (1988), discussed below, made it quite clear that the attorney general's decision not to seek the appointment of an independent counsel is *not* reviewable in any court.

5. See, for example, *In re Sealed Cases No. 98-3077*, 151 F.3d 1059 (D.C Cir. 1998); *In re Sealed Case No. 99-3091*, 192 F.3d 995 (D.C. Cir. 1999).

6. Former Solicitor General Archibald Cox, for example, who first investigated President Nixon, was an active Democrat.

7. See, for example, "The Borking of Starr," *Wall Street Journal*, March 11, 1998, p. A20, accessed on 1998 Westlaw-WSJ 3485801; Government Press Releases by Federal Document Clearing House, March 19, 1998, accessed on 1998 Westlaw 7322335, "Radanovich Urges Reno to Support Starr."

8. Yet the attorney general has *refused* to appoint an independent counsel in several serious matters relating to allegations of campaign finance illegalities, even when the director of the FBI has urged her to appoint an independent counsel. At other times she has objected to any expansion of the counsel's jurisdiction, even when the courts have eventually ruled that her position was legally in error. See, for example, Terry Eastland, "How Justice Tried to Stop Smaltz," *Wall Street Journal*, December 22, 1997, p. A19, cols. 3–6.

Although the White House has often complained that the Justice Department should not have assigned the Lewinsky perjury scandal to Judge Starr, Janet Reno has never suggested that she should not have assigned that case to him. Instead, she has, once again, been silent.

9. Reprinted in, for example, "Let Starr Do His Job," *Wall Street Journal*, March 11, 1998, p. A20, accessed on 1998 Westlaw-WSJ 3485802. See also, "Starr Power: Former Attorneys General Bemoan Smear Campaign," *Telegram & Gazette* (Worcester, Mass.), March 15, 1998, p. C1, accessed on 1998 Westlaw 2728164. Griffin B. Bell served President Jimmy Carter; Edwin Meese III was appointed by President Ronald Reagan; Richard L. Thornburg worked for both Reagan and President George Bush, and William P. Barr served in the Bush administration.

10. Don Van Natta Jr., "White House's All-Out Attack on Starr Is Paying Off, with His Help," *New York Times*, March 2, 1998, sec. A, p. 12, col. 1.

11. See, for example, Deborah L. Rhode, "Conflicts of Commitment: Legal Ethics in the Impeachment Context," *Stanford Law Review* 52 (2000): 269. Professor Rhode, who teaches at Stanford Law School, was senior counsel for the Democratic members of the House Judiciary Committee during the impeachment proceedings involving President Clinton. As she attacks the independent counsel and others, she admits that her "[p]ersonal involvement in a partisan proceeding inevitably shapes perceptions." Ibid., 271.

Consider also another example of an academician who was quick to come to the aid of the president and to attack those on the other side. In June 1998, an administrator at Pace University posted this message on an ethics list serve, an electronic bulletin board that was widely circulated to academicians:

> For those who are interested in a highly scholarly, balanced, more-in-sorrow-than-in-anger, presentation of (a) evidence that significant leaking has occurred from Judge Starr's office; (b) evidence that he has failed to adequately investigate and police this conduct; and (c) an analysis of the ethical implications of (a) and (b), you might want to contact Prof. Ron Noble of NYU Law School (another colleague of Judge Starr) and ask for a copy of the paper he delivered recently at the Philip Blank Memorial Lecture on Professional Ethics at Pace Law School. Prof. Noble, former Chief of Staff in the Crim. Div. of DOJ and Undersecretary at Treasury for Enforcement, presented a cogent, quite compelling lecture that included a lot of information I have not heard elsewhere. The paper will be published this fall in the *Pace Law Review*.

However, the paper was not published in the fall of 1998. Nearly a year later, an August 3, 1999, e-mail from the Pace Associate Dean for Clinical Education (sent in response to my query) confirmed that the article will never be published. Although those comments will never be officially published, and thus will never be documented, they were widely distributed as "true" and "objective."

On June 10, 1998, I mailed Professor Noble a letter that quoted the posted message and said,

> I would like very much to have a copy of your paper. If Associate Dean Merton's summary of what you said is correct, you have made a very serious charge.
>
> I happen to be a special consultant to the Office of Independent Counsel and I know that various people have claimed that our office has engaged in leaking but all of the judges who have examined the issue have found no leaking from our office. Of course, that does not stop people from making claims that are not based on fact.
>
> Perhaps you know something that the judges supervising the grand juries do not know.
>
> Thank you very much. I look forward to your reply.

Letter of June 10, 1998, on file with the author. I sent that letter to Professor Noble yet again on August 4, 1999, over a year later. I still have not received a reply. Clearly, it is easier to make serious charges than to document them.

12. See, for example, *Jones v. Clinton*, 36 F.Supp.2d 1118 (E.D. Ark. 1999), holding the president in contempt for misrepresentations, under oath, in his civil deposition. He subsequently paid a fine of more than $90,000. *Arkansas Democrat-Gazette*, July 30, 1999, p. 1.

13. Judge Wright repeatedly came to that conclusion in her contempt decision, a ruling President Clinton did not appeal. She said,

> [T]he record demonstrates by clear and convincing evidence that the President responded to plaintiff's questions by giving false, misleading and evasive answers that were designed to obstruct the judicial process.

Jones v. Clinton, 36 F.Supp.2d 1118, 1127 (E.D.Ark. 1999). Ibid. at 1131: "[I]t simply is not acceptable to employ deceptions and falsehoods in an attempt to obstruct the judicial process. . . ."

Judge Richard Posner's book, *An Affair of State* (1999), offers "scathing criticism of virtually all participants in the drama." George Priest, "Trial by Senate," *Wall Street Journal*, September 14, 1999, p. A20, accessed on 1999 Westlaw-WSJ 24913620 (reviewing book). Judge Posner concludes that "Clinton's violations of federal criminal law . . . were felonious, numerous, and nontechnical." Judge Posner came to the decision that the president was guilty of repeated perjuries, witness tampering, suborning, and obstruction of justice.

14. Theodore B. Olson, "The Law Liberals Finally Learned to Hate," *Wall Street Journal*, February 24, 1999, p. A18, accessed on 1999 Westlaw 5441966.

15. David Rogers and Glenn R. Simpson, "White House Memo Makes Case for Clinton," *Wall Street Journal*, December 9, 1998, p. A3, accessed on 1998 Westlaw-WSJ 18995067. Clinton's lawyer went on to argue that the president's assertions were not perjurious because people who heard him "knew what was meant."

16. The most recent example is that of Judge Walter L. Nixon Jr., whom the House impeached and the Senate removed because he lied, under oath, about asking a local district attorney (a state official) not to prosecute a businessman's son. *Nixon v. United States*, 506 U.S. 224 (1993). Note that the federal judge had no power over that state official; the federal judge was not convicted for "abusing" his office; and his lie did not occur in his capacity as a federal judge but in his capacity as a witness.

17. Laurie Kellman, "400 Scholars Dismiss Clinton Impeachment Case," *Washington Post*, November 7, 1998, p. A3, accessed on 1998 Westlaw 22534048. See, for example, ibid., "'There's nothing official about his misconduct,' University of Texas law professor Douglas Laycock said."

18. Professor Susan Low Bloch, Letter to the Editor, *Washington Post*, November 22, 1998, p. C6, accessed on 1998 Westlaw 22536608.

19. "Don't Let the President Lie with Impunity," *Wall Street Journal*, December 10, 1998, p. A22, accessed on 1998 Westlaw-WSJ 18995174.

20. Many members of the academic community supported President Clinton in his successful effort in the Senate to avoid removal from office after the House impeached him. We know that the Senate has removed judges from office because of perjury having nothing to do with their judicial functions. Yet some academicians argued that the House should not impeach a president for private conduct, such as cheating on taxes. One argument, by University of Chicago law professor Cass R. Sunstein, is especially noteworthy: Assume that the "President murders someone simply because he does not like him. There is no political motivation; the dispute is entirely personal. This is a hard case [in which to justify impeachment] under the analysis thus far." Nor did it become easier to justify impeachment after his further analysis. Cass R. Sunstein, "Impeaching the President," *University of Pennsylvania Law Review* 147 (1998): 279, 313.

21. See, for example, Theodore B. Olson, "The Law Liberals Finally Learned to Hate."

22. *Jones v. Clinton*, 36 F.Supp.2d 1118, 1130 (E.D. Ark. 1999) (footnote omitted).

23. Editorial, "Mr. Clinton and the ABA," *Washington Post*, August 11, 1999, p. A18, accessed on 1999 Westlaw 23297444, noting, "President Clinton's own lawyer described his testimony as 'evasive, incomplete, misleading, even maddening.' Is that the sort of respect for court proceedings that the ABA wishes to encourage in its membership?"

24. Editorial, "Mr. Clinton and the ABA."

25. Judge Wright said, "There is no need to engage in an extended analysis of the President's sworn statements in this lawsuit. Simply put, the President's deposition testimony regarding whether he had ever been alone with Ms. Lewinsky was intentionally false, and his statements regarding whether he had ever engaged in sexual relations with Ms. Lewinsky likewise were intentionally false, notwithstanding tortured definitions and interpretations of the term 'sexual relations.'" *Jones v. Clinton*, 36 F.Supp.2d 1118, 1130 (footnote omitted) (E.D. Ark. 1999). The judge also ruled that the "President's testimony at his deposition that Ms. Lewinsky's denial in her affidavit of a 'sexual relationship' between them was 'absolutely true' likewise was 'misleading and not true.'" Ibid.

26. See, for example, Nat Hentoff, "What About Ethics?" *Washington Post*, August 21, 1999, p. A19, accessed on 1999 Westlaw 23299164, quoting from ABA reference and noting that President Clinton was "honored" to be the ABA keynote speaker.

27. Michael Hill, "Business Students Get Ethics Lesson at Prison; MBA Candidates Must Visit Convicts to Receive Degrees," *Baltimore Sun*, May 9, 2000, p. 1B. In this case, MBA students visited the prison to meet white-collar criminals and "hear cautionary tales of what can happen if they take their degrees and run in the wrong direction." That was not the purpose of Ms. McDougal's speech to the ABA.

28. Speech of July 7, 2000, New York City (emphasis added).

29. Speech of July 7, 2000, New York City.

30. Letter from Louis J. Freeh, Director of the FBI, to Kenneth W. Starr, October 19, 1999.

31. *Hogue v. Neal*, 340 Ark. 250, 12 S.W.3d 186 (2000) (per curiam), holding that the executive director of the Arkansas Supreme Court Professional Conduct Committee and the committee had a "mandatory duty" to process the professional misconduct complaints against President Clinton.

32. Michael Rowett, "Ethics Experts' Views Differ on Clinton Case," *Arkansas Democrat-Gazette*, June 11, 2000, p. A1. This story noted, "A review by the *Arkansas Democrat-Gazette* of the committee's 33 other disbarment complaints since 1990 showed that 23 of them include allegations of violating the same two rules cited in Clinton's case."

33. David E. Rovella, "Clinton Has New Nemesis: Bar Prosecutor's Case for Disbarment Has Worrisome Strength," *National Law Journal*, July 17, 2000, pp. A1, A7, quoting Dershowitz.

34. Ibid.

35. Those *Standards* are reprinted in Ronald D. Rotunda, *Legal Ethics: The Lawyer's Deskbook on Professional Responsibility* (St. Paul: ABA, West Group, 2000), pp. 961–1042.

36. The article appeared on April 27, 2000, in *WorldNetDaily*; available at ⟨http://www.worldnetdaily.com/bluesky_bresnahan/20000427_xnbre_should_cli.shtml⟩. I could not find the article, or anything else on *WorldNetDaily*, after an extensive computerized search of the news media using Westlaw or Lexis. However, I did find the article by searching the World Wide Web. The ABA disclaimer that follows in the text probably served to give the article more attention than it otherwise would have received.

37. ABA Center for Professional Responsibility, *Center Membership News*, vol. 5, no. 4 July 2000, p. 4 (emphasis added).

38. The ABA was anxious to emphasize that the ABA has not "expressed an opinion as to how the President's case should be resolved." Ibid. The standards provide, for example, that disbarment is appropriate if the lawyer "knowingly violates a court order," "with the intent to obtain a benefit for the lawyer or another . . . and causes . . . potentially serious interference with a legal proceeding." Standard 6.21. Standard 6.11 also recommends disbarment if the lawyer "makes a false statement" or "submits a false document" (the Lewinsky affidavit), and causes "potentially serious injury" or "potentially adverse effect on the legal proceeding." Factors that aggravate and "may justify an increase in the degree of discipline" include "dishonesty or selfish motive," a "refusal to acknowledge wrongful nature of conduct." In their filings before the Arkansas discipline committee, the president and his lawyers insisted that he testified "truthfully" (even if his answers were misleading). The president has "substantial experience in the practice of law" [he is a former law professor, former attorney general of Arkansas, and a former practicing lawyer]. Standard 9.22(b),(g), and (i).

39. DNA testing has been used during the last decade. Since 1994, pretrial DNA testing has become "commonplace." Laurie P. Cohen, "Reasonable Doubt: Someone Who's Guilty Would Never Want DNA Testing, Right?" *Wall Street Journal*, July 12, 2000, pp. A1, col. 1, and A12, col. 1. The president was surely familiar with DNA testing before his recent statements supporting it; after all, the FBI used DNA testing to connect the president to Ms. Lewinsky.

40. Patrick H. Caddell and Marc Cooper, "The Death of Liberal Outrage," *Wall Street Journal*, December 23, 1998, p. A14, 1998 Westlaw-WSJ 18996658. Patrick Caddell was a pollster and strategist in the presidential campaigns of George McGovern, Jimmy Carter, Gary Hart, and Walter Mondale. Marc Cooper is contributing editor of *The Nation*. They explained the legal academy's silence as an effort to get a Democratic president elected after 12 years of Republican presidents.

41. "What's New," *Wall Street Journal*, August 3, 2000, p. A1, accessed on 2000 Westlaw-WSJ 3038982.

42. "President Clinton yesterday delayed a federal execution scheduled for Saturday by at least four months, giving attorneys for a Texas murder convict more time to argue for clemency and postponing a potentially troublesome political issue for Vice President Gore until after the November election." David A. Vise, "Clinton Delays Execution under New Clemency Rules," *Washington Post*, August 3, 2000, p. A2, accessed on 2000 Westlaw 19622332.

43. The political timing was so obvious that the *Washington Post* titled one article, "Clinton Halts Execution until Federal Clemency Policy Is Set; Delay Could Ease Potential Campaign Dilemma for Gore," by Charles Babington and Bill Miller, *Washington Post*, July 8, 2000, p. A02, accessed on 2000 Westlaw 19618345.

44. David S. Cloud, "President Is Likely to Decide Clemency Case after Election," *Wall Street Journal*, July 10, 2000, p. A6, accessed on 2000 Westlaw-WSJ 3035775.

45. 518 U.S. 727, 116 S. Ct. 2374, 135 L.Ed.2d 888 (1996).

46. 521 U.S. 844, 117 S. Ct. 2329, 138 L.Ed.2d 874 (1997).

47. 119 S. Ct. 1923 (1999).

48. 120 S. Ct. 1878 (2000).

49. Administrative regulation set these hours between 10 p.m. and 6 a.m.

50. The administration also lost important cases in the lower courts. See Timothy Lynch, "Dereliction of Duty: The Constitutional Record of President Clinton," *Capital University Law Review* 27 (1999): 783, 786–97; Floyd Abrams, "Clinton vs. The First Amendment," *New York Times Magazine*, April 27, 1997, p. 10. At the same time, the administration had some First Amendment victories. In *National Endowment for the Arts v. Finley*, 525 U.S. 569, 118 S. Ct. 2168, 141 L.Ed.2d 500 (1998), for example, the Supreme Court upheld a law enacted in 1990, but only after reading the law in a way that avoided the constitutional issue and interpreting it to be almost meaningless. Still, the point is not to count administration victories. It is to illustrate that the bar was essentially uninvolved in opposing Clinton administration legislation that the courts held in violation of the First Amendment.

51. *Pratt v. Chicago Housing Authority*, 848 F.Supp. 792 (N.D. Ill. 1994).

52. Quoted in Kevin G. Salwen, "White House Allows Searches without Warrants in Public Housing," *Wall Street Journal*, April 18, 1994, p. A16.

53. Ibid.

54. Jean Christensen, "Police Sweeps: Should Wrongs Take a Right? Public Housing Security Begs Debate," *Minneapolis-St. Paul Star-Tribune*, April 30, 1994, p. A4, accessed on 1994 Westlaw 8454417.

55. *Pratt v. Chicago Housing Authority*, 848 F.Supp. 792 (N.D. Ill. 1994), granting a preliminary injunction and holding that tenants in the Chicago Housing Authority were likely to succeed on their claim that a policy authorizing nonconsensual searches violated the Fourth Amendment.

56. *South Dakota v. Dole*, 483 U.S. 203, 107 S. Ct. 2793, 97 L.Ed.2d 171 (1987).

57. See, for example, A. M. Rosenthal, "Seeking Domestic Tranquility," *New Orleans Times/Picayune*, April 22, 1994, p. B7, accessed on 1994 Westlaw 3580704.

58. See, for example, Susan N. Heman, "Come Out with Your Rights Up!" *Newsday*, April 20, 1994, p. A36, accessed on 1994 Westlaw 7433149 (op-ed by professor opposing the president's proposal).

59. Michael Briggs, "Cisneros Sets 10-Day Goal for Sweep Plan," *Chicago Sun-Times*, April 9, 1994, p. 3, accessed on 1994 Westlaw 5562736: "Albert Alschuler, a University of Chicago Law School professor, said that one way the Clinton administration might overcome constitutional problems with sweeps would be to suggest that housing authorities reserve in leases the power to conduct unannounced sweeps of apartments."

60. Marianne Means, "Slick Willie Finds the Constitution an Inconvenience," *Seattle Post-Intelligencer*, April 22, 1994, p. A14, accessed on 1994 Westlaw 6119510.

61. Nat Hentoff, "Just between You, Your Doctor, and the Police."

62. Pete Yost, AP Wire, "Coalition Says FCC Rules Invasive; Privacy Groups, Industry: Limit Data Sent to FBI," *Cincinnati Enquirer*, May 20, 2000, p. A3, accessed on 2000 Westlaw 10082327; *Associated Press Wire Service*, May 19, 2000, accessed on 2000 Westlaw 20910474

63. Neil King Jr. and Ted Bridis, "FBI's Wiretaps to Scan E-Mail Spark Concern," *Wall Street Journal*, July 11, 2000, pp. A3, A6, col. 3, quoting Mark Rasch. See also Nick Wingfield and Don Clark, "Internet Companies Decry FBI's E-Mail Wiretap Plan," *Wall Street Journal*, July 12, 2000, p. B11A; Nick Wingfield, "ACLU Asks Details on FBI's New Plan to Monitor the Web," *Wall Street Journal*, July 17, 2000, p. B7, cols. 4–6.

64. Nick Wingfield, Ted Bridis, and Neil King Jr., "EarthLink Says It Won't Install Device for FBI," *Wall Street Journal*, July 14, 2000, p. A16, col. 4.

65. "Washington Wire, Untapped Source," *Wall Street Journal*, July 14, 2000, p. A1, col. 5.

66. Ted Bridis, "Updating of Wiretap Law for E-Mail Age Is Urged by the Clinton Administration," *Wall Street Journal*, July 18, 2000, p. A3, cols. 1–2.

67. *Wall Street Journal*, June 28, 2000, p. A1, col. 3; Pete Yost, AP, "Reno Defends Position on Fund-Raising Issue; Independent Counsel to Investigate Gore Not Needed, She Says," *Charleston Gazette & Daily Mail*, June 28, 2000, accessed on 2000 Westlaw 2615084.

68. Excerpts from Vice President Gore's Justice Department Interview, *Washington Post*, June 24, 2000, p. A6, col. 5 (emphasis added).

69. See, for example, Robert Sedler, "The Unconstitutionality of Campus Bans on 'Racist Speech': The View from Without and Within," *University of Pittsburgh Law Review* 53 (1992): 631.

70. In 1995, despite First Amendment objections, the ABA narrowly passed a resolution "condemning discrimination in the practice of law 'by words or conduct' on the basis of race, sex, socioeconomic status and other categories." Francine Schwadel and Amy Stevens, "Legal Beat," *Wall Street Journal*, August 10, 1995, p. B7, accessed on 1995 Westlaw-WSJ 9895572. In 1998, the ABA added that prohibition to its Rules

of Professional Conduct. *ABA Model Rules of Professional Conduct*, Rule 8.4, Comment 2. *ABA Center for Professional Responsibility, Annotated Rules of Professional Conduct*, 4th ed. (Chicago: ABA, 1998): 584.

71. Quoted in, for example, A. M. Rosenthal, "On My Mind: The Three Questions," *New York Times*, September 18, 1998, sec. A, p. 29, col. 6.

72. Martha Sherril, "Grave Doubts" (Sen. Bob Kerrey Interview), *Esquire* 125, no. 1 (January 1996): 86.

73. Originally published in *Slate Magazine*, an on-line publication, and repeated, for example, in, Editorial, *The Detroit News*, January 18, 1997, p. C14, accessed on 1997 Westlaw 5575950.

15. The Media and the Cultural Institutions

David Horowitz

The question before us is whether the guardians of the law have failed to defend the rule of law during the Clinton presidency. More specifically, the question before me is whether the media and cultural institutions, which would normally be expected to help defend the rule of law, have failed. I will limit the focus of that question to the events surrounding the impeachment of the president. Obviously, there will always be individuals and sometimes even democratic majorities who fail to respect or defend the rule of law. The betrayal of the democratic order by the people itself is always a possibility, of course, and the Founders were keenly aware of the paradox that the sovereign people might be a threat to their own rights. That is the rationale behind the constitutional framework. The system of checks and balances inherit in the separation and division of powers is intended to respond to and counter that threat.

In addition to the checks that are built into constitutional government, however, voluntary associations such as political parties, colleges and universities, the media, and religious and cultural organizations have a responsibility to help preserve and protect the system of government that ensures the freedom in which they function. That is simply part of the eternal vigilance that is the price of freedom. How did those institutions acquit themselves in the main crisis associated with the Clinton presidency?

Let me preface my answer with the candid observation that many of those institutions have suffered an appalling decline over the last four decades. They have been systematically subverted by an anti-democratic, anti-American Left whose clear purpose is the destruction of the framework designed by America's Founders. The war on "European" America, on the American heritage, and on the American legal system is now four decades old and its battles have inflicted incalculable damage on the moral and legal fiber of this

231

nation. Our once liberal universities have been thoroughly politicized and intellectually debased by the authoritarian Left during those years. In the impeachment proceedings, many played a despicable, partisan role. As for the Democratic Party, since 1972 it has been similarly suborned. During impeachment, it failed to produce even a handful of statesmen who were ready to rise above party, whose efforts might have spared the nation its year-long ordeal.

The Clinton presidency has been a devastating experience for the nation's institutions and the mental health of its people. Not all of the damage was ideologically motivated, although ideologues most certainly made it possible. To the long-term political offensive was added the contingent fact of a chief executive whose personal problems and criminal irresponsibility have been the cause of much of the damage. But that was damage inflicted out of the passions of self rather than from any political or ideological agenda as such.

I have been asked to address the question of how and why the media and the cultural institutions failed to defend the moral and political principles that constitute the rule of law underpinning the nation. In truth, I have to say that I believe that at least some of those institutions acquitted themselves, if not admirably, then as well as one has a right to expect, given that they are inevitably political institutions as well. In particular, as best as we can tell, every facet of the president's sordid misdoings was eventually reported in the national media. Moreover, 119 newspapers and press institutions, including such sympathetic organs as the *New York Times*, the *Los Angeles Times*, and the *Washington Post*, did call for Clinton's resignation. Hollywood, which off screen was Clinton's cheering squad and principal base of "moral" support, produced on screen such implicitly anti-Clinton parables as *Air Force One* and *Independence Day*, in which men of honor and courage occupied the presidential office. Hollywood was also responsible for *Saving Private Ryan*, a tribute to the patriotic generation of World War II and to their dedication to duty, honor, and country. It also produced an epic paean to the rule of law, *Amistad*, which was about slaves whose rights were defended by principled public servants and the American system of justice. Hypocrisy, the 17th Century French epigrammatist La Rochefoucauld said, is the homage vice pays to virtue. In sum, I think it is a tribute to the American people that at least some of the institutions of the media and the culture acquitted themselves with a measure of honor in this mess.

It will be objected, however, that that is all well and good, but the president escaped formal sanctions—and the media, in particular, did not clamor for impeachment or conviction. In my view, that objection begs a more important question. Since impeachment is a political process, the Senate's failure to convict Clinton following his impeachment by the House needs to be seen as a political failure. Given the unwillingness of the American people to support the impeachment of their president, a reasonable argument can be made that a responsible press should not have supported impeachment. Perhaps also a responsible Congress should not have voted to take the fateful step to impeach, or, having voted to impeach, should not have voted to convict.

Just what are the political consequences of convicting and removing a president that the sovereign people have elected and wish to see serve out his term? Would not those consequences—bitter and perhaps irreconcilable divisions in the electorate, a thirst for retribution continuing into the next generation, a sense of betrayal and a breaking of trust—merit a second thought about proceeding along such a path, however legally warranted? Might not pursuing a course that was not politically viable have caused an even greater injury to the rule of law in the long run?

I believe such a course would have led to those kinds of consequences. Thus, I am thankful that Bill Clinton was not removed—and not simply because, as a Republican, I would not have wanted to see Al Gore in the White House a full year-and-a-half before the coming election. Given the failure of the Republicans to convince a decisive majority of the American people that the president's removal was required, the political ramifications of such a removal would have been to throw the nation into a constitutional crisis. No believer in the rule of law could wish for such a result.

What then was the cause of the political failure? Recent polls show that 49 percent of the American people now believe that Clinton should have been impeached—up from 40 percent during the impeachment process itself—while 44 percent would still oppose impeachment. That shift has taken place without political pressure from either side since impeachment has been a dead issue for more than a year now. Even at the time of the most heated debates, however, the American people believed that Bill Clinton was corrupt, and many despised him as a person even though they did not want him removed from office. Most Americans believed he was guilty of perjury. Many would not invite him to their homes for dinner. But they also did not want him impeached.

Clinton's escape from judgment was achieved because he based his defense on conservative principles and because Republicans were largely silent for eight months, enabling him to define the issues in a manner favorable to his case. When Republicans did finally find their collective voice, they talked past the immediate concerns of the American electorate and based their prosecution on issues that were too complex for the public to digest.

For eight crucial months, between the time Monica Lewinsky surfaced and President Clinton admitted their relationship, Republicans said relatively little about the developing sex scandal. Unbeknown to many of them, their leader, House Speaker Newt Gingrich, was himself conducting an adulterous affair, which was not a secret to the White House and its occupant. Perhaps that influenced the silence. We do not know.

Presumably, the Republican silence was based on two calculations: hope that the other side would self-destruct, and fear that Republicans could not handle the issue without shooting themselves in the foot. In fact, the two calculations had the same reasoning behind them: Republicans were afraid to fight the political battle. It was because Republicans did not trust themselves to frame the scandal to their advantage that they put their hopes in a Democratic implosion. Whatever the explanation for the Republican silence, however, the consequences of that silence for the impeachment process were immense.

While Republicans said nothing, the White House launched its own national campaign to define the issues for the American public. In political war, if only one side is shooting, the other side will be dead soon enough. While Republicans vacated the battlefield from January to August, the White House was able to define the issues of the scandal and thus establish Clinton's defense—on conservative grounds the American public was likely to accept.

Most crucially, the president's allies portrayed him as a victim of government abuse and thus as a defender, ironically, of the rule of law. They defined the issues surrounding the investigation as government invasion of privacy and government prosecutors out of control—growing conservative concerns. When Americans responded to that appeal, that should have been cause for conservative satisfaction, not dismay. Thus, it is not the American people that Republicans should blame for the failure to remove the president. They should blame their own political ineptitude in framing the issues.

When Republicans finally did make their case, they built their arguments on legal grounds that were either unintelligible to most Americans or had been rejected by them because they were based on liberal principles they themselves opposed. Thus, although impeachment is a political process conducted by the legislative branch, Republicans singularly failed to focus on the *political* case for removing the president. (The China foreign policy scandal would have been one possible avenue to pursue.) Instead, they relied on interpretations of the law—on abstruse legal arguments arising from the failed Paula Jones suit. It was radical sexual harassment law, allowing the court to investigate the personal sexual histories of defendants in sexual harassment cases, that led to the discovery of Monica Lewinsky. Yet sexual McCarthyism—a charge Democrats successfully used to damage the Republican prosecutors—was an invention of the radical Left. Ironically, with Republicans embracing their enemies' philosophy, sexual harassment laws framed the entire impeachment debate. Those were laws designed by radical feminists that conservatives had always opposed.

Thus, the impeachment debate revolved around such questions as, "Was the president's testimony in a sexual harassment case material?" "Was testimony in that case about matters that should be private?" "What constitutes perjury?" "Are civil cases of perjury normally prosecuted?" "What is obstruction?" "What are impeachable offenses?" "Has the bar for an impeachable offense been set high enough in this case?" Those were questions only constitutional experts and trial lawyers could properly discuss with any claim to authority, which is why they filled the evening talk shows. Because the debate was legalistic, many people found it complicated, irrelevant, or just plain confusing, particularly since Republicans were also reminding them that impeachment was a political process and political jurors would render the verdict.

In other words, Republicans chose to fight on grounds on which the public could not or would not follow them. Because the *legalistic* arguments of the Republicans failed to gain traction with a majority of the public, the Democrats' *political* arguments prevailed. The president's privacy had been invaded; government prosecutors had abused their power; and a sex act was no reason to remove a president the people had elected. A skeptical public was easily persuaded that the president was a victim of partisan attacks.

In the end, the impeachment debate was framed by the Democrats. And sound Democratic political strategy was buttressed by a full-employment economy, a soaring Dow, positive social trends (declining crime rates, increasing morality indexes), and no clear political case for removal. In such circumstances, the public's (conservative) response of sticking with a twice-elected sitting president was perfectly understandable, even reassuring. It was also consistent with respect for democratic principles, based on the sovereignty of the people, which is a key element of the rule of law, even if not the only element.

The lesson, therefore, is plain. If the rule of law is to be sustained, and if no one is to be above it, then we cannot rely on law alone to carry the day. Law is brought to life in the political process. Those who would preserve the rule of law, therefore, must attend to that process.

Contributors

Lillian R. BeVier is the Henry L. and Grace Doherty Charitable Foundation Professor of Law at the University of Virginia School of Law, where she teaches constitutional law, intellectual property, real property, and torts. A graduate of Smith College and the Stanford Law School, where she served on the *Stanford Law Review*, BeVier practiced law in Palo Alto, California, before joining the academic world. She serves on numerous boards and testifies often before Congress.

C. Boyden Gray is a partner at the Washington, D.C., law firm of Wilmer, Cutler & Pickering, where his practice focuses on a range of regulatory matters with emphasis on environmental issues, biotechnology, trade, and the management of risk. A graduate of Harvard College and the University of North Carolina Law School, where he served as editor in chief of the *University of North Carolina Law Review*, Gray clerked for Chief Justice Earl Warren of the U.S. Supreme Court. He served as legal counsel to Vice President George Bush and then as White House legal counsel under President Bush.

David Horowitz is president of the Center for the Study of Popular Culture and is a best-selling author and editor. He is a graduate of Columbia University and the University of California at Berkeley. During the 1960s he was a leader of the New Left as editor of *Ramparts* magazine. In the 1970s he withdrew from politics to write. His *Destructive Generation: Second Thoughts about the Sixties*, coauthored with Peter Collier in 1989, chronicled the legacy of the New Left. Horowitz's political journey is recounted in his autobiography, *Radical Son*, which the Free Press published in 1997.

Douglas W. Kmiec holds the Caruso Family Chair in Law at the Pepperdine University School of Law, which he assumed in 1999 after nearly two decades of teaching at the Notre Dame University

Law School. A graduate of Northwestern University and the University of Southern California Law School, Kmiec served Presidents Reagan and Bush as the head of the Office of Legal Counsel in the Department of Justice. He was a White House Fellow and a 40th anniversary Distinguished Fulbright Scholar. He is the author of numerous works and coauthor of three recent volumes on the Constitution.

Robert A. Levy is senior fellow in constitutional studies at the Cato Institute and adjunct professor at the Georgetown University Law Center. He earned a B.S., M.B.A., and Ph.D. from the American University and then founded CDA Investment Technologies, Inc., a major provider of financial information and software, serving as CEO until 1991. After selling his business, Levy earned a J.D. from the George Mason University School of Law, serving as chief articles editor of the law review. He clerked for Judge Royce C. Lamberth of the U.S. District Court and Judge Douglas H. Ginsburg of the U.S. Court of Appeals for the District of Columbia Circuit.

Timothy Lynch is associate director of the Cato Institute's Center for Constitutional Studies and director of the center's Project on Criminal Justice. A graduate of the college and the law school at Marquette University, Lynch has written on a range of issues but has focused recently on the American criminal justice system. His 1997 study for Cato, "Dereliction of Duty: The Constitutional Record of President Clinton," was widely cited as the first serious compilation of Clinton's assault on the rule of law.

Theodore B. Olson is a partner with the Los Angeles law firm of Gibson, Dunn & Crutcher, serving in its Washington office since 1984. A graduate of the University of the Pacific and the law school at the University of California at Berkeley, he was head of the Office of Legal Counsel in the Department of Justice during President Reagan's first term. He was counsel to President Reagan on several matters, including the Iran-Contra investigation and prosecutions. Olson is president of the Washington, D.C., Lawyers Division of the Federalist Society. He argues often before the U.S. Supreme Court.

Roger Pilon is vice president for legal affairs at the Cato Institute, where he holds the B. Kenneth Simon Chair in Constitutional Studies and is founder and director of Cato's Center for Constitutional Studies. A graduate of Columbia University, he holds an M.A. and a Ph.D. from the University of Chicago and a J.D. from the George Washington University School of Law. Prior to joining Cato he held five senior posts in the Reagan administration, including at the State and Justice Departments. He has taught philosophy and law and was a national fellow at Stanford's Hoover Institution.

Bill Pryor is the attorney general of Alabama. A graduate of the University of Louisiana at Monroe and the Tulane University School of Law, he served as editor in chief of the *Tulane Law Review* and clerked for the late Judge John Minor Wisdom of the U.S. Court of Appeals for the Fifth Circuit. In private practice in Birmingham from 1989 until he became attorney general in 1997, Pryor also was an adjunct professor at the Cumberland University School of Law.

Ronald D. Rotunda is the Albert E. Jenner, Jr., Professor of Law at the University of Illinois College of Law and a visiting senior fellow in constitutional studies at the Cato Institute. A graduate of Harvard College and the Harvard Law School, where he was a member of the *Harvard Law Review*, he clerked for Judge Walter R. Mansfield of the U.S. Court of Appeals for the Second Circuit. Rotunda practiced law in Washington, D.C., and served as assistant majority counsel for the Watergate Committee and as special counsel to Independent Counsel Kenneth Starr. He is coauthor of the five-volume *Treatise on Constitutional Law* and author of *Modern Constitutional Law*.

Nadine Strossen is president of the American Civil Liberties Union and a professor at New York Law School. A graduate of Harvard College and the Harvard Law School, where she was a member of the *Harvard Law Review*, she practiced law in Minneapolis and New York City before joining the academic world. Strossen has received numerous awards. She was twice named one of "The 100 Most Influential Lawyers in America" by the *National Law Journal*. Her book, *Defending Pornography: Free Speech, Sex, and the Fight for Women's Rights*, was named a "notable book" of 1995 by the *New York Times*.

Fred Thompson, senator from Tennessee, has served in the U.S. Senate since 1994. A graduate of Memphis State University and the

Vanderbilt University Law School, he was an assistant U.S. attorney, minority counsel to the Senate Watergate Committee, and special counsel to both the Senate Select Committee on Intelligence and the Senate Committee on Foreign Relations. He is an author and has acted in 18 motion pictures. In the Senate Thompson was elected chairman of the Governmental Affairs Committee, which was chosen by the Senate leadership in 1997 to conduct an investigation into alleged improper or illegal activities associated with the 1996 federal campaigns.

Daniel E. Troy is a partner at the Washington, D.C., law firm of Wiley, Rein & Fielding, where he specializes in constitutional and appellate litigation. He is also an associate scholar at the American Enterprise Institute. A graduate of Cornell University and the Columbia University School of Law, where he served on the *Columbia Law Review*, he clerked for Judge Robert H. Bork on the Court of Appeals for the District of Columbia Circuit. From 1987 to 1989 Troy served as an attorney-adviser in the Office of Legal Counsel of the U.S. Department of Justice.

James Wootton is president of the U.S. Chamber Institute for Legal Reform. A graduate of the college and the law school of the University of Virginia, he joined the Reagan administration in 1981, becoming deputy administrator of the Justice Department's Office of Juvenile Justice and Delinquency Prevention in 1983. In 1986 Wootton was appointed to the Legal Services Corporation as director of Policy, Communications and Legislative Affairs and was later named counselor to the president.

John C. Yoo is a professor at the law school at the University of California at Berkeley, where he teaches constitutional and foreign relations law. A graduate of Harvard College and the Yale Law School, where he served on the *Yale Law Review*, Yoo clerked for Judge Laurence H. Silberman of the U.S. Court of Appeals for the District of Columbia Circuit and Justice Clarence Thomas of the U.S. Supreme Court. He was general counsel for the Senate Judiciary Committee and has written widely in the area of foreign relations law.

Cato Institute

Founded in 1977, the Cato Institute is a public policy research foundation dedicated to broadening the parameters of policy debate to allow consideration of more options that are consistent with the traditional American principles of limited government, individual liberty, and peace. To that end, the Institute strives to achieve greater involvement of the intelligent, concerned lay public in questions of policy and the proper role of government.

The Institute is named for *Cato's Letters*, libertarian pamphlets that were widely read in the American Colonies in the early 18th century and played a major role in laying the philosophical foundation for the American Revolution.

Despite the achievement of the nation's Founders, today virtually no aspect of life is free from government encroachment. A pervasive intolerance for individual rights is shown by government's arbitrary intrusions into private economic transactions and its disregard for civil liberties.

To counter that trend, the Cato Institute undertakes an extensive publications program that addresses the complete spectrum of policy issues. Books, monographs, and shorter studies are commissioned to examine the federal budget, Social Security, regulation, military spending, international trade, and myriad other issues. Major policy conferences are held throughout the year, from which papers are published thrice yearly in the *Cato Journal*. The Institute also publishes the quarterly magazine *Regulation*.

In order to maintain its independence, the Cato Institute accepts no government funding. Contributions are received from foundations, corporations, and individuals, and other revenue is generated from the sale of publications. The Institute is a nonprofit, tax-exempt, educational foundation under Section 501(c)3 of the Internal Revenue Code.

CATO INSTITUTE
1000 Massachusetts Ave., N.W.
Washington, D.C. 20001